Praise for

Writing from Left to Right

"Serious-minded elected officials must separate the wheat from the chaff. That is why Michael Novak is indispensable. His genuine civility and humility, clarity of thought, willingness to be challenged by facts, and love of America are evident to all who know him and therefore rely upon him . . . Michael Novak is an American treasure."

—Dan Lungren, former U.S. Congressman and California State Attorney General

"Few men have combined the life of the mind and the life of action as completely, and consequentially, as Michael Novak. We see him, in this exhilarating memoir, moving naturally between philosophy and statecraft, collaborating with the deepest thinkers and boldest leaders of age. With George McGovern and Ronald Reagan, with Gabriel Marcel and John Paul II, Novak is always teaching and always learning. Watch closely and you will learn his secret: He grasped early on that the human person is the subject, not the object, of history and politics. Readers who pick up *Writing from Left to Right* expecting a partisan trope will be surprised and edified."

—Christopher DeMuth, distinguished fellow, Hudson Institute

"One of America's greatest moral philosophers—the theologian of democratic capitalism—relives not only his own intellectual journey, but that of America: from the turbulent 1960s and '70s, through renewal in the 1980s, and into an uncertain future in which his wisdom can be our guide. An enriching experience to read."

—Morton Kondracke, *Roll Call*

"This book is essential reading for anyone who wants to understand the politics and intellectual debates in the United States over the last half century. The evolution of Michael Novak's thought illuminates the changes the country has undergone as well as the fundamental moral and strategic issues we will face in the decades ahead."

—Carl Gershman, president, National Endowment for Democracy

"Michael Novak's life could have made a novel—seminarian, witness to Vatican II, equally in the thick of the radical politics of the 1960s and the resurgence of conservatism in the 1980s, a favorite of John Paul II, an advisor and often friend to leaders as different as Robert Kennedy, Ronald Reagan, Margaret Thatcher, Bill Clinton, and both Bushes; and yet also a theologian and public intellectual whose books have influenced countless lives, including mine. His gentle voice comes through on every page of this recounting of a remarkable life."
—Charles Murray, W. H. Brady Scholar, American Enterprise Institute,
and author of *Coming Apart and The Bell Curve*

"The 'journey from liberal to conservative'—this is the familiar saga of some New York Jewish intellectuals who made that journey half a century ago. Michael Novak's memoir is by an eminent Catholic intellectual, from a very different social, ethnic, as well as religious, background, who arrived at the same destination about the same time. It is a riveting tale of the events, characters, and, more important, ideas that helped shape his world—and ours."
—Gertrude Himmelfarb, author of *The People of the Book*

"An engaging, personable, and personal account of a muscular intellectual. Michael Novak draws us into the events and ideas that propelled his evolution in politics and economics. His insights and analysis are honest and help explain our nation's recent social, political, and economic history. On a personal note, Michael knew my dad very well and understood his essence—Jack Kemp was always a quarterback. I heard my dad praise Novak's work many times, and Michael and Karen were like family."
—James Kemp, president, Jack Kemp Foundation

Writing from
Left to Right

MY JOURNEY
FROM LIBERAL
TO CONSERVATIVE

Michael Novak

IMAGE

New York

Published in the United States by Image, an imprint of the Crown Publishing Group, a division of Random House, Inc., New York.
www.crownpublishing.com

IMAGE is a registered trademark, and the "I" colophon is a trademark of Random House, Inc.

Grateful acknowledgment is made to the following for permission to reprint previously published material: McGraw Hill: excerpt from *A Time for Truth* by William E. Simon. Copyright © 1978. Reprinted by permission of McGraw-Hill Education. Paul Adams: excerpt from the blog *Ethics, Culture, & Policy,* http://ethicsculture.blogspot.com. Reprinted by permission of the author.

The author wishes to thank the following publications for allowing him to excerpt and adapt material from his previously published articles: *American Spectator*: "He Called Me Friend" (July/August 2011). Reprinted by permission of the *American Spectator.* Carnegie Council for Ethics and International Affairs: "Underpraised, Undervalued System" first published in *Worldview Magazine* (July/August 1977). Reprinted by permission of Carnegie Council for Ethics in International Affairs, www.carnegiecouncil.org. *Commonweal Magazine*: "Marcel at Harvard" (October 5, 1962) and "Humphrey at Stanford" (March 24, 1967). Reprinted by permission of *Commonweal Magazine.* Dow Jones & Company, Inc.: "Breakthrough in Bern" first published in the *Wall Street Journal* (June 4, 1986). Reprinted by permission of Dow Jones & Company, Inc., as administered by the Copyright Clearance Center. HarperCollins Publishers: "Athensbury" first published in *Religion as Story*, edited by James B. Wiggins, copyright © 1975 by James B. Wiggins. Reprinted by permission of HarperCollins Publishers. *National Catholic Reporter*: "Vietnam Peace Candidate Bucks the Odds" (August 16, 1967), "Coups and Countercoups Are Bought with Money" (August 23, 1967), "Lieut. Commander Thong Was Killed Last Night" (August 23, 1967), "How to Cheat in an Election" (September 6, 1967), and "Dwight Hall Owen Jr." (September 13, 1967). Reprinted by permission of *National Catholic Reporter,* Kansas City, Missouri, www.ncronline.org. Transaction Publishers: the 2002 Introduction to *The Open Church,* the 1995 introduction to *Unmeltable Ethics,* and excerpts from *Choosing Presidents* (1991). Reprinted by permission of Transaction Publishers. *The Weekly Standard*: "The Last Liberal: Sergeant Shriver's Life and Times" (May 24, 2004) and "The Victorian Lady: Margaret Thatcher's Virtues" (April 22, 2013). Reprinted by permission of *The Weekly Standard.*

Library of Congress Cataloging-in-Publication Data is available upon request.

ISBN 978-0-385-34746-4
eISBN 978-0-385-34747-1

Printed in the United States of America

Jacket design by Jessie Sayward Bright
Jacket photograph: Paolo Gaetano Rocco/Getty Images

10 9 8 7 6 5 4 3 2 1

First Edition

For Karen,

my axis, my love,

at my side through all these adventures,

loved by all who met you.

Contents

part three:

CULTURE TRUMPS POLITICS AND ECONOMICS

Acknowledgments

There is no way this book could have been written or completed without the assistance, in matters both of detail and of large design, of Elizabeth Shaw, my long-distance research assistant in Arlington, Virginia. Elizabeth was indefatigable in helping me find records and check facts and numbers, but more than that in the heavy editing involved in making substantial cuts to keep the book within an appropriate size. My good editor Gary Jansen suggested the shrewd strategic decision to focus on economics and politics rather than make it an all-around memoir. Loretta Barrett, longtime literary counselor and literary go-between (formally, agent), nurtured me all the way through with encouragement, hopefulness, and advice both strong and true. In the book's early stages, Mitchell Boersma was also of important assistance, and Arielle Harms was a tremendous help in reviewing final proofs. And many, many others read earlier drafts, made good criticisms, and offered suggestions.

God bless you, one and all!

Ave Maria, Florida
January 21, 2013

Prologue

This book is about political and economic upheavals between the years 1960 and 2005, and the navigation through heavy waves that many of us chose. This is not just my story, but the story of hundreds of thousands, even millions. Many more are likely to join us over the next decade. Reality does not flinch from teaching human beings hard lessons.

One of my first political involvements was to prepare a lyrical speech—I suggested the "New Frontier" as a theme—for a Democratic aspirant to the U.S. Congress from New Jersey, who wanted to invite John F. Kennedy to campaign for him, and to have his own high-toned talk to impress the senator. I wrote the talk, but the Kennedy team never came to Paterson. I sent the speech to Boston anyway. The nominating convention was a little less than two months away, so I suspect the Kennedy team had already chosen the theme themselves. But the effort did have some interesting repercussions among the local union leaders and city hall "realists" in New Jersey.

During the early 1960s, Tom Hayden and the Students for a Democratic Society used an article of mine from *Harper's* alongside their own founding documents. A bit later I began writing about the war in Vietnam, first defending it, then slowly becoming more critical of it—and then even more critical of the anti-war movement itself.

From 1965 on I found myself out in California as an assistant professor at Stanford, just as the Berkeley radicals were coming into full throat, and conscientious objector rallies were heating up at Stanford. My dear Karen and I attended one peaceful march in Oakland that turned mean, and we were very nearly arrested.

By the beginning of 1968, Bobby Kennedy called me to San Francisco, as the first person (so I was told) he would meet with when opening his California campaign. He had two messages: that an article of mine, "The Secular Saint," had moved him to step up and finally jump into the race; and that he now needed my support among young people in the West. A bit startled, I said I needed twenty-four hours to clear some obstacles, but—yes.

I had loved Bobby's brother Jack and was still desolate after his sudden bloody death. (The murder of my own brother in Bangladesh followed two months after Jack was slain.) I was in Rome for the Vatican Council on November 22, 1963, and that night we few Americans huddled together with other Americans—my stricken wife, Karen, and I ended up at dinner with John Cogley (who drafted Kennedy's address to the Protestant ministers in Houston) and Michael Harrington (author of *The Other America*). The four of us could barely talk, we felt so empty, so plunged into the Absurd.

I then watched supportively as President Johnson launched the War on Poverty, and then the big push on the civil rights revolution (which had begun under President Kennedy and Martin Luther King).

I was still at Stanford the night that Bobby Kennedy was shot. (I had been invited to fly with him and his family to the Los Angeles hotel that night.) Just two months earlier, on April 4, Martin Luther

King had been struck down in Memphis. An awful spring. An awful year. An awful five years.

A longtime supporter of Hubert Humphrey (a hero to my father-in-law, who was the Iowa Democratic Party committeeman), I had been horribly embarrassed by a speech Humphrey gave at Stanford on the war in Vietnam. That crushingly miscalculated speech and the immense disgust that followed led me to promise myself that I could never vote for him for president. Internally, I moved left of left. By August 1968 I was working with Harris Wofford at Old Westbury, the new experimental college of the State University of New York. Harris had been Sargent Shriver's point man in the Peace Corps; he was later elected U.S. senator from Pennsylvania. He was a decent, generous, and spirited man.

In 1970 the great and wonderful Sarge, a truly good, large-hearted, and—if it's not too much to say—even saintly man, asked me to come with him on his national campaign to elect Democratic congressmen, and we traveled together to thirty-nine states. Two years later I was on the campaign plane with him again, in 1972, having shown up at his home with a draft of his acceptance speech when he got the nomination to be George McGovern's running mate. I had already written speeches for McGovern. Throughout the campaign I came to admire both men greatly. It didn't hurt that both were fans of *The Rise of the Unmeltable Ethnics,* but it was the sheer goodness of their characters that won me over. Both were war heroes. Both were modest, not self-promoting.

Through a mutual Baptist friend, Jimmy Carter came to see me in New York late in 1975—it was his very first campaign trip there, and we spent all day in Queens (Archie Bunker country), and then drove in for his first ever talk in Manhattan. Afterward I wrote a piece that turned out to be the first coverage of him in the national press, and it went into all the early press books of the campaign.

In 1976, for foreign policy reasons, I decided I could not support

Carter after all, and I began campaigning for Senator Scoop Jackson in Pennsylvania. At the convention in New York I was in Scoop's hotel room on standby, in the event that Jimmy Carter telephoned to ask him to be his running mate (the senator had been tipped off that he was one of two finalists).

By 1979 Carter's foreign policy weaknesses tempted Muslim rioters to take hostage many Americans at the embassy in Iran. Domestically, Carter was forced by the economic "stagflation" to speak of American "malaise," but he then irrelevantly campaigned against millionaires and "three-martini lunches."

I learned a lot from that campaign, and even more from the next twenty-five years of the greatest prosperity ever experienced in human history. I saw the force of ideas in that campaign and the political battle that followed. The sunny Ronald Reagan (coming into office in the wake of Margaret Thatcher and Pope John Paul II) was a good deal shrewder and his ideas were stronger and deeper than the press and his opposition had bargained for. The facts of America's rapid revival forced me to change my approach to economic policy, from Democratic welfare designs to the creation of new industries and millions of new jobs. For the first time, against my presuppositions, I saw the contributions to the common good made by the founding of a few million new small businesses. "Entrepreneur" went in my mind from being a slur to being an indispensable vocation for the benefit of the poor and unemployed. To have employees you need employers.

Further, Ronald Reagan's determination to take the "Kick me!" sign off the backs of Americans (he picked up the phrase from a speech of Jeane Kirkpatrick's at the 1984 Republican National Convention on the San Francisco Democrats) and his new toughness in working every single day to bring down the Soviet Union taught me an ancient lesson again: *Si vis pacem, para bellum:* If you wish for peace, prepare for war." I learned from Reagan's clearheadedness about two terms Americans in their moralism like to avoid: "self-interest" and "power." I saw how his hard-minded thinking about ridding the world of nuclear weapons outflanked the Soviets by building superior power and through American inventiveness. (His threat of "Star Wars" was taken with deadly seriousness and shook them to the bottom of the Soviet treasury, even while many of my old liberal friends ridiculed it.)

For some years, meanwhile, William Simon, Jack Kemp, Vin Weber, and many of their friends were awakening me to a new way of thinking about economics, as approached through foresight, enterprise, initiative, and risk. I witnessed with my own eyes the almost immediate results of the switch from Carter's economic policies to Reaganomics. I could see close at hand the jump in morale among young entrepreneurs (including graduate students suddenly grasping that they could start new businesses of their own). I saw with my own eyes the effects of Reagan's creative tax and regulatory regime, which was designed to propel a burst of millions of new small businesses, along with an unprecedented explosion in employment. I watched as wholly new technologies such as computers, cell phones, genetic therapies, and fiber optics came into being. Reagan's capital gains tax cuts enticed the investments that ushered in a new Electronic Age, replacing the Machine Age. This was a prosperity that, to my surprise, lifted every boat, from the bottom up. The numbers and proportion of the poor dropped; the median income rose; more than ever before, many married-couple families among blacks earned more than $50,000 a year. I had not expected any of that. My aim on the left had been to help the poor—I now began to see a better way to do that.

President Reagan twice asked me to be his ambassador to the UN Commission on Human Rights in Geneva, and then to take on a related assignment a few years later at the Bern Round of the Helsinki Talks (that year focusing on "openness" among societies).

Although I was a rank amateur and made lots of rookie mistakes, I must have done something well: In later years, the presidents of the Slovak Republic, the Czech Republic, and the Republic of Poland awarded me the highest medal those countries can give a foreigner, in large part for that work.

Reagan had also appointed me to the Board for International Broadcasting, the governing body responsible for Radio Free Europe and Radio Liberty (since 1994 the body has been known as the Broadcasting Board of Governors), and then Bill Clinton reappointed me. I may have been one of the longest serving board members ever (eleven years), and I gained invaluable insight into how Communist countries actually worked—and into the impending breakdown of Communism. First the Berlin Wall came down in the epoch closing year of 1989. Then the Soviet Union collapsed in 1991. My friends in Prague sent me a big Soviet flag they tore down from their building as soon as the Russian soldiers left for home (speedily)—and I hung it in my office for a while, with joy.

Bill Clinton had befriended me (he befriended everybody) about a month before taking office as president, and we worked together on more than one small project—for one, arranging for him to meet with Václav Havel on the Old Bridge across the Charles in the Old City and to play his saxophone to an adoring world press. The aim was to let Havel make the case directly to Clinton for moving the Radios from Munich to Prague. Clinton supported the move when few in his administration approved. It saved the U.S. government a small fortune, and it brought the Radios closer to their audience on the other side of the old Iron Curtain. The Radios sponsored all sorts of new activities—for example, seminars for journalists trained under Communism but now working in free countries on how to choose their stories on their own and how to develop them without being told in advance what to write.

Clinton imitated much of the Reagan economic program, raising taxes only a little actually, and he kept the economy strong and vital. Yet his one flaw was not paying attention to developing threats. (His focus was domestic; he did not see the connection between international strength and domestic progress.) There are always wars in human history—new ones, generation after generation—because wars spring from the human heart itself (as Saint Augustine taught back in the fifth century). Peace never lasts. This time, the original and founding dream of one Muslim empire was being stirred by a minority of radicals, a minority that was passionate and constantly active. These radicals eventually saw the United States as their greatest obstacle: the fount of all the dreadful perversions of modern secular culture—the "Great Satan."

Eight months after George W. Bush took office in 2001, the plotters struck. It was a particularly peaceful, blue-skied September day. Thank God, Jack Kennedy championed the U.S. Special Forces, then called the Green Berets, giving them immense public support (not to say romance), political impetus, and the financial wherewithal to expand. In them the United States had a world-class, small-team fighting force, ready for instant worldwide action. Presidents George H. W. Bush and George W. Bush had much need of them. I supported both Iraq wars, for reasons discussed below. Both were necessary if young Muslim males were to turn their energies from resentment and destruction toward working for prosperity and the expansion of the human rights of Muslims. I attribute the later outbreak of democracy movements around the Arab world to the passionate discussions of liberty that distinguished the struggles in Afghanistan and Iraq. The Arab Spring was only a first wave; it was almost certain to fall short, but there will be many future waves. Human rights are natural rights, and universal, and nothing drives their necessity home like suffering under oppression.

Finally, I have lived long enough to see economic errors repeat themselves over and over. Dostoyevsky predicted this: Humans claim to want liberty but then shuck it off when its attendant responsibilities become irksome. I have come to judge "progressivism" itself to be a well-intentioned but deadly error. It overrates human innocence and goodness and underrates human weakness and preference for getting things for free rather than as a result of arduous work. It claims to want equality, but it does not grasp how that demand undermines the motive for initiative and hard work. It is a form of statism, trying unsuccessfully to drape the smaller garments of small government and liberty around its gigantesque frame. And the trouble with statism is that it works only until the state runs out of other people's money. By 2013 the United States has done that. Most government spending today is financed by debt, most of it owed to foreign powers. That is a symptom of the greed of progressives, feeding boundless appetites for utopian schemes, to be paid for at the severe expense of future generations. I find this disgusting. For me it is just plain stealing from our grandchildren. I can hardly face my own, Emily and Stephen, Wiley and Julia. Our generation's thievery from our children is perpetrated in the name of the unprecedented "compassion" of our generation—a compassion that we ourselves are not paying for.

I am glad that I am in my eightieth year and will not live to see the suffering, and perhaps bitterness, of these grandchildren. How they will despise us!

A philosopher and theologian by training, I grew up with a deep interest in how ideas change history—and how history changes ideas.

Providence—held by America's founders to be that "Great governor of the universe"—arranged that I should live through movements both from history to ideas and from ideas to history.

At eighty I look back over the events I have witnessed, and I revisit the lessons I learned the hard way. Events and facts forced me to change my mind about the ideas with which my education imbued me, eager pupil that I was. I worked out my changes of mind publicly in articles and books. As my new direction became clear, I lost many close friends. My phone stopped ringing. Angry letters from dear friends pleaded with me to desist. I was shunned at professional meetings, even by the closest of old colleagues. Some refused to appear with me ever again on any academic program. This was a common experience among those of us who moved from left to right in our time.

Why? Because the two metaphysical beliefs of the Left are that *progress is unstoppable,* and that *progress means always turning left.* Any turning toward the Right contradicts this metaphysics and must be shunned.

Even today, when feelings have mellowed, old acquaintances josh me for having changed my mind on several key matters. I josh them back: "How on earth, seeing what we saw, living through what we lived through, did you *not* change? I thought the rule was open-mindedness, revision as facts warrant, and fresh judgments of reality."

Many persons today are again wrestling with political and economic beliefs they have long held and are beginning to drift away from them.

I may be quite wrong in how I dealt with my own doubts and inquiries during my adulthood. Perhaps the record of how I believed, and then doubted, and found what seemed to me a better way to reach our goals may help others to avoid mistakes I made and take better and surer steps on their own. In heavy seas, to stay on course it is indispensable to lean hard left at times, then hard right. The important thing is to have the courage to follow your intellect. Wherever the evidence leads. To the left or to the right. "The first moral obligation is to think clearly."

part one

Left Turn

1

A Snapshot of My Left Turn, 1967

One pivotal scene at Stanford University in February of 1967 may plunge the reader into the political turmoil of that time. Vice President Hubert Humphrey—an old hero of Karen's and mine (and of her politically savvy father), and an old Niebuhrian realist himself— came to Stanford to give a major speech on the war in Vietnam, just as support for the war at home was tottering.

That there would be a protest on Stanford's campus when Humphrey showed up went without saying. Yet a number of us, to one extent or another anti-war and moved by the anxiety about the futures that gripped many of the young men in our classes, tried in vain behind the scenes to make the imminent protest peaceful and dignified. My own favorite maxim in those days came from Albert Camus, and I quoted it often: "I should like to love my country and still love justice." Several of my professor friends and I wanted to have the American flag on our side and appeal to American principles and rhetorical traditions. We thought it very wrong to alienate the vast American middle. Most of Middle America did not like this war, either, and wished *their* sons did not have to go fight in it, so far away. And most did not like the strutting South Vietnamese generals who were running the country after the assassination (with President Kennedy's connivance) of Diem, the legitimate leader of that time. It was a mistake, we thought, to drive Middle America away. For the Left, it was only decent to reason with the American public directly, facing both the ugliness of the situation and the hard necessity to block China's ancient ambitions in Southeast Asia.

So let me now describe what happened on Humphrey's visit.*

The campus prepared for Humphrey's visit for more than a week. But even a month before, at the end of January 1967, a group of students from various religious groups had collected funds to send two professors to the Washington mobilization of the Clergy and Laity Concerned about Vietnam. They then sponsored rallies and smaller discussions on campus. The radical students were discouraged and relatively quiet. Thus, just as Humphrey arrived, leadership in the anti-war movement had passed to moderates and newcomers. A hastily organized faculty committee urged as many persons as possible to greet Humphrey in strict silence, wearing white armbands, and pledged neither to applaud nor to boo. Student groups—not consulted about this proposal in advance—held strategy meetings of their own. The radicals had collected a file on Humphrey's speeches and insisted that the vice president no longer heard alternatives but only emitted propaganda. They were insulted that he was being offered a university platform, thus lending Stanford's prestige—*their* prestige—to such propaganda. The moderate students, together with the hastily organized faculty group, argued that militant protests *antagonized* public opinion. A young man with a soft Georgia accent, who had recently resigned from the ROTC, was especially persuasive in arguing that demonstrations should be "effective" and

---

*For fuller descriptions, on which I base this account, see the two books I wrote just after that time, *A Theology for Radical Politics* and *Politics: Realism and Imagination;* and also my letters to my family at the time.

"designed to persuade the uncommitted, not alienate them. I know what the people back home think," he said, "when they see pictures of wild demonstrations."

In the end, ecumenism triumphed: all anti-war groups would work together. The night preceding Humphrey's visit, an all-night teach-in was held. As usual, all the radical students were there, but relatively few moderates. Early the next morning, crowds gathered outside Memorial Auditorium. Although students and faculty were admitted one by one through a single door, where identity cards were checked, the 1,700 seats inside were filled in fifteen minutes; many of the about a thousand students and faculty who wore white armbands and had pledged silence did not get in. (Although official denials were forthcoming, many thought at the time that the auditorium had secretly been packed through other doors.) When Humphrey entered, those in the front rows (mostly senior university people and guests) rose as one man, and the ovation of the unpledged overpowered the silence of the pledged. Humphrey began his address to a tense, divided university audience by honoring them with their recent appearance on the cover of *Time* magazine as members of "The Now Generation." His glib, insensitive speech was met with incredulity, then disgust, and finally outrage by many of those who until that moment had considered themselves moderates.

About sixty radical students rose to walk out just after Humphrey began to speak, to demonstrate that they knew he would voice no honest opinion. Others, persuaded by the moderates, had decided "to give the vice president of the United States a chance." They sat quietly for almost twenty minutes while Humphrey evaded the question of the war in his prepared remarks, tried to portray himself as a former radical from Minnesota, which he was, and then nationally as a founding leader of Americans for Democratic Action (ADA), the left wing of the Democratic Party. When three selected panelists finally brought up the question of the war, Humphrey spoke of it in terms that well-read students knew were mere simplicities. When he claimed that the university community *supported* the war, almost two hundred others—many of whom had not intended to walk out—rose and quietly filed out. Outside, listening by loudspeaker, students and faculty evaluated every sentence, some shouting "Shame!" or "Lie!" at his succession of simplistic statements. A serious, reasoned, complex talk about the war would, that day, have persuaded many at Stanford. The anger that Humphrey generated—oblivious to his own ineptitude—turned scores of heretofore inactive students into militant opponents of the administration.

Humphrey appeared at a window after the speech. Those outside cried "Shame! Shame!" A crowd gathered to let Humphrey know the insult he had delivered, and to let him feel their detestation of the murder and destruction committed in their name in Vietnam. ("We do not bomb civilians," Humphrey had answered indignantly. "But you can't put a bomb in a barrel.") As the Secret Service whisked Humphrey to his car fifty yards away, students came running, shouting, "Shame!" and, from the more angry, "Murderer!" Two prostrate protestors were moved from his unmarked path by police. No one touched Humphrey or his car. The shoving and the running, less rough than in a crowd after a football game, nevertheless conveyed a sense of stampede and an electric passion of outrage. A Secret Service man kicked over a rancid can of beer and thought someone had thrown a container of urine at him. Humphrey was still speaking bitterly of his Stanford experience a year later.

President Sterling of Stanford apologized—not to the university for the vice president's performance, but to Mr. Humphrey for the university's behavior. There had been no violence, no riot, nothing but the excitement of running and voicing "Shame!"—and an utterly shameful example of government propaganda. President Sterling then took the extraordinary measure of sending a letter to every person at the university "out of a deep concern for the preservation of free and civilized debate." The debate, some students felt, had not been free; it was, on Humphrey's part, a mockery of civilized discourse: he was using the platform of a great university to clothe the government's policies with respectability. There was no arrangement of any kind for genuine cross-examination by the university community—nothing like the freedom of the Oxford Union, for example. The helplessness of the United States Senate regarding U.S. foreign policy was experienced at Stanford that day in February. The moderates felt betrayed. The radicals said: "We told you so."

2

Never Forget
Where You Came From

Three brief stories from my youth bear heavily on my political views from then until now. The first is from 1939, when I was six years old. My father and I were in the almost empty living room of our new home, stacking books in the bookcases on either side of the fireplace. We were just putting the bright crimson Harvard Classics onto the shelves when the music on the radio was interrupted by a newsflash announcing the Nazi invasion of Poland. It meant the beginning of the long-dreaded war. "Listen closely, Mike," my father said. "It's going to change your life."

Nazi tanks (we saw the film clips later) were rolling across the border and bent-wing Stuka aircraft were strafing peasants on the roadways and bombing everything that moved. My dad was probably thinking that before long he would be called into the army—it was obvious that it would be a long war. He continued his quiet advice: "Study all you can about the Nazis and the Communists. These will be the two movements that will shape the next forty years."

The second event occurred when I was going on eleven. I was at the Saturday matinee at the movies when the news reel popped up on the screen. I was horrified to see dead bodies being slung into rows of trucks at a concentration camp out in the countryside of southern Germany. Human beings being slung like sacks of sand— that shook me deeply and frightened me.

The third story grew out of happy, boisterous times at Uncle Johnnie's and Uncle Emil's. There were always eight or nine kids my age and younger running noisily up the stairs, shouting and laughing all the while, hollering over the shoulder challenges to one another, and sometimes running out into the backyard underneath the grape arbor to pause for a rest. Every Slovak family had a grape arbor and made wine in the fall. Hollyhocks and huge sunflowers blew majestically in summer winds. Both Johnnie and Emil worked at Bethlehem Steel—Johnnie as manager of the open hearth Monday through Saturday, Emil somewhere along the line. Emil's second finger had been cut off by "some gol-danged unstoppable machine" at work; he swore a blue streak, as happy as he could be. Emil took no guff from politicians, whom he roundly disliked (except for his son Georgie, who was an elected officer in the union local). His other son, Frankie, was drafted into the army and became one of the headquarters' cooks and personal cake baker for General Eisenhower in Britain.

In later years, when journalists wrote about "Americans," I tested each of their sentences against the views of my uncles. The journalists almost never described the America of Johnnie and Emil. The categories in the journalists' heads did not include my uncles. In some ways Johnnie and Emil were the most liberal FDR Democrats that you ever met, and patriots (our family fought in successive wars) and churchgoing in their gruff and unsentimental way. They were family men, and moral, and they liked their beers with a good rich head, the stronger the taste the better. Emil's boys went hunting with him, and Emil would have withstood the thumbscrew rather than give up his faith. He figured God could stand his cussin' and his bluster, even if the pastor didn't much like it. From him I derived my "Uncle Emil test" for judging politicians and elites. He looked on the youngest of the Novak boys, my dad, with special fondness, maybe because he looked at "Mickey" as a thinking man with ideas of his own and a love for books. Uncle Emil didn't share that love, but he paid it great respect. They were half-brothers—after Emil's mother died, his father had married for a second time, and Mickey and Johnnie were born of that second union.

All four of my grandparents came to America from farming villages about twenty miles apart in rural Slovakia, along the "Amber Way" in the county of Spiš (pronounced *Spish*), where the family worked as serfs on the land around the great castle there. After 1939 that region fell under Nazi, then Communist, occupation and was walled up behind the Iron Curtain for nearly fifty years. The family in Slovakia and the family in America exchanged letters once or twice a year, and almost always my mother tucked a five-dollar bill into her envelopes to them. When I finally met them in the 1970s, none of the Sakmars (my mother's side) in Slovakia remembered receiving any money in family letters—which were opened and screened by the secret police.

In the spring of 1900 my grandfather Ben, then sixteen, set out by foot for Bremerhaven to find his ship for America. The whole parish said a rosary on his behalf behind the church, set high up on a ridge that faced west. Before he left, alongside the road through the family fields, Ben had affixed to a tree a ten-inch crucifix under a slanted roof he had made himself. When I visited the village in 1974 it was still there, except that the road no longer passed that way. The tree stood in the middle of a great field of barley waving in the breeze. From my youth I had felt tied to the fate of my relatives overseas, to some degree responsible for the future of the little mountain nation, where we could trace family roots back to about A.D. 1260. This early bond enabled me from across the ocean to feel like a distant cousin to the great hero of that region, Karol Wojtyla, introduced to the world as Pope John Paul II when he was ushered out on the balcony of St. Peter's in 1978.

It also impacted my political views that I was born and nurtured in Johnstown, Pennsylvania. Johnstown lies deep in a valley of the Allegheny Mountains between Pittsburgh and Altoona. Along the valley floors below the surrounding hilltops flow two rivers spread out like the letter "Y": the Conemaugh and the Stonycreek, which meet at the point and flow together toward Pittsburgh. From the time of the Civil War onward, Johnstown's iron and steel mills and surrounding coal mines made the city an innovative industrial powerhouse on the western frontier, which would shortly lose its eminence to Andrew Carnegie's Pittsburgh farther west. In 1889, a massive flood overwhelmed downtown Johnstown. When a dam broke, the city was buried under a wall of water thirty feet tall that struck the city like an enormous wave. Of the town's approximately 28,000 inhabitants, some 2,600 perished in hours. Nearly all the buildings on the valley floor were smashed to smithereens.

By rights the city should have died then, broken in spirit by the sudden violence. But a hundred years later people were still singing "The Johnstown Polka" (which celebrates "the city with a will"). The town had been reduced to nothingness; thousands despaired, but most Johnstowners kept coming back. They rebuilt the downtown, making it much better than before, only to have it once again submerged by the flash flood of 1936, and then again during the near-monsoon of 1977. The thin soil on the hillsides can absorb only so much water until a thousand brooklets and rivulets run down into the valley from every side. The narrow rivers along the "Y" can overflow rather quickly, and then be thrown back by the narrow gap between two gateway flanks of the unyielding hills.

Just growing up in that town taught me about the nothingness that underlies all things, the immensity of human suffering, and the need to dig deep for the steady will to create anew. For me the destructiveness that hit all of Europe in 1939 was like that: the darkness . . . and the need to build from bottom up a new civilization. The biblical *creatio ex nihilo* has never been just a metaphor for me. It is a fundamental law of life, not least for a writer facing a new, cold, and empty page.

3

Political Beginnings

I spent the years from my fourteenth until my twenty-sixth birthday apart from "worldly affairs"—preparing, I hoped, to help change human affairs as they then were by studying to become a priest of the Congregation of Holy Cross. These studies took me from Pennsylvania to Indiana, Vermont, and Massachusetts, and then to Rome, Italy, and Washington, D.C. In those years I got a good whiff of American electoral diversity and a strong taste of Italy's serious struggles (almost to the death) between the Communist Party and the Christian Democrats. Most of my fellow seminarians—nearly all, as far as I could tell—were Democrats, often enough from union backgrounds.

In January of 1960, after a long and painful struggle in mind, heart, and conscience, I judged that my true vocation was in lay, not priestly, life. One motive was to write fiction, another to become more closely involved in the war of political ideas. Whatever one might say about earlier centuries, in the twentieth century certain ideas catalyzed huge political eruptions, terrors, persecutions, and wars. Intellectual life in our time was not wholly cerebral and remote: For millions it meant death.

On the smoking ruins of Europe and Asia after World War II, *how* to build a humanistic culture was not clear. Even in the more placid times of life at home in my twelfth or thirteenth year, my father told me, "Mike, never argue religion or politics. No one ever changes his mind. It's never worth it." But it did occur to me that if politics and religion evoke such powerful passions, there must be one helluva career in that.

I discovered some of that passion, too, in my work with dying cancer patients in Rome in 1957. The smell of the place was foul beyond foul. Each week some of the patients who had been there the week before had died, and new ones had been brought into their beds. Nearly all were from the countryside, with no place else to go for care. Several were ardent voters for the Communist Party. The sight of my collar and cassock when I arrived each week was enough to set them off on a political tirade: first, about injustices the capitalists inflicted on the poor; second, about the injustice of the diverse fates that God meted out to individuals—individuals like themselves. Why *them*? Disease had taken the lung of one, the nose of another, the innards of the stomach of a third, the lower lip and part of the chin of another. They spat an ugly spittle. The odor on their breaths was sulfuric. They had come to this hospital to die, and they knew it, but many did not accept it.

My job was to bring them kindliness, a smile, gentleness, sometimes a caress on the forehead. To talk and josh with them. To come to the bed of one particularly passionate comrade and raise my fist in the Communist salute (he grinned and saluted back). To stop for prayer and a blessing for any who asked.

One begged me to cure him. "Saint Francis Assisi did it; why can't you? If you wanted to, you could."

I stayed in the seminary another eighteen months, until I completed my January exams at Catholic University in Washington, D.C. While there, I learned to love that beautiful city, and I felt obscurely that my destiny might one day bring me back there for a long time, the way French novelists and philosophers and playwrights were drawn to Paris, or Italian writers to Rome.

After acute inner turmoil and suffering in Washington (the pain I cannot exaggerate), I broke the hearts of a great many people— and my own lifetime image of myself—by deciding that I could not, really could not, become a priest. It was wrong. It was not what God wanted of me. I simply had to go.

Who knew where?

I left the seminary for home and then took a train to New York City—with a hundred dollars in my pocket from my father, and my first brown suit (not black) in a dozen years. My heart was singing out with joy to be back in the world, doing what I should be doing.

As long as I had been reading autobiographies of writers I had dreamed of living in New York in a garret apartment with only my typewriter, living in loneliness, and doing the hard work of writing. *Now* I could live out my dream for real. I was deliriously happy.

New York, New York! It is the dreamland for artists of all kinds from all around the world. Somehow I didn't have much fear about moving up in their ranks. There was no way to know how deep my talent ran, or how extensive it might be. Somehow I knew I had been given the duty to excel. My danger lay on the other side: perhaps I wasn't really as good as I imagined. The idea of a great test ahead heightened my excitement.

Back when I was in school, at the beginning of every football game I took my place near the end zone to accept the opening kick-off and tried to make myself as nervous as I could. I pranced up and down, did some bends and stretches, practiced a shifty move or two.

I wanted my adrenaline up to perfect pitch when the whistle blew, the leather was kicked, and the fluttering ball came down swiftly out of the blue sky in the glint of the sun.

So it was on the train to Manhattan. By the time we reached Newark, the adrenaline was pretty high in my chest. I could hardly hold myself in my train seat. At Penn Station I practically bolted out of the train, down the long, noisy ramp, and up the escalators, emerging on Seventh Avenue to head downtown.

I had a room arranged at Leo House on Twenty-third Street, a small apartment house built by German immigrants for welcoming German newcomers in the nineteenth century. The cost might have been even less than $10 per week. I couldn't open the drawer of the dresser beside the bed without lifting my feet out of the way up onto the bed. Besides that, when I came in at night and switched on the lights, at least half a dozen startled cockroaches ran for hiding places. There were too many to kill, and the supply seemed endless, so any hope of ridding my place of them seemed pointless. I was particularly disgusted by the ones on my bed and pillowcase. I had to hope that they would not run up on a sleeping body that twisted and turned a few times a night. Yet somehow this repulsive sight made me glad. *Haec olim meminisse juvabit,* I remembered from my high school Latin: *Someday the memory of these things will fill you with joy.* I really was in New York. I really was accepted now—by the cockroaches. I belonged.

Near the end of my stay at Leo House, I found out whence the endless supply of cockroaches had emanated. The blind man from the Punjab, tall and sweet-tempered, had moved out, and the doorway to his room, across from mine, lay open. There on the crud-stiffened floor was a dish for his dog's food, unclean, encrusted—and covered with roaches. There were so many roaches circling around on the floor in that room that one could not have stepped in without crushing some. They made the floor swirl with repulsive movement. Once that room was cleared out and thoroughly fumigated, the numbers of roaches in my room diminished markedly, but by no means did they die out. Residents of New York are exceptionally hardy, even the resident roaches of New York—*especially* the roaches of New York.

The first thing I did was finish my first novel, *The Tiber Was Silver,* and, luckily, Doubleday picked it up on my first try at finding a publisher. *Tiber* was no big financial success, yet it was published in French by Fayard—and every single dollar in those days kept me alive and at work. I think it sold 30,000 copies, mostly in paperback.

Next I wanted to turn my attention to informal reading in politics, sociology, and economics—all fields in which, beyond some basics, I felt weak, given what I wanted to do. Therefore, I leapt at a chance to write speeches for a new Democratic candidate for the U.S. Congress from Paterson, New Jersey. An old buddy of mine from the high-school seminary at Notre Dame during the years 1947–48, John Holley (who used to say he was related to Damon Runyon), called to offer me a job. A tall, heavy, soft-spoken, and soft-hearted lawyer from northern New Jersey, he was the campaign manager for an aspiring Democratic congressman in a solidly Republican district, an unusual candidate who shall remain nameless. This candidate was ambitious. He thought 1960 would be a good Democratic year, believed Jack Kennedy would be the Democratic presidential candidate (when not everybody did), and wanted to attract Kennedy's help by making a couple of "eloquent" speeches ("a cut above the average, a speech that stands out"). Maybe he could even draw Kennedy into coming and speaking on his behalf during the campaign. After a conversation with the two of them, I started to work immediately on a speech. John and the candidate liked it, but they had to walk it by their other campaign leaders, the guy from city hall in Paterson, the AFL-CIO guy, the woman from the teachers' union, the guy from the NAACP, and assorted others. A more hard-assed and hardheaded group would be tough to assemble. I met with them in one of the city offices.

The speech was on the "New Frontier," and it was about how, while the last eight years had been comfortable and safe, the old pioneering spirit had been lost—the sense of adventure, the dreaming of big dreams had gone awry. How it was time to open up a new frontier, stir America's young, and inspire a nation to lift its head and follow its early destiny. The hardened veterans listened. "Paterson ain't Harvard!" one of them said. "Not gonna go over too good in my shop." "My guys are gonna whistle and hoot. They want bacon. They want meat and potatoes. They want more money." "Some of the teachers will like the lilt, but what the hell does it mean for them?"

I would have been pretty deflated—everything they said was true—but the candidate said he wanted to give the speech anyway and send it up to the Kennedy camp. His other speeches would concentrate on the things all politicians did, he said, but the important thing is the new spirit that's in the air. The country is tired. People want to feel their hearts stirred again. Kennedy will mean youth. He will bring spirit.

"What makes ya think that Kennedy is gonna win?" one thick fellow (who hadn't shaved that day) asked pretty acridly. "My guys tell me it's gonna be Humphrey. We need a winner—not a playboy that's never worked a day in his life. Humphrey is who we're going for."

Riding back to New York on New Jersey Transit, I felt pretty much at a loss. The only kind of speeches I knew how to write were the frilly kind guys like them didn't like. Well, I reasoned, that's why the candidate hired me, isn't it? Something different. Something fresh. Still, a lot of my earlier inspiration was *phzzing* out of me pretty quick, like air through a busted tire valve.

I still sent my speech to Archibald MacLeish, the Harvard poet and director of Kennedy speechwriters, who replied with a hand-written thank-you note and asked me to keep sending him things. I'm not sure he even read the speech; he probably just handed it off to another hard-boiled aide, who aimed it at the round file cabinet in the corner.

You can imagine my jubilation, my feeling of triumph, when the whole country was roused by the New Frontier speech that Kennedy gave at his address after his nomination. But the first and overwhelming feeling of exultation I felt was that a *Catholic* had been nominated for the presidency of the United States. Oh God, standing right there in the cafeteria of the Harvard Law School, how I identified with all the parochial school kids I had known! Especially with all the Irish kids—we used to run home together after school to avoid being beat up by the larger body of public school kids from two blocks away. This was in McKeesport, Pennsylvania—Andy Warhol's hometown—where we moved after my dad's second promotion; I went to eighth grade there. (It was there that I won the Irish Day hundred-yard dash at Kennywood Park, under the name O'Novak.)

It was a great day to be a grandson of Catholic immigrants.

But it was also a great day to imagine the faces of that candidate's advisers over in Paterson. He soon called me over for a meeting with his team. It was astonishing how much they had learned to like the idea of the New Frontier since a month or so earlier when I had presented it; now they thought it was brilliant. Politics 101: Ain't nothin' like success. Guys who said "it" couldn't be done beforehand always end up after "its" success patting you on the back to remind you how much they were rooting for you.

And Politics 102: Never be intimidated by the experts.

By the way, I never imagined that my text actually had anything to do with the final Kennedy address. It was rejoicing enough just to see that I had been on the same wavelength, without any coaching. That gave me a bit of confidence in my own instincts, and a sense that I could read underlying currents as well as the best.

WELL, THAT WAS THE extent of my beginnings in politics. Basically, in New York I learned the meaning of chutzpah, and I picked up a little of it. There was also the aspect of the *literary* war of political ideas. In New York I got to meet the editors of practically every magazine of opinion—at least the more liberal ones.

I was the typical Catholic grandson of immigrants who worked in the mines, and I had a cousin who was a load boss in the United Steelworkers. Across-the-board Democrats, all of us. Some of the editors were Ivy League Protestant (but usually lower-class), some were Jewish, but they all had the young Americans' spirit of joy in their bloodstream.

They were at the head of the liberal ranks—or wanted to be. They didn't like the rich, the owners, the corporate executives. For them, "Republican" was a dirty word. It was used like an ethnic word, too, but it wasn't *our* ethnicity.

It is notable that I did not try to call on *National Review* or, on the other side, *The Nation.* Concerning the latter, the situation of my family in Slovakia prevented me from wanting to help those even remotely sympathetic to the Far Left (whose most dynamic ideas spring from socialism and its ideal of equality and building up the central state—that is, *egalityranny*).

In regard to *National Review,* I did admire its status as an "aginner" and its brio. But I did not like the way it stood in the way of progress, shouting "*Stop!*" And I thought it warned "Red!" a little too often, too, and did not grasp the distance between the ideals of the Democratic Party and those of communism. For Democrats of that generation, "liberty" was still a stronger idea than "equality."

I confess to having had a secret sympathy for conservative ideas like those of Edmund Burke, or even fighters in the trenches such as Whittaker Chambers. In the symbolic war between the comparatively dumpy Whittaker Chambers and the neat, tailored look of Alger Hiss, Chambers seemed a bit closer to my family than Hiss. The underdog seemed at first a bit outmatched by the aristocratic elite—a little like the guys in the mills and mines of Johnstown compared with the managers of Bethlehem Steel up on the hill in treelined Westmont.

These were not just ethnic or class feelings. Since childhood I had been studying in my youthful way the brutal ideologies of the twentieth century, and I had taken sides against the socialists—without a whole lot of sophistication, but with a long learned unwillingness to give up common sense.

I'LL SHARE ONE OTHER highly "realistic" experience of politics during my time in New York. In late July 1960, when it was apparent that the candidate I'd been working with was not going to pay me, my friend John Holley, who had gotten me into this, honorably came to my assistance. We had a meeting with the candidate. Polite, but no dice. He was having trouble meeting campaign costs himself. For my part, I needed to earn a living and had spent a lot of hours producing speeches for him. He said he hadn't used most of them. John said that was beside the point. Had Mike done what you asked? Yes. Then pay up.

John Holley was a big man whose face flushed bright red under any excitement at all. When John turned to me in the car, his face was flashing like police lights. "Have to sue the bastard, Michael. Not to worry, I'll represent you in court, won't cost you a penny. Bald-faced injustice drives me crazy. Especially injustice to my friends."

I have two memories of the trial. First, the sheer ruthlessness of the candidate's attorney attacking my past innocence and impracticality in the seminary, my inexperience in politics, my betrayal of a friend by demanding money when he had already done me a big favor by bringing me into the action, and on and on. I had no idea a plaintiff would have to sit there and hear this. With a suddenly icy heart, I thought: What can the jury do except believe this? They don't know me from Adam. This attorney has made me out to be a really worthless lowlife.

Next the candidate's attorney put me under close questioning. I decided I would stifle my impulse to protest; I would be calm and give honest, straight answers but correct him quietly where he told out-and-out untruths. Afterward I thought I had done very poorly by letting the big man swing away at me.

Then, during the recess, that lawyer came over to John to ask for a settlement out of court. "How much?" John asked. They set a price. John looked at me. I said it was about all they owed me. Enough. We shook hands.

What a thoroughly unreal experience! John explained to me that my character had shone through, and the jury seemed to be on my side. Sure could have fooled me! I never quite trusted courtrooms again. One begins with a blank slate—no truth or facts at all on it—and then is the victim of a savage attack, with mud and more mud being thrown. How on earth can anyone defend himself against that? Well, a jury of twelve sensible people must be persuaded, and jurors may also hate the mudslinging, which they too may have experienced. And sometimes some of them defend the attacked one as if they were in his shoes. Amazing to me, our jury got it right, based on very little from me. Still, the whole iffiness of the thing scared me.

It perhaps goes without saying that for a young man of twenty-six with a long career of celibacy behind him, I spent a good bit of my energy looking for Miss Right. I kept dating eagerly, one neat girl after another. After Leo House, I found a clean, quiet room in the home of an Irish family near Fordham. My third-floor room was almost as small as my room at Leo House, but it smelled starched and clean, and the walnut floors shone. My landlady, Mrs. O'Neill (not her real name), watched over my comings and goings with a smile in her eye. I liked the Irish very much, having grown up with so many of them, and I had learned from them to hold my own in banter and to end my sentences with the upward intonation of a question. Mrs. O'Neill got a kick out of that.

One evening, as I was descending the stairs for an evening out, kindly Mrs. O'Neill strolled out of the kitchen, gently rubbing a glass with a dish towel. "Going out with a girl tonight?" she asked, with a gleam in her eye.

"Not just one girl, Mrs. O'Neill—three! My friend had four tickets for the theater, and invited two friends from Boston. Three girls and me! What do think of that, Mrs. O'Neill?"

She worked on her glass a moment. Then she smiled, and said: "Well, it does say, 'Blessed art thou among women!' You be careful now, won't you? Seeing all these girls night after night."

"Say a Hail Mary for me, Mrs. O'Neill!" I said as I closed the door with a happy grin on my face.

Blessed art thou among women. I love that and quote Mrs. O'Neill to this day.

WHILE IN NEW YORK I decided to apply for grad school. It was plain to me that writing was no way to earn a living all by itself. One would have to be editing, or publishing, or employed by a university. A man could write on the side as industriously as he could, but to live he would have to find a steady (if modest) income.

With all my chutzpah—and my innocence about this world—I applied only to the philosophy programs at Harvard and Yale. I was accepted at both, but I received an additional scholarship at Harvard that tipped the scales. My thinking was that I would read fiction and poetry and plays all my life, but only in grad school could I get a foundation in philosophy that would (eventually) help me to think my way through modernity, as well as ancient and medieval thought. My dream was to build a bridge, beginning with practical things. If ethics is a branch of politics (as Aristotle proposed), that might be a good place to begin.

The chairman of the department in my first interview told me that the selection committee had been especially interested in the fact that I wanted to work on the philosophy of God. "The last grad student who did that," he said with a twinkle, "never finished his work here. He lost his faith. We'll be very interested in how you do."

4

At Least a Little *Veritas*
at Harvard

I won't say too much about my personal and religious adventures at Harvard, except for a few words at the end of this chapter. Suffice it to say I found the university exciting except for one thing: The philosophy department (during my two years there) was dominated by an extremely dry and infertile emphasis on symbolic logic and language analysis, in sheer detachment from the massive turmoil of the twentieth century. "Real" and "person" are key terms in metaphysics and philosophical anthropology, but they were not exactly hot subjects in Harvard philosophy during those years.

John Rawls arrived just as I was leaving, and his arrival, no doubt, helped to brighten things. Henry Aiken, the existentialist and phenomenologist, had been nudged out (so I was given to understand) and was now over at Brandeis. Men like Robert Nozick and Robert D. Putnam, the authors of *Anarchy, State, and Utopia* and *Bowling Alone,* respectively, were not yet around to open up a more earthy approach—and Robert Putnam was in government, not philosophy. Later, too, Hilary Putnam came to the philosophy department with his love for symbolic logic and cognate fields, but he branched out into humanistic concerns in the "I-Thou" school of Rosenzweig, Buber, and Lévinas. I am sorry I missed that.

To be sure, several of the professors of philosophy in the terms that began in 1960, 1961, and 1962 were neither logicians nor materialists. Daniel Williams, a dear man whose model and love was David Hume ("Saint David Hume"), relished metaphysics, if only as a fitting backdrop to Hume's skepticism. Rogers Albritton, a student of Wittgenstein (even down to his mannerisms), was fascinated by Wittgenstein's hints at metaphysics. However, he seemed more careful about guarding his own standing in language and logic. Roderick Firth, the ethicist, was bright, chipper, and almost traditional in his predilections. He respected Aristotle and very much liked the nineteenth- and twentieth-century Brits and Americans who kept "the Aristotelian persuasion" deep in their more narrow empiricism. The closest he came to helping me shape my own views was teaching me about the device of the "omniscient observer" in ethics. Imagine winning the approval (or disapproval) of an ideal observer, from whom nothing escapes attention, and who is not deceivable about the circumstances, intentions, and motives of an ethical action. I ran into Professor Firth a decade later when I was living on Long Island, and he congratulated me on recent articles he had admired. His was a much appreciated kindness.

But the tone of the place, which dominated even these stalwarts, rang aloud with language, logic, and anti-metaphysics. "Soul" was a word frowned upon. The questions that most grabbed me, especially those concerning God, politics, and the social sciences, were absent.

In those days the great sociologist David Riesman (author of *The Lonely Crowd*) was a mind saver for me and later became a fast friend, mostly through his extraordinary multi-page, single-spaced correspondence, dictated through his tireless secretary. Stephen Graubard, editor of *Daedalus,* befriended me and invited me to write for him. Within the department itself I felt great sympathy from Professors Williams and Firth, and even Albritton. But on the questions that most preoccupied me, especially about being, reality, and God, I had to write a handprinted card to put on the wall just behind my desk that said: DON'T THINK. I felt reduced to trying to endure the department.

I must say, however, that I was able to turn at least five of my term papers into refereed articles in major philosophical journals. I also made a bad mistake: While still a graduate student, I published two books. Young scholars, listen up: This is a dumb thing to do. You are only asking for trouble. In graduate school, your whole life and focus is best directed at graduate studies.

Harvard brought me a most wonderful thing—one of the greatest intellectual encounters of my life: I met the penetrating French playwright and existentialist philosopher Gabriel Marcel. Henry Aiken, chairman of the department before fleeing to Brandeis, had invited Marcel to give one of Harvard's most coveted lecture series, the William James Lectures. However, when the appointed year and date arrived, Aiken was gone, and the rest of the department pretty much left Marcel to himself. I don't recall seeing any philosophers present except at the first lecture, when they introduced Marcel uneasily.

You may wonder what an encounter with an existentialist has to do with politics. The subject of Marcel's series was "The Existentialist Background of Human Dignity." That question, it turned out, went pretty much to the heart of what was later referred to as the "Human Rights Revolution." Marcel was far closer to the philosophy of the playwright-protestor and later president of the Czech Republic, Václav Havel, and more amply grounded in a humanistic politics, than anyone else in the philosophy department at Harvard. He fanned the sparks in me of a lifelong interest in the "person"—an understanding quite different from that of the "individual." One can point to a schoolchild's yellow pencil as an "individual" thing. But "person" points to a creature able to reflect on her own past, approve of some parts of it, disapprove of others, and choose among various roads into the future. In other words, "person" means an individual being who is conscious, choosing, and self-directing.

Just before I met Marcel, an article of mine was published in *Harper's* in the fall campus edition of 1961. The article assigned to me was "God in the Colleges," and it set out my contemporaneous experience of Harvard and similar campuses. I later heard that my essay played a small part in influencing the drafting of the Port Huron Statement by Tom Hayden and other founders of the New Left. It certainly showed my readiness to hear Marcel. The conclusion of that article bears repeating here:

> "God is dead. . . . What are these churches if they are not the tombs and sepulchers of God?" Nietzsche asked. But much of Western humanism is dead too. Men do not wander under the silent stars, listen to the wind, learn to know themselves, question, "Where am I going? Why am I here?" They leave aside the mysteries of contingency and transitoriness for the certainties of research, production, consumption. So that it is nearly possible to say: "Man is dead. . . . What are these buildings, these tunnels, these roads, if they are not the tombs and sepulchers of man?"
>
> God, if there is a God, is not dead. He will come back to the colleges, when man comes back.

Gabriel Marcel spent himself at Harvard conscientiously, generously, and with humor greeting others, and thoroughly enjoying his lectures. He was aging then and not so hale. Those of us who saw him closely sometimes feared for his health. He went as far away as California; other times to Texas, Pennsylvania, New York, and elsewhere. He spoke, in English or French, to large groups and to small seminars. He came back to Harvard fatigued, for he did not sleep well on trips or find rest on planes. He tried to keep up with a mounting correspondence; he tried not to turn down too many requests for his time; and he tried to make himself *disponible*—a term he used to name his highest idea of virtue: *disponibilité*, the virtue of making oneself available to any who need help. First of all, it means giving a fellow human full attention, showing a willingness to help, walking the extra mile. His was a very philosophical way of describing what religious persons of many faiths regard as loving your neighbor as yourself. It is a quite natural virtue, practiced by atheists of a certain disposition as well as by devout Jews and Christians— even those who do not pass through synagogue or church doors. Marcel, after all, was a professional philosopher, not a theologian.

There is a story that provides penetrating insight and is at the root of what Gabriel Marcel had to say at Harvard. Until her death, the story goes, Marcel's wife delighted in preparing his typescripts; she kept his papers in order and saw to it that the needed lecture was in his briefcase as he prepared to leave. But one day as he sped on a train to an important lecture, Marcel discovered that his wife had put the wrong typescript in his briefcase. His first thought was of her, and he told his companion: "I'm so glad she isn't here; she would feel so bad."

It was obvious in reading Marcel's work and in meeting the man himself that for him persons were the most important "facts" in the universe. His first thought was habitually of persons; later he thought of things. Rather than insert himself into the scientific viewpoint according to the positivist's program, Marcel insisted on keeping himself outside the scientific viewpoint and within the broader framework of a questioning intelligence, a framework more person centered. A person, he said, cannot be exhausted by a list of objective descriptions; a person cannot be summed up in a series of file cards. In the William James Lectures, he told how his experiences with an information service for dislocated persons and their families in 1914 taught him the difference between *factual descriptions* and *persons*. Meeting at last with the men (or with their families) whose lives he had first met on index cards, the stunning difference shocked him into awareness. Their human reality went beyond the very long lists of facts written down on those much thumbed through cards. For Marcel, philosophy begins with wonder; but the wonder primarily concerns the mystery of the person and of person-to-person communication.

Marcel brought new light to daily experiences, such as recognizing the "presence" of other persons and "encounter" with another person—in other words, not just a passing, inattentive moment with another human being, but something more. He drew attention to the difference between sitting between two people on the subway for an hour—treating them without recognition or interest or attention—and the act of having a memorable exchange of personal qualities. He recalled paying attention to no one in the subway car until, when exiting at the train door, he paused to let a woman in a blue raincoat go first. She invited him to go first. Neither acceded—until at the same time they both did. Their eyes met, they both laughed, and each got a glimpse of the other's personality and manner. An hour later, by accident, the two met again in a room of the art museum, and each recognized the other—not as if they were like any other person milling in the room, but as if each had exchanged a fragment of his or her personality with the other before. They both smiled in recognition.

When someone ceases being just an "it" to you and appears, even for a moment, as a "thou," someone already known to you even in the slightest way, you have stepped from the realm of *objects* into the realm of *persons*. You have already glimpsed the almost bottomless possibilities of memory and experience known to that other, as well as the liveliness to new possibilities that will shape that other in the future. You have allowed a "thou" to become present to you, internalized in you, no longer a blank thing but a person reflecting, choosing, living.

Marcel spoke at Harvard of other experiences in his life that, step-by-step, led him to formulate his own "concrete philosophy." He spoke of his family, of his early idealist phase. When he spoke simply and frankly before this Harvard audience of his conversion to Catholicism, the effect, for some of us, was like that of witnessing the inauguration of President Kennedy: in spite of ourselves, and to our own surprise, we experienced a joy and a release of feelings long buried. Marcel conveyed the directness of an intelligent and faithful European Catholic, and he awakened—just by his presence and his words—the echoes of a long, solid tradition. In the light of Marcel's own history, the scientific atmosphere of Harvard seemed suddenly inadequate, and the concrete intellectual histories of the individual men in the departments seemed as significant as their "objective conclusions." The timidity and unreflectiveness of American religious people seemed irksome. Marcel seemed to pay so much closer attention to the important little details of life.

Locke and others in the English empiricist tradition give primary attention to sense data and sense experiences. Marcel gave primary attention to fuller and richer experiences than that—the exchanges of personalities that occur in everyday life, in the encounters to which we are open with others. Both approaches begin with the real, but their understandings of what is real are quite different.

Gabriel Marcel won great affection and esteem at Harvard. Then in his seventies, Marcel was short in stature; he must once have been robust. His unruly white hair or, outdoors, his battered felt hat, made him seem somehow innocent and approachable. In the lapel of his blue suit he wore the red badge of the Legion of Honor. The first night I met him, at a cocktail party just after his arrival, he sat near the doorway of the room, surrounded by a small circle of graduate students and faculty wives. He held his hands in front of him on his strong black cane; his eyes blinked and lines creased his face as he concentrated. His smiles radiated a relaxation and warmth that made brightness come from his face. He listened closely, and always as he answered it was the man speaking; it was not the position, not the pose.

When I joined the group and, in a lull some time later, asked him a question about Claudel, his eyes flashed. He replied that for him Claudel was one of the two or three great figures in French letters in our century, perhaps the greatest. He talked then of Péguy, and Bloy, and Camus, and Gide, and Maritain, and Bernanos—whose *Diary of a Country Priest* Marcel himself had discovered and championed while he was working as a reader at a publishing house. (Camus and Gide were atheists, of course, not Catholics; but they were men of deep questions and broad human sympathy.)

Afterward he took me to dinner, to speak more of that wonderful age for Catholicism in French letters. Then we walked slowly back across a dark Harvard Yard to his room. He stopped often, turning his back against the strong October breeze and the leaves it was already carrying. He held on to his green felt hat. His leg, the one injured in an auto crash some eight years earlier, pained him from time to time, he confided. It made it necessary for him to stop and rest. At his suite in Grays Hall, even before taking off his coat, he limped to his bedroom, bringing back a packet of pictures of his grandchildren, about whom he had just been talking with much pride and affection.

Using a thick rectangular magnifier to help his right eye, he sat deep in an easy chair to read *The Funeral Pyre* to me. It was one of his favorites among his plays, and in spite of his eyes watering from the effort, he read it intensely and dramatically to the end. When he finished, he blinked at me from under the circle of light from his lamp. He sat in silence for a while, much moved from the play's shattering revelation of a lived lie. I was, too; I did not want to speak.

As I rose to leave, we shook hands. "Tonight," he said, "I think we have had an encounter. I think so. Don't you?" The words touched me deeply because they voiced the inner thoughts of us both. "*Voilà!*" he said.

For me it was pointedly instructive, on a first, shy meeting with a great philosopher, to begin not with words but with the experience that the words were about. Thereafter, to learn his thought would be to complete the analysis of such experience, to render it in words. But meeting a person (any person) is so rich that at first one is without the desire for words.

Marcel's James Lectures, while sounding to auditors looser and less pointed than his best work (a later reading, we thought then, might alter that judgment), addressed the crowning question of our century: *On what intellectual grounds do we say that man has dignity?* In the unfailing moments of genius in his series of lectures, Marcel pushed us closer to an answer. Human dignity springs from the inexhaustibility of the human person, outrunning scientific descriptions and human verbalization. Our scientific apparatus plods along behind, machinelike, working out the techniques for inquiring further, like the useful drudge that it is. From every other thing in the universe, the human person is distinct. While alive, the human person is never complete; the person is always "becoming." The human person is a creator, a chooser of new directions.

Fundamentally, however, Marcel's answer does not lie in a book of lectures; it lies in concrete living. The greatest argument in favor of Marcel's purposes, methods, and worldview is that, though arduous, they can be lived—in love, in personal relations, in scientific or technical work—at no diminution to our scientific aspirations. Marcel was among those teachers of men in whom we do not have to distinguish *salva* human fallibility: what they say from what they do. He was a rich teacher.

Another of my great intellectual mentors—Reinhold Niebuhr—was introduced to me at the Harvard Divinity School, although mainly through his writings. Before coming to Harvard I had written a review of one of his early books on irony and tragedy, which came to his attention—and he was surprised and pleased to receive such attention, as he told me when we later met, from a young Catholic scholar. It soon became my aim to write my doctoral thesis on Niebuhr's Christian Realism and his (implicit) use of Aristotelian practical wisdom. Thus, I was determined to read every word Niebuhr ever wrote, including his journalism and ephemera.

I found Niebuhr's political realism—his reliance on Saint Augustine's City of God versus the City of Man, his "pessimistic optimism" (to coin my own term)—very useful for my own developing political philosophy. I wanted to model myself on Niebuhr in two chief respects: his realistic resistance to utopianism, and his habit of unmasking the pretensions of elites—in particular, the so-called political reformers. Niebuhr had begun his professional life (in the first years after the First World War) as a pacifist, only slowly finding realistic reasons for rejecting that position. As a young pastor in industrializing, tension-filled Detroit, he had learned the distinct difference between voiced intentions and real interests. He had broken with the chief journal for which he then wrote, *The Christian Century,* because of its refusal to take the rising realities of Hitler's Germany seriously and its dreadfully imprudent resistance to American "rearmament," and its failure to imagine the awful World War II to come.

Niebuhr fought his intellectual battles not only in the pages of the weekly journals but also in more probing and more lasting theological and philosophical books. He became the teacher of two generations of political leaders: both Protestant activists as well as "centrists" and "realists" such as Arthur Schlesinger Jr. and James Reston of the *New York Times*. He always served as a gadfly of the Left, stirring it to do better, and to do it more realistically. He tried to draw attention away from voiced moral intentions and toward power and interest. American Protestants, he found, were unusually uncomfortable talking about power. High rhetoric about moral hopes was their self-disguising convention.

Niebuhr's realism, by contrast, affirmed that it is much harder than facile preachers recognize to reach a moral judgment about a political decision. For example: Should the United States go to war against Adolf Hitler—or choose pacifism as the more moral course? Niebuhr's considered advice was do not ask *first* what we *should* do—especially in the context of national powers and interests. Instead, allowing for what needs to be changed, Niebuhr insisted, first get settled on these points:

1. What are the institutional, political, and material *interests* involved?
2. What *powers* are arrayed? What are the limits and weak points of each? Who is likely to prevail? At what costs?
3. What *resources of ethical analysis* do I have at hand in the tradition that I choose to live by (nihilist, relativist, secular humanist, Jewish, Protestant, Catholic, or other)?

Here Niebuhr proposed that his new school of *Christian Realism* contributed several distinctive moral axioms, based on its fresh vision of the human self. The self is not purely good, but flawed, often moved by passions and illusions, and is faced with highly contingent choices amid the turmoil of the dramas of history. Among these axioms are:

1. Expect that every man sometimes *sins*.

2. Expect that every man also has the capacity to *act virtuously* (just not on every occasion), and allow for the power of God's own effects on history and human lives to confer on weak humans the ability at times to rise even to heroic heights.

3. Expect the laws of *irony* to operate. (One's stated motives are not always one's unexamined, baser aims; and human actions nearly always end in unintended consequences.)

4. Expect to feel the bite of the laws of *tragedy*. Tragedy flows from overlooked human weaknesses that turn high hopes upside down and bring disappointment and even desolation to ballyhooed purposes.

5. Know that *decision makers for social and political bodies* must take into account factors that an *individual* dealing with another individual does not normally have to consult. In one's political role, one represents many others and cannot merely decide according to one's own familiar, personal preferences.

6. Know that in social and political actions, an agent delegated with authority commits an entire institution to long-term future actions, an institution of larger power, broader scope, and greater longevity than his own personal life—and this *difference be-*

tween public duties and personal inclinations is often
keenly felt by the agent.

7. Know that our actions in history seldom work out
as we innocently would hope. Even so, we are responsible for protecting our actions from some *un-
anticipated* (but not unheard of) *future ill effects.*

In Niebuhr's thought and practice, *experience* teaches us by our
own mistakes and those of others. Experience builds up in us a set
of internal warnings and probing sensors that instill in us a kind of
"practical wisdom," a rather tacit way of knowing what to expect. In
practice, so many unexpected things go wrong, and so many surprises barge in, that there seem an infinite number of ways to err—
and only one way to succeed: getting all significant details correct
in advance, by a kind of learned instinct. On the other side, practical wisdom sometimes counsels: Act while the iron is hot; strike by
surprise and from a surprising direction. Over the years, Niebuhr
suggested, always *take counsel* with the most experienced, wisest persons you know, those who have been through such decisions many
times. Sometimes a man's "best friends," long dead, can teach him
only through books. Even so, read and imbibe the wisdom to be
wrested from their experiences. Few are better teachers than the ancient Greeks and Romans—and the players of the biblical dramas.

There was another virtue Niebuhr insistently taught: a certain
humility before the awful contingencies of human action in history.
Nearly all great leaders have prayed for a clear head, alertness to
changes in circumstance and probabilities, firmness under criticism,
and the courage to bear up under adversity. One should prepare
oneself for the ironies and tragedies that characterize human lives—
words that much helped me on my thirty-two-day voyage into the
heart of the Vietnam War years later.

Harvard also gifted me with one other, most central, encounter—
the axial point of my life. On a blind date in Harvard Square in
March 1962, I met Karen Laub, my future wife. In the first minute
I saw that she was the woman I had been waiting and praying for.
Out of prudence, I waited another nine minutes before I allowed my
mind to close on my future course of action: "Yes, she's the one. We
are meant to be married." Of course, I didn't tell her, and it took a
full year of waiting until she reached a similar certainty.

When we met, Karen was an art instructor at Carleton College
in Minnesota. She was also a painter and a printmaker and had
studied with Oskar Kokoschka in Austria and Mauricio Lasansky at
the University of Iowa. Lasansky was for decades the top printmaker
in the world. Kokoschka loved how rapidly Karen was progressing
(on her own) and was astonished by her originality, virtuosity, and
courage. He awarded her one of the prizes at the end of his summer
session, and he told her privately she could be "the next Picasso"—a
praise that Karen held over my head, to my pleasure, all our life.

In the fall of 1962 Karen moved to Cambridge to work with a
well-known Boston artist who had a print studio downtown. The
following spring, after twelve long months of sweet yet turbulent
courtship, I proposed to her, and she, at last (as she wrote her mother
at the time), had "run out of reasons for saying 'no.'" It then took
us very little time to get married, and on June 29, 1963, we became
man and wife in Assumption Church in Cresco, Iowa, in the diocese
of Dubuque. I was so, so lucky.

Now, you may wonder what all this has to do with my political
education. You might underestimate what politically aware states
such as Iowa and nearby Minnesota have to teach. The East Coast,
they aren't. Pennsylvania, they aren't. George Laub, my father-in-
law, a hulking country lawyer (six foot four inches, and a minimum

of 275 pounds), was a jovial, gregarious man, known to everyone in the county—indeed in the region. For some years he was the Iowa committeeman for the Democratic Party—he had chaperoned Harry Truman on his famous rail trip though Iowa in 1948, his little Karen getting to sit on the president's knee on the flag-draped platform of the last car, shyly waving to the crowds. In later years George ran twice for U.S. Congress in his district, centered on Waterloo to the west. His opponent was the most conservative member of Congress, H. R. Gross, who years later ended his long career never having been defeated. My father-in-law modeled himself on his neighbor just to the north, Minnesota's Hubert Humphrey. It was too bad H. R. beat back George's two challenges.

Once, when Karen and I were driving up to Carleton, we passed a huge billboard sitting in the cornfields. Against a deep blue background, a campaign slogan in white highlighted with a touch of red shouted out: SMITH DOESN'T JUST SAY HE'S CONSERVATIVE . . . and listed his convincingly right-wing credentials. In Pennsylvania and Massachusetts, I had never seen such stress on being conservative. Out our way, the stress was on labor, FDR, progress. Even the Republicans were "moderates" all. We used to say that Democrats set the agenda, and Republicans merely cautioned "not so much, not so fast, not now." Out in Iowa, George Laub, who was very progressive, had to show he was conservative enough, and sensible, and a good fellow to work with.

It must be said that George would have wished that Karen hadn't married someone from outside Iowa—someone who was also an ex-seminarian and was studying the history and philosophy of religion. He didn't much like the East, Harvard, or eggheads studying metaphysics. He had been hoping for a young lawyer to inherit the distinguished firm he had built up over the years. Later he sometimes introduced me to others as "my son-in-law, the celestial physicist." He was inordinately proud of Karen, as I was. But I inferred that he had much opposed her going east to become "a professional art-ist," a term that summoned up in his mind barefoot, stringy-haired, loose-living bohemians living in Greenwich Village. He thought she should settle down instead as a good wife and mother and part-time artist in Cresco, Iowa—at least when we were courting, Karen hinted that was her father's vision. In fact, she had already come close to being engaged to a young man attending law school who shared that vision. Worse for me, she loved this young man (to a degree I didn't know), which put me in a battle to woo her away. It was a battle worth all those long months.

After I did not pass my comprehensive exams in the spring of 1963 (I felt certain the hated logic had done me in), the chairman of the philosophy department called me in to tell me that I had done well enough that he and some of the other faculty had gone to the Divinity School to discuss transferring me to a recently established program in the history and philosophy of religion, jointly adminis-tered by the philosophy department and the Divinity School. The Divinity School had accepted the proposal. The downside was that I would have to take two more years of coursework, but my scholar-ships would stay intact. I could also have a semester's leave to observe the second session of the Second Vatican Council from late Septem-ber until early December in Rome.

I swallowed hard at having to do two more years of coursework. This would be the fourth consecutive two-year sequence of course-work I would do in graduate school—two years in Rome, two at Catholic University in Washington, two in the Harvard philoso-phy department, and now two more in the Divinity School. My most ardent desire was to write novels. I was being courted to move back to Pennsylvania to run for the local congressional seat against a long-seated Republican incumbent. I now had the responsibilities of a newly married man. In the end, I decided that, oh well, I would come out a more richly *educated* man, and I took the deal.

That is how my beautiful young Karen and I got to take our second honeymoon in Rome that fall, which led me to begin writing for journals all across the world—articles from a layman's point of view on the day-by-day course of that most dramatic big Council of the century, only the twentieth in 2,000 years. Some 2,600 bishops from every part of the world flew in to sit on bleachers in rows inside St. Peter's. The West's oldest living institution struggled to renew itself and gain a fresh start before a new millennium approached. Karen and I had a blast.

By surprise, I inherited a contract for a book on the session, which had to be completed six weeks after the Council session adjourned early in December. Karen worked on her seventeen great classic prints based on "The Apocalypse," the first such series since Albrecht Dürer's in the fifteenth century. Karen pushed hard in December to get this immense work done, and I worked like crazy, too—with two stenographers and one editorial assistant—to get the manuscript of *The Open Church* (Macmillan, 1964) to New York City by January 16, 1964.

5

The Second Vatican Council, Second Session

The experience of living in Rome from September through December of 1963 during the second session of the Second Vatican Council was the next important part of my political education. The West's oldest living institution was undergoing a painful *aggiornamento* (bringing the Church up to the present day). Together with the youngest ever president of the United States (elected at age forty-three), and the burgeoning civil rights movement in the American South, a new spirit was stirring in the world—and new hope that cracks might eventually appear in the ice of the Cold War, hope seldom seen since World War II.

After our wedding that summer, Karen and I had put more than $2,000 in cash in the bank, thinking this: A worldwide Council of the Church takes place on average only once a century. How could we, a young writer and artist, possibly be absent? Karen, who loved Rome more than any other artistic home, and I with my fond memories of Rome and my vocational preoccupations in the history and philosophy of religion—how could we possibly be absent? Unforgivable! I asked Karen if she would consider taking a second honeymoon in Rome until at least mid-January, and her mischievous eyes lit up. She had promised herself before marriage that she would not go back to Europe until she could go with a husband who loved art. Karen went right to work planning the autumn. She took charge of working out our sea passage and ordered a Volkswagen Beetle from the factory in Wolfsburg, West Germany.

Karen also started immediately on sketches for a long series of lithographs she would complete in Rome. For my part, I bought all the books that had been published in English, French, and Italian on the first session (1962), and I also pulled out the young Lord Acton's personal report on the First Vatican Council (in 1870), which would be my measuring rod. We had nine days aboard ship to look forward to.

Once we took to the sea, Karen began writing longish letters on our trip for the *Cresco Times–Plain Dealer.* She was a vivid writer, and the joy she took in detail after detail is still a pleasure to read.

> Our ship, the SS *Provence,* left promptly from Pier 13 in New York at 3:30 p.m. on September 3, 'mid much confetti, tearful good-byes, and the noise of a rousing shipboard band. Ben, Michael's younger brother who is at Penn State, saw us off, and your [her father's] beautiful 'Bon Voyage' corsage cheered us. It was a deep purple orchid which lasted for five days and was admired by all. It was a perfect complement for our dressy evening dinners.

Karen especially loved the dances held each evening after dinner. Since I was not a dancer, far too self-conscious and stiff, I encouraged her to dance with others, and she did so with gusto. She described very well, too, her awful sickness during the second day, how she took to our tiny stateroom and sweated, twisted, and turned in misery.

After two days she came out on deck for the rest of the trip, and the fresh air brought her to full vitality. We had one of the best times of our lives.

When we were two days out from Europe, just when I was running out of the reading I had brought from home, the ship closed its library. The only thing there I had found to read the day before was a biography of a leader I truly disliked: Richard Nixon. Karen laughed out loud when I showed her the book. I forced myself to read it, lest I die of boredom. Yet I did learn more about conservatism in America than I had known before—and glimpsed a view of the world quite different from my own. Unexpectedly, however, I found some of Nixon's perspective disturbingly similar to my own. For instance, I sympathized with plain, ordinary working people more than with university and Hollywood elites. And my relatives were a lot more likely to be cops or soldiers than young urban professionals. And I did not find the press evenhanded, although as a Democrat I was happy it wasn't.

THE WONDER OF ROME in 1963 was the intensity of conversation—at dinners, at cocktail parties, on long walks, sitting on benches in some age-haunted park with the warm sun on one's arms. We met with bishops, journalists, illustrators, editors, friends of friends. Everybody in the world, it sometimes seemed, was passing through the city and wanted to take us at least for a drink (plus an earful of free background or even theological tutoring). Why not? There passersby might run in to John Cogley, Robert Kaiser, Walter Lippmann, Michael Harrington, ambassadors from around the world, magazine publishers, documentary makers, movie stars, architects, and hundreds who did pencil sketchings or watercolors. Our centrally located home at the Pensione Baldoni (near the Castel Sant'Angelo, once Hadrian's tomb) became a haunt of some of the Americans at Vatican II.

Bishops were streaming in from every diocese in the world, accompanied by little swarms of black-cassocked experts, often bright and upcoming priests (each bishop was allowed to bring two). The future Cardinal Bernardin was one who visited in our pensione. We found it a bit comical to watch all these important bishops, princes of the Church in their own dioceses, used to being chauffeured in shiny black cars, now forced to climb in and out of crowded school buses with everybody else, or else travel in chartered buses from some hotel or other. They looked like an army of Santa Clauses being bused round at Christmas to all the department stores. Packed in with brother bishops in the buses, they looked more like schoolboys than muckety-mucks. The bright violet robes they wore, which back home stood out wonderfully against everybody else, here were part of a dense crowd, like a fraternal guild from the Middle Ages.

It was somehow reassuring to see bishops so humbled. They themselves felt it, and for the first time recognized in the flesh what an immense worldwide fraternity they were part of. By the hazards of the alphabet and their personal months of service, they found themselves in their assigned seats (crowded into St. Peter's in the bleachers built just for this splendid four-year occasion). One could easily be seated next to a bishop from Nigeria on one side and a bishop from Malaysia on the other. They discovered beside them men who were, like them, not specialists in theology, and were as friendly, as modest, and as besieged with similar headaches as they were. Many took up a correspondence with these distant friends that lasted a lifetime.

Vatican II was front-page news around the world. If the most time-encrusted and hidebound institution in the world was examining its own conscience, instituting reforms, and taking in large gulps of fresh air, well then, any institution in the world could do so. And *should*—that seemed to be the subtext. Camelot in the United States, the young president—the whole world seemed to be in the grip of the "new" and "rebirth" and "change" and the "now." It was the most intense and electrifying and, yes, loving and kindly atmosphere I can remember or even imagine living through again. Somewhere I have a photo of one the most recalcitrant, flinty, and hard-nosed of the American Catholic priests on the conservative side beaming and, with a shy smile, eye-to-eye with the once rabidly anti-Catholic Paul Blanshard. The two of them looked like the best of newly met friends, like fresh roommates together for the first time. Those were the days when, as the joke went, the new rubrics called for referring to Beelzebub as "our separated brother."

But the main business occurred in the long morning sessions of debate within the walls of St. Peter's, where argument and counterargument went on day after day, according to the agenda. On some days a secret written ballot vote was taken: *placet* (yes), *non placet* (no), or *placet iuxta modum* (a lukewarm affirmation). And every day at noon, down the broad Mussolini-built Via della Conciliazione, there was an English-speaking briefing on the morning's discussion on the Council floor, with crisp outlines of the chief points made and ample time for journalists to raise questions. At first, there was still considerable suspense about which "side" would win and on which major issues. As time went on, this pattern was almost always in evidence: the forces on the side of reform and renewal received well more than half the vote—not quite two-thirds but verging on it. The suspense then became how large the margin of difference would be. The more solid the vote, the better the chances of its governing the final Council documents with strong language.

Issue, of course, differed from issue. Some were more about practice and pastoral concerns: Should the language of worship be the local vernacular, or should it remain the "one and universal" language of Latin? Others were about some of the deepest questions of theology: What sort of community is the Church? What is the relation of the authority of all the bishops bound in one universal communion to the designated authority of the Bishop of Rome, the pope, the "first among equals"? How far toward Protestant pluralism can the Catholic Church move and still retain the strength of its unity? The Catholic Church has been from the beginning a pluralistic unity, not only of Rome and Constantinople, but also the special rites of Alexandria, Antioch, Ethiopia, the Maronites, the Chaldeans, and others who were colorfully visible at the Council.

It was during the second session that the balance of bishops tilted decisively toward what in journalistic shorthand we ink stained wretches called the "progressives" in the Church. Their adversaries were the "conservatives"—or even the "archconservatives," the "traditionalists," or the "party of fear."

These opposing camps could be distinguished more theologically, based on their fundamental conceptions of doctrine in history. One party liked to think of the Church as eternal, unchanging, bound forever to its basics. Yet often they understood these "basics" in the idiom of the sixteenth and the highly defensive subsequent centuries. In *The Open Church* I coined the term "nonhistorical orthodoxy" to describe this view. The alternative view, I ventured, is best understood as the tendency to take all definitions and even key terms in their own originating context. In most ways, those glibly called "progressives" were actually striving mightily to go back to beginnings, and apply the slow, evolutionary steps of the Catholic "development of doctrine" (John Henry Newman's phrase) in response to the new questions of each new age, era by era. In some ways, the progressives were the true inquiring, probing traditionalists.

On the one side, serious men stressed the eternal, nonhistorical, essential character of the Catholic faith: true today, yesterday, and for all times—the one eternal Church, holding to the same essentials from age to age. On the other side, serious men stressed the hazards, limitations, and glories of the existence of the Church in time with its struggles, its internal doubts and conflicts and the temporal resolutions thereof, its ability to see only a limited number of the facets of truth, given the limited development of language, concepts, and accumulated insights at any one particular time—the adventure of partial understanding, hard-won clarifications, and sudden conceptual breakthroughs that set the whole context in a new framework, a larger paradigm.

A number of intellectual breakthroughs were required—sometimes simply the study of historical materials never dwelt on before—to distinguish, for example, the many differences in the meaning of the word "grace" among disparate writers, at different times, in different contexts. To understand the living, historical meaning of terms requires historical knowledge of an extraordinarily learned kind; it is not simply given by consulting a dictionary put out at a certain time and place. At various historical periods, humans may have struggled to articulate the same truth in different ways. Yet it is as wrong to concentrate solely on the accidents of history while overlooking the essential continuities as it is to do the reverse.

On the other hand, merely to concentrate on the conceptual essentials, while missing the adventure of how these were arrived at by historical creatures of flesh and blood, is often to come away with a merely "notional" understanding of the essentials. One memorizes the definitions given in dictionaries or serious textbooks. But one loses the blood, sweat, and guts of the intellectual battles through which, one by one, the elements of those essential things came to be recognized, in all their developing historical fullness. Some proposed developments of doctrine, true enough, turn out later to have been wrong, since they embody a deceptively hidden logic that works its way out only over generations. Discernment is needed, as well as humility and long prayers to the Holy Spirit for warding off falsehood masquerading as legitimate development.

An observer should not miss the fact that each side in the dispute between the nonhistorical and the historically minded has something powerful to communicate, and that each of us, without exception, is *capable* of discerning the merits of both. But that in turn always requires great expenditures of patience and goodwill. Still, when one group of serious thinkers leans toward the essential and nonhistorical side and a rival group leans toward the existential and historical, they are likely to give quite dramatically different twists to virtually every argument they consider.

EVEN TO THIS DAY, I meet Catholics who disapprove of my rightward turn, especially in politics and economics, but who smile and say, "But one thing I really like of yours is *The Open Church* and that stuff on nonhistorical orthodoxy. Great stuff."

Nonhistorical orthodoxy came to be widely accepted as a highly useful interpretive key in thinking through what exactly separated the two main tendencies of the Second Vatican Council. In this I had a comparative advantage over other public interpreters of such matters: I had studied quite recently under teachers who were the supreme models of the at first overpoweringly strong, and later the weaker, of the two main historical tendencies at the Council. I had already been thinking through for myself the chief divisions between the two schools among my teachers. I liked and admired all of them enough to rule out the possibility that there was some special moral fault weakening one side and some special moral virtue bolstering the other. Now, in God's eyes it might have been true that the "conservatives" were the more saintly party and the "progressives" the more self-indulgent (and even vain) party. I don't give much weight to that either way, for the issue was not who had the higher morality or superior saintliness. Rather, the difference fell out along an *intellectual* divide. Who gave the better account of our faith?

Even at Vatican II, the straightest road ahead was not by way of simpleminded "progress" but by an ever deeper probing of tradition. The fundamental struggle was getting to the living core of tradition—to love the past in order to help it find new but traditional forms of living faithfully in the present. That was the "spirit of Vatican II." It was truly, deeply, probingly more traditionalist than the so-called conservatives, whose tendencies were formed by the most recent four centuries. It was also many times more two-sided than today's progressives, who cannot even admit that Bishop Karol Wojtyla and the priest-theologian Joseph Ratzinger were among the deepest and most influential progressives of Vatican II. The decisive difference is that today's progressives think of the tradition and authority of the pope and the bishops with considerable hostility. The true progressives at Vatican II did not. For almost all, the experience of Vatican II gave them new respect both for the living power of tradition and the authority of all the bishops of the world in union with the Bishop of Rome. So it has been for two thousand tumultuous years. The way the Catholic Church works in history is quite humble, among imperfect and even fault-laden humans, moving (often much too slowly) along a sinewy path in the jungle, where patches of light only occasionally break through the darkness.

SOME REALLY HISTORIC DECISIONS lay ahead as October 1963 spread its cooling arms over the city. Our new generation had an unusually hopeful view—almost a utopian view—and a supreme self-confidence in our superiority over all previous generations. We were guaranteed to suffer a very great fall and an immense disappointment. I remember feeling from the very first a sense of bitter irony and impending disaster. Both Karen and I, in our different ways, could not help having a rather darker view of life than most. We always expected the worst—but then were delighted by the little things that turned out beautifully.

Perhaps the greatest of all decisions to be made by the Council was to define how the "People of God" (the Council's new way of speaking about the Church) down through history had vaguely, hesitatingly, but consistently thought about the relation of the primacy of the Bishop of Rome (Saint Peter and his successors) to "the Twelve" (the College of Bishops throughout the world). The People of God had always thought of itself as an institution, a community, not simply a collection of individuals. For example, when Judas betrayed "the Twelve," the institution could not be set straight until a successor was elected, thus keeping the original "Twelve" intact. The point is not the number twelve, but the sense of a whole in need of completion. As the generations went on, the College of Bishops would inevitably grow larger and larger. A little more than a century after Christ's death, shrewd observers would marvel at the fact that in so short a time the Church had spread all around the Mediterranean, which was then the whole of the "known" world. From the second century, great Catholic teachers were speaking of a "universal" people (that is what "catholic" means), made up as *one wine* "from many grapes," *one bread* "from many grains of wheat."

The Council in effect proposed an image of concentric circles— one people given their unity by being loyal to a visible institution, led across the centuries by worldwide ecumenical councils that gather all the bishops together around the pope. If for at least a hundred years (since Vatican Council I), more attention had been concentrated on the pope, the one Bishop of Rome, *the* traditional sign of unity among the people, Vatican II restored the image of the pope as working with and through the whole communion of bishops worldwide. Vatican II took care to emphasize the unique role and perspective of that one Bishop of Rome among others—and in so doing took conscientious care to be faithful to Vatican I. But the Second Vatican Council did help to contextualize the emphases of the First Vatican Council, and to grasp the whole in which the separate parts and roles are made one. It defended the unique, living principle of the whole people: unity with the Bishop of Rome. It defended the unique role of the pope, even while noting that his distinctive role was to bond together the larger unity of the College of Bishops, spread throughout the entire inhabited world and plainly witnessed in action in the bleachers inside St. Peter's.

Much of the "progressive" world, both outside and within the Church, shot right by this fundamental continuity of Vatican II with all its predecessors. It missed the tremendous historical depth of the research contributed by theologians of the earlier twentieth century, who had launched a mighty movement they themselves called "recovery theology" (*ressourcement*)—a sustained probing into the sources of Catholic life, an intensely conservative work, propelled by love for the deepest living streams of the older Catholic traditions. To climb up to *aggiornamento* (today) one must first reach for strength in yesterday.

Within a few years after the Council, I found myself reacting more and more negatively to the large faction of the "progressives" who failed to grasp the truly conservative force of Vatican II—its revival of ancient traditions, its sharper disciplines, its challenges to mere worldliness and mere politics. I began moving from left to right in restoring real contact with the actual texts of Vatican II. Even at the Council, the progressives seemed to be dividing into two parties—one modeling Church on the most recent and new thinking of the age, the other steadily deepening the balanced official texts of the Council. One took strength from the enthusiasms of the secular press, the other took strength from the contrarian, countercultural voice of ancient truths of great importance today.

In other words, my first movement from left to right began in religion. It went slowly at first. This move did not begin to creep into my political and economic principles until my experiences at Stanford, in Vietnam, and at SUNY Old Westbury.

My favorite saying from Vatican Council II was "All things human, given enough time, go badly." In not a few respects, Vatican II did go badly, especially inside the Church among priests and nuns and in the ranks of its educational and journalistic elites.

On balance, Vatican II had enormously beneficial fruits for the Church and for the world. But it carried within it its own personal tragedies and institutional ironies. The gargoyles of the ancient fountains of Rome once again observed with sardonic irony another generation come and go, now down Rome's twentieth-century streets, but not nearly as glorious as they thought themselves, not nearly as pure and sinless. And yet, in the words of William Butler Yeats, the mouths of the gargoyles might also have been babbling: "Everything we look upon is blest." The Holy Spirit really did permeate Vatican II even more deeply than many so earnestly prayed for.

On November 22, four friends and I burst back into our pensione, only to find Signorina Baldoni somberly but loudly shushing us, ostentatiously drawing me aside. Karen had stayed behind that afternoon to take a nap (she had not been feeling well). The Signorina had convinced herself that Karen was pregnant, so in a loud whisper she said we should not disturb "Signora Karen." Then she whispered that President Kennedy had just been shot in the head in Texas. She shooed us into the corner room to watch the television. The TV picture was fuzzy, and the American anchors and announcers were still in a state of confusion and uncertainty—some with

choked-up voices, all trying desperately to maintain their compo-
sure and a suitable solemnity. What was happening in Texas just at
noon was reaching us in the early evening in Rome. We felt sick to
our stomachs.

For weeks we had convinced ourselves that we were witnessing
the threshold of a new era, a long awaited time. Even the more cynical European journalists had been writing about the hopefulness of
a new, young president of the United States appearing at the same
time as a new rebirth of the Catholic Church. Everywhere it had
seemed like the beginning of a New Age. And now . . .

John Cogley of the *New York Times* telephoned the pensione.
He had just turned on his TV. He was stricken almost too deeply
to talk. Three years before he had been summoned to work with
the nominee in mid-1960 to co-write his crucial Houston address
to a group of Baptist ministers. Many of the latter had grown up
thinking that Catholics were of the devil, the Whore of Babylon, the
whole raison d'être of the abrupt turn by the Protestant Reformation
back to "real Christianity." Many of them thought (and preached)
that a Catholic in the White House would start work on a tunnel to
the Vatican and bring the country to decadence. Kennedy's chances
to carry the South in the 1960 election were doomed if this bigotry
went unchallenged, so Kennedy had decided to meet it head-on,
right in the open. Now just over three years later, he was dead. He
would have no further chances—not at anything, anything at all.

In 1961, when my younger brother Richard, a newly minted
Catholic priest, was sent down to Georgia on a brief summer assignment, he was partly amused, partly horrified, when little children
timidly approached him to ask if they could have a look at his devil
tail, which they had been told every priest kept hidden under his
cassock.

When the Baptist ministers had assembled in Houston, Kennedy
walked into that auditorium to face the lions directly, with calm and

clarity. John Cogley had come to feel like a brother to the soon-to-be president.

Cogley had felt, as I had there at Harvard on Kennedy's Inauguration Day, a great lifting of weight off his shoulders, an unexpected rush of release, the experience of a new birth, politically and culturally. Both of us had rejoiced in the subsequent celebrations of "Camelot"; ironic and silly as the idea was, it was contagious. Now we felt only the senselessness of the television set in front of us, one scene being replayed over and over, as the open convertible pulled slowly around the circle in Dealey Plaza in Dallas. The head of the president snapping forward, his collapse, and Jacqueline Kennedy bending over him. This squalid killing. Death. Our own youthfulness slipped away, never to return.

Karen was awakened by the commotion. She was, with all her inner sense of death and absurdity, as desolate as the rest of us.

My brother Dick's senseless murder in Bangladesh only two months later knocked both of us down again. We had taken a plane from the Old Continent on January 16, the same day (unbeknownst to us) that Father Dick, all of twenty-seven years old, was being knifed to death in East Pakistan. It was the tail end of a month of Muslim-on-Hindu violence. Thousands of Hindus were slain; some rivers became choked with their bodies. Months afterward Dick's head was found by a Bengali detective along one of the riverbanks. The detective told me of this in person some years later at the opening of the Father Richard Novak Memorial Library at Notre Dame College in Dacca.

Both Dick and I, after studying the questions raised by Thomas Aquinas in his long dialogue with Muslim scholars some seven hundred years before, had committed ourselves in college—we were both studying to become priests—to bridging the gap between Muslims and Christians. Dick really tried to do something about it; he volunteered to go to a Muslim country and learn Arabic. He had wanted to become the newest—and, if possible, the best—interpreter between the two traditions. His self-sacrifice was one of the first fruits of the Council.

Father Richard had very quickly become a champion of independence for Bangladesh while he worked among both poor villagers and his students (and their families) at Notre Dame College—which was attended by many who later moved into the ranks of their new nation's elite, including a future ambassador to the United States who invited me to the embassy in 1996 to speak his praise of Father Richard. He gave credit to Father Richard for the national prize he won in logic, which launched his career. I ran into similar testimonies from prominent Bengalis down the decades. I think Dick will one day be declared among the martyrs of the Church, and that, one day, the Bengalis themselves might put up a small monument to him. Fifty years after his death, he is still remembered there—even revered. *Laus Deo!*

6

At Stanford, Turning Left

While attending the Second Vatican Council, Karen and I took some marvelous trips. We visited Assisi, for one, with Robert McAfee Brown, the famous theologian from Stanford University, and all autumn we had dinner with him often. This is the reason why, early in 1965, I was invited to interview for an opening in the nascent religion department at Stanford. Bob was a student and colleague of Niebuhr—he even owned a summer cabin near the Niebuhrs in western Massachusetts, not far from Stockbridge. Some people thought Bob was the nearest thing to a successor to Niebuhr, or even the legitimate heir. It was fun to team-teach with Bob, as we did maybe twice over the next nine quarters. It was a chance for me to learn about a whole new world of people, arguments, and ideas. Karen was also happy to be in the company of both Bob and Sydney, his very practical and activist wife.

I really loved teaching at Stanford. I loved everything about it. Those three years were among the happiest of my life. They were happy from the first moment that Karen and I, stopping off in Iowa, climbed into a brand-new, fully loaded station wagon (a white Plymouth Fury), which her father bought for us as a wedding present.

Surrounded by the scents of a new car full of comforts, Karen and I were in love with each other and eagerly expecting our first child early in December 1965. It was August as we headed across South Dakota's baked prairies toward Mount Rushmore, then on out to Wyoming. We glided by in awe at the Rockies above us and the light-shafted national forests along the highways.

The Stanford campus is surprisingly lovely, even when you visit it for the second, third, or even hundredth time. The air of the valley is the softest air on earth, bearing the light fragrance of orange, lime, and lemon trees. The Palo Alto air rests gently on one's arms, as if at a lower air pressure.

Karen found a new home for us close to the public swimming pool and the public library, graced with both orange and lemon trees in the small backyard. It seemed heavenly, and we began preparations to make a down payment. We had our first real home—albeit without any furniture yet.

The first course I taught at Stanford unexpectedly marked a big turning point in my future political development. The course was on Aristotle's *Nicomachean Ethics* and Thomas Aquinas's commentary on it some sixteen centuries later, together with the addition by Aquinas of the central concept of *caritas* (the special love that constitutes the inner life of God, and is infused into those open to it by his free generosity). Aristotle had written that *phronesis* (practical wisdom) is the inner spring and dynamism of all the virtues. Aquinas agreed with regard to the natural virtues. But Aquinas knew that Christianity infuses nature with *caritas* (God's own loving grace, offered to humans who accept it), which acts in much the same way but is led a bit more by the loving will than by the intellect alone. *Caritas* pushes the intellect where it hesitates to go, and yet it needs the intellect to criticize it and keep it honest and real. To be sure, Aristotle *almost* recognized an analogous role for the heart, the will, the longing for the good. Aristotle saw that one's instilled self-governance of natural appetites—and even one's inclinations in friendship and eros—pulls at one's intellect. He defined the kind of intelligence that operates in ethics as practical intelligence rectified by goodwill in action: *recta ratio agenda* (reason in action, guided by our goodwill).

The highest joy of that course was reaching the point in Aristotle's back-and-forth ascent of the mountain, trying to winnow out what practical wisdom actually *is*, when he at last turns to lessons learned from sports. Exemplifying practical wisdom is to get all points, factors, and nuances of doing exactly the right thing in the right way in the right circumstances—as an archer, drawing upon his thousands of experiences in shooting his bow, at different distances and angles and in different winds, takes accurate measure of the tensile strength of this string, the heft and smoothness of this arrow, and the power of this bow, *and hits the mark*. Scores a bullseye. *Thunks* the arrow right into the center of the target. To do so, the archer has to get everything right that might affect that singular shot.

I LOVED MY STUDENTS at Stanford. Each year I probably taught a fourth of all the undergraduates. Each quarter, in addition to a small seminar, I also offered a lecture course in the largest lecture hall on campus, Memorial Auditorium ("Mem-Aud" in the catalog), usually frequented by 250 to 300 students. One of the most popular of these courses was "Belief and Unbelief," and another favorite among the students was "Christianity and Modern Literature." The course that did most to shape my own slowly developing political principles was "Christian and Secular Ethics," which allowed me to treat the works of Reinhold Niebuhr extensively, especially *Moral Man and Immoral Society*. On the secular side, I lingered on my Harvard favorites, Albert Camus and his secular saint, Dr. Rieux of *The Plague*. In a way I didn't then foresee, both of these writers became models for my slow turn from left to right. Niebuhr was the very model of slowly moving from left to right—not so much in economics, it's true, nor in party sympathies. But from utopianism, for sure. Camus, too, was working his way out of utopianism to a hard-earned realism.

Albert Camus wrote eloquently about the intellectual proximity of the serious believer and the serious atheist: "What do they lack but churches, these atheists of our generation, men of rare compassion, to distinguish them from being Christians?" (my paraphrase). There are saints among both believers and unbelievers who give up their lives to help suffering humankind. Other witnesses, both believers and unbelievers, have made much the same point about experiences they lived through in Dachau, Buchenwald, and Auschwitz—and in the vast, shadowy, and much less studied Gulag archipelago. Under persecution, belief and unbelief can be quite close. No one sees God; one feels no lift to the heart.

At Stanford I encountered again a young woman whom I had met in Boston when I was lecturing over at Newton College (run by the elite Madames of the Sacred Heart). Her name was Kathie Mulherin, and I hired her to help me with typing and some light research. Kathie later wrote a piece for *Commonweal* that chronicled the radicalization of former moderates and conservatives at Stanford, citing my own case as an example. As I recall, she emphasized that I was temperamentally conservative, while being driven more and more in a radical direction by the force of reasoned arguments and harsh experiences.

For example, Karen and I (virtually alone among Stanford faculty) went with some of my students to a protest in Oakland, across the bay, at the regional office of the Selective Service. Our purpose was to offer moral support to those who wanted the option of conscientious objection to this particular war. The protest was to be nonviolent, but the city police turned out in full battle array, and the mood grew hostile and edgy. A few activists threw their bodies down in front of the advancing police line and were treated to a taste of rude, unforgiving force. Most of us, including Karen and me, stood back against the Selective Service building, out of the way of the advancing police. That day was an ugly one. We were glad to stand by our young friends in their hour of need—and glad also that, for all but a few purposeful activists, the day went safely enough.

The radicalization of more and more students occurred with every fresh event in the chain of absurdity, pose, and half-truth that characterized American political life during those days. In October 1967 Karen and I, along with more than a thousand Stanford students, traveled to Oakland to watch long lines of marching policemen advancing against fellow students, their feet falling heavily in the street and the sun gleaming from their helmets. Together we saw the naked force on which "law and order" rested, and we saw whose law and order it was: cop after cop had a prosperous pot belly and blue eyes, and the plainclothes inspectors, captains, and FBI photographers wore the same haircuts and suits as congressmen, businessmen, professors, and the active military. Several dozen students and two faculty members who "sat in" in protest spent ten days in the Santa Rita prison in October, and some served harsher sentences of twenty days in December. They experienced the stupidity, petty cruelty, and viciousness of the county prison system, and they became friends with the blacks and the poor who were fellow prisoners.

Meanwhile, the government had begun to put Stanford draft resisters in jail. The new draft policy showed Washington's contempt for pragmatic administrators and student radicals alike. A war against the Johnson-Humphrey version of the American way of life seemed to become more necessary every day. Student conversations turned to a probable guerrilla war in America's cities coming soon, along with acts of sabotage. An ROTC building was burned to the ground at Berkeley in January. Within a week, bright flames licked the wooden Navy ROTC structure at Stanford. The arson, officials noted grimly, was skillfully executed. Booklets from Canada explained how to make Molotov cocktails, use explosives, and set fires. Students whose humanistic convictions had once made them believe that killing was immoral had been placed in the position of being forced to kill anyway—either in Vietnam or at home, either Asian peasants or American whites. Most Stanford radicals remained pledged to nonviolence; however, the number of those who crossed the line toward violence (at first only in principle) seemed to increase monthly.

It was much easier to lecture on Kafka to Stanford students then than it had been just a few years earlier. Madness, nihilism, suicide, revolt were daily, nerve-jangling issues. The tortured characters of Dostoyevsky's *The Possessed* no longer seemed remote and abnormal. The choices of Bonhoeffer, Camus, and Sartre against a different sort of tyranny had become models to consider fearfully, because one's own future was at stake. Education had become a *serious* business.

I moved from Niebuhrian Christian Realism to a guarded support of radical students. I was born with a conservative temperament, but I tried hard to inspect opposing arguments closely. Reluctantly at first, I concluded that at key places those who were part of the New Left had better arguments, which the Old Left was not successfully rebutting. To explain the details of this shift here would take up an awful lot of space. The example of how I changed my judgment of the war in Vietnam *twice* may give an indication. The record of these changes can be traced through my articles in *Commonweal* and the *National Catholic Reporter,* my most frequent outlets during those days.

As that war heated up during the Kennedy years, I supported the Kennedy effort, fortified by reading the three book-length reports on the war that became available while I was still at Harvard, including David Halberstam's *The Making of a Quagmire.* Halberstam was already becoming famous for his fearless criticisms of the Kennedy effort in the *New York Times.* All those criticisms and more were fleshed out in his book. Yet even he, its tartest critic, concluded that Vietnam was a war worth fighting—only in a more competent way. His conclusion greatly influenced my first judgment.

Given my temperament and my attachment to Niebuhrian realism, I was becoming a neoconservative before that at first tiny movement was named. In 1965 I wrote an article on Vietnam called "Our Terrorism, Our Brutality," which argued that reports from the shifting battlefields gave a picture of a very ugly war in which enemy combatants were mingled with civilians—a war without front lines or massed armies (except on very few occasions). We all wished we did not have to fight such a war, and that it would soon be over. But we were right to fight it, I announced, except not with any sense that we could do so in innocence. I faced how bad things were but still came out in favor of the war.

However, I became more critical of the war as I learned more and more about it. In 1967 Robert McAfee Brown, Rabbi Abraham Heschel, and I contributed a chapter each to criticizing the war in a pamphlet called *Vietnam: Crisis of Conscience,* published by a group called Clergy and Laity Concerned about Vietnam, among whose founders were Martin Luther King and a number of the mainline clergy of Manhattan. One of our aims was to call into sharp focus the communal implications of both Jewish and Christian faith. Faith that focuses solely on individual judgment about the moral life of individuals falls short of biblical faith. Sometimes the prophetic teachings of the Bible must also be called upon in moral judgment of political matters, too, as in fact they always have been, as against slavery and segregation, and in regard to some of the nation's wars such as the War of Independence, the Civil War, the Spanish-American War, and World War II. The American political conscience was again at a crisis point regarding Vietnam.

I judge that my essay in that book was the most guarded and historically meticulous of the three. In the end I resolved, using the just war theory, that the war in Vietnam was not justifiable on all four required counts: just end, just means, sufficient grounds for hope of victory, and morally proportionate means. The United States may have had good cause to enter the war—to protect the legitimate independence and the liberties (partial but real) of South Vietnam. The pro-war case rested in part on the assertion that, in direct violation of the Geneva Accords, there was an active but surreptitious move southward of overwhelming numbers of North Vietnamese troops. I laid out the case made by Theodore Draper's long article in *Commentary,* that the evidence then visible in Vietnam did not support that assertion. But I had never been there myself.

By the end of the war, it had become clear that Draper and I had been wrong. A great North Vietnamese invasion of the South had in fact been taking place, more rapidly as time went on. It became starkly visible when, after the Americans left Saigon in ignominy, the disciplined, uniformed troops that marched into the city were crack North Vietnamese divisions, not pajama-clad guerrillas. I had allowed myself to be deceived.

My position gradually became this: Although the initial U.S. war aim had been correct, Vietnam was not a wise place to launch a huge jungle war. A distant nation could deploy hundreds of thousands of men in those jungles and take huge losses without success. And among popular opinion, some of the U.S. methods and means seemed to be self-defeating. Thus did I put realism at the service of the (modified) radical position. I did not trust the "real" radicals, who seemed often to be in contact by telephone with leftists overseas. I was not a socialist; concern for the fate of my family still in Slovakia deterred me from that.

Not until 1968 did I finally reason that one of the justifying causes for a just war was increasingly tenuous. The jungles of that distant battlefield more than 8,000 miles away and the close-in nature of the daily combat (right into cities themselves) made success far less likely. By then I was arguing that the United States should work toward a reunification of North and South Vietnam on solid human rights principles. Most of the people in the South who were ardently opposed to the Communists were Catholics who had been driven out of or had fled the North; they longed for a just and safe reunification. Of course, this turned out to be utopian: *if only* such idealistic aims were in fact rooted in realities on the ground. American will had weakened, and the North Vietnamese seized the victory. My determined attempts at realism were not hardheaded enough.

Nonetheless, with each year that passed I became more and more dismayed with the impersonality of the draft lottery—its excruciating effect on young men trying to plan for and be serious about the course of their futures—and the lack of candor, even the doubletalk, of those charged with leading the war. I feared the radical left, but even more I resisted the "pragmatic" and in part self-deceived liberals.

I ended up arguing that we Americans would be held morally responsible for how we withdrew from the war, as well as for how we had gotten into it and how we had fought it. Our great task was to negotiate an accord between North and South Vietnam that would not allow for the enslavement of the South. But that enslavement is what actually happened. Those film clips of thousands of South Vietnamese fleeing their own beloved lands on rickety boats, robbed and raped by pirates all along the way, desperately seeking freedom, haunts me still.

The American anti-war movement had shed many tears over the treatment of the South Vietnamese people during the war; it evinced no concern at all about their far more brutal fate once the United States withdrew. Joan Baez, the great folk singer of the time, was a noble exception. She did protest against the North Vietnamese beatings, torture, and "re-education" camps. As for me, I learned a sharp lesson about the double standards and moral unreliability of the political left.

My concluding reflection on the Vietnam War, after the fall of Saigon in 1975, was that the Soviets and the Chinese would interpret the collapse of American resolve as a characteristic national weakness. They would use surrogates as full-time burglars, going down the hallways of the world systematically looking for new rooms to break into. Soon enough Angola, Grenada, Afghanistan, Syria, Iran, Chile, Nicaragua, and El Salvador followed. Refugees from such places poured into the United States and Europe.

It was indeed an ugly time. Even then, I came out of it feeling that I had not been as steady in my thinking as I would have liked to have been.

7

Thirty-Two Days in Vietnam to Cover the 1967 Election

I flew to Saigon in early August 1967. My son, Rich, was twenty months old, his sister Tanya was expected to arrive in two months. Karen wore a worried look as I departed.

I thought I must see the country for myself. Besides, three Stanford students (Dwight "Dee" Owen, Tom Fox, and David Truong, the son of that year's presidential candidate, Truong Dinh Dzu) were already in the country, as was Don Luce, leader of the International Voluntary Services (IVS) at Stanford. They all wanted me to experience for myself the salient facts on the ground, which they thought were not being reported accurately.

Dee was working with the Revolutionary Development Team (probably under the CIA) in Quang Ngai in the North. Tom was working as a civilian volunteer in Tuy Hoa, a village near the coast of central Vietnam. David Truong's family invited me to travel with his father's campaign both in Saigon and up-country. Don Luce offered me housing in the Saigon house of the IVS. I was certain to see a large portion of the country and have access to experienced guides and translators. Since I had written in support of the war based largely on David Halberstam's book from the battlefield, I was sympathetic to our military in the field and their mission, but I was not certain that our military strategy was right.

Traveling beside me on the last leg of the plane trip to Saigon was the young Jonathan Schell, who was later to become famous for his vivid report from Vietnam, *The Village of Ben Suc,* detailing the massacre of villagers by an American patrol led by Second Lieutenant William Calley.

Every few days I filed reports for the *National Catholic Reporter* by mail. They usually appeared two weeks later. Let me here condense some of these salient steps in my political education.

As a newcomer on the scene, I found Vietnam a hall of mirrors. I could never be certain on whose side my informants were. For example, a man who gave me a ride on his motorbike from downtown to the IVS residence told me his name was Thac and showed me papers purporting that he was an appointed electoral officer in a large hamlet just outside Saigon. For what purpose—to discredit elections or to discredit the army officers representing General Thieu and Colonel Ky of the current government, I could not tell—he explained to me how, as an electoral official, he would cheat. He would get the government total up to a high proportion of the vote, no matter what actual votes came in. He told me no one had asked him to do this, but he knew the government expected it of him, and his job was at stake. He also told me he was a Catholic; he said that most of the Catholics had fled North Vietnam, really hated the North Vietnamese, the Vietcong, and the Vietcong guerrillas, and supported the government.

Thac said that most people would not vote. "Say in my hamlet there are 1,000 voters. Maybe 600 will vote—maybe 200 for Thieu-Ky, 200 for Huong, 200 for I don't know. Then I add 300 for Thieu-Ky. Nobody know. Thieu-Ky get 500 votes. It look like ninety percent of people vote. Nobody know." The original ballots were destroyed immediately after the count.

Thac told me that during the previous year's election for Constituent Assembly, he went to vote late in the day. A friend of his was the official in charge. "You are a dutiful citizen," his friend commended him. "You are only the thirteenth person to vote all day." (There were more than 200 voters in the hamlet.) "It was late," Thac continued, "so I was surprised to read next day that, in the official count, between 80 and 90 percent in my hamlet cast votes. You see?" he said. "It is easy."

Later that night, Thac unexpectedly came back to the IVS residence and showed me an even fuller batch of his official papers, but he asked me never to use his name in what I wrote. "I am not afraid," he said. "If you write a good article, I will have done something for my country." But whom was he actually working for?

A few days later I headed up north to one of the most hotly contested provinces in Vietnam, Quang Ngai. Dwight Owen, one of the Stanford students who encouraged me to see Vietnam for myself, had invited me for a visit. People in the regional development teams, like Dee, scorned the massive military operations, preferring to live with the people, teaching and encouraging them right on the spot. They trained them to protect themselves by setting up night ambushes in the surrounding jungle against Vietcong marauders, and they also helped to improve the schools and local agriculture. When I arrived, Dee said a battle had just occurred on the seacoast (the part of the province he was responsible for) the night before. He was about to drive off in his jeep to check it out and gestured for me to jump in. I lifted my knees to adjust to the sandbags that covered the whole floor of the jeep. Turning toward me he smiled wanly: "Land mines."

On our way out to Junk Base 16 on the coast we paused at an

open-walled but well-roofed school, of which Dee was very proud. "The men of the village just completed it. I brought them the materials myself. Neat, isn't it?" The teacher waved when she recognized him, nodded to the class, and in unison they shouted out a happy greeting. As we rounded a sweeping bend, the road bounced us pretty good, and the smell of the sea reached us.

Junk Base 16 was one of the most heavily fortified strongpoints on the Quang Ngai coast. It was defended by 118 men from the Vietnamese navy, along with five U.S. naval advisers. At night the navy's armed junks patrolled the coast, trying to intercept fishing vessels bringing supplies to the Vietcong. The previous night, when fifty of the complement of junks and half the men were at sea, the base had been all but destroyed by a force of at least 200 Vietcong opening fire. It was 3:00 a.m. The reduced defensive force held the swarm off for about ninety minutes before being overwhelmed. One Vietnamese officer, who was the first man to flee, was still shaking the next day, unable to hold steady.

Dee and I dismounted from the jeep and walked up to an American assessment team. The highest ranking American adviser, a lieutenant colonel, estimated that the mine field surrounding the camp had been defused. The machine guns of the night sentries had been sabotaged in advance; several sentries were found dead at their posts, some with jammed guns. A blast had blown the eight-inch concrete wall of the command post outward, as if a bomb had been planted in advance. The commander had been killed, but he previously had good relations with the VC. One of the Americans wondered aloud whether he had crossed them.

The assessors found sixteen of sixty-eight defenders dead, with about thirty-five wounded. About twenty of the women and children on the base were also dead. The dependents' quarters were leveled, but the main camp, though torn up, was still standing, and the officers' quarters, though ransacked, were virtually untouched by fire. The highest ranking American adviser had been killed. Another American had been blinded as he escaped from his bunker, but he somehow found his way through the barbed wire and over the embankment to the water. When he was found hours later in the junk of a fisherman who had picked him out of the water, his face was covered with wood splinters.

As the day waned, hundreds of villagers fled the area by foot, bicycle, and Lambretta scooters. Others fled by fishing boats up the river channel in order to get closer to Quang Ngai City. Our interpreter, a twenty-six-year-old student at Saigon University, told us the villagers resented both the South Vietnamese and the American troops, who couldn't defend them, as well as the VC who had attacked them.

Obviously this attack was about more than Vietnam's presidential election. One woman at the base, when asked what she thought of the upcoming election, had to be told what an election was.

My first night back in the compound in Quang Ngai, Dee and his friends put me in a stucco building about ten yards from their quarters. One slid a loaded rifle just under my bed and put a revolver in my hand. "If anybody knocks on your door, even staff members you recognize, do not answer them and do not let them in. We're close by. You're protected by the heavy wall from the street outside. Get a good night's sleep."

I sat on the bunk and assessed my surroundings—not far enough away from the wall to be safe from a grenade. I didn't sleep well that night.

The next day Dee invited me to go with him on a night ambush, assuring me it was usually boring. He did say that every so often his eager bunch got into a mean firefight. He also forewarned me that the Vietcong had put a bounty on his head. At six foot five, he was referred to in Vietnam as "Mr. Tall." His invitation stirred dreams I'd had ever since I was a boy. But when I measured myself against the task, I feared I lacked training with weapons and tactical behavior. I told this to Dee and said I thought it would be foolish for me to go with him—but after I left Quang Ngai, I regretted not having gone.

When I said good-bye to Dee the next day, he was sleepy from the night ambush. I told him I might go with him next time. Meanwhile I had to get back to Saigon to spend three days with presidential candidate Dzu, who wanted to take me along on his campaign back into remote villages outside the northern perimeter of the capital. It was heavily Buddhist territory—and very fertile in votes for him. I told Dee I would come back after spending three days with the campaign.

I need to mention that some years later, Mr. Dzu's son David Truong, the Stanford student, was arrested for espionage. In Vietnam I learned that there were many people playing both sides as a self-defense. Back in Saigon, I asked the middle-aged Vietnamese interpreter for the *New York Times* how he had learned such good English. He told me he had begun studying English when he saw the French defeated at Dien Bien Phu in 1954. On a whim I asked him what he was studying now. He answered, "Chinese."

Back in Saigon, it was taken for granted that the team of Nguyen Van Thieu, the chief of state, and Nguyen Cao Ky, the premier, would win easily. I was lucky to be able to focus on at least one of the challengers. Through his son, I was able to stay in Mr. Dzu's home for some days, and when on the third day I came down with diarrhea, his beautiful wife took care of me. I formed a good impression of Truong Dinh Dzu and his party, the People's Unified Front. Some observers ranked him as the second or third most serious civilian candidate. I had seen in the villages that Dzu had strengths among the Buddhists, and he had taken pains to get in writing a pledge to support him from each of the Buddhist leaders of the region.

The symbol of the People's Unified Front was a white dove. Dzu's campaign platform proposed that South Vietnam, not the United States, should lead the way in negotiations with Hanoi, which would give rise to the premise for a gradual withdrawal from South Vietnam of both U.S. and North Vietnamese forces.

In Saigon, both Vietnamese and American reporters shrugged when asked about the prospects of Dzu's candidacy. But Dzu was not a nobody. He had an extensive law practice, including a large American clientele, had been close to but not involved in every Vietnamese government during the past ten years, and had the asset of having served time in solitary confinement under the cruel regime of Ngo Dinh Diem. A Vietnamese newsman described him, half deprecatingly, as "our only candidate who speaks fluent English."

Dzu told me that his plan foresaw the withdrawal of approximately 50,000 American troops yearly over eight years. His aim in negotiations with Hanoi was the eventual reunion of North and South Vietnam. "We do not wish," he said, "to inherit the fate of Germany and Korea. We wish to show the way to a peaceful settlement of national reunification."

Dzu told me that he thought the South Vietnamese government, which "invited" the American presence in Vietnam, should request the Americans to stop bombing the North and to allow secret North-South discussions. He suggested that it wouldn't be difficult to arrange open contact with Hanoi, the Buddhists, and other Southerners. He argued that the South Vietnamese could negotiate with their own countrymen far better than the Americans could. "This is the first war the Americans ever fought for nothing," he told me.

One of Dzu's persistent themes was that the North and South

were one nation, not two; reunion was inevitable and "blessed by the stars." Dzu was matter-of-fact about taking the stars seriously. A learned astrologist had told him he would be president of Vietnam before he was sixty years old. He was sure.

After three days in the field with Mr. Dzu, watching him visit for long periods with the Buddhist monks in many villages, I hurried to get back to see Dee, as I had promised.

At the huge military base at the Saigon airport, I had signed up as "press" for a ride to Quang Ngai. After a wait of some hours, a gruff sergeant barked out the names of six or eight men, myself included, who were now authorized to board the last plane to Quang Ngai. I asked him if I had time to duck back into the departure hut for a Coke. He said, "Make it quick. Run." No sooner did I exit from the sandbagged hut with my Coke, running all the way, than I saw my plane lumbering down the runway. The SOB had done that deliberately.

It took a while to hitch a ride back to IVS for the night. I had some dinner and then wrote to my wife. I told her my intention to go back to Quang Ngai City to see Dee. I didn't mention any ambushes. The day before my letter reached her, she had heard the news of a Stanford student killed in Quang Ngai. Now she panicked.

When I finally arrived in Quang Ngai the next afternoon, the driver sent to pick me up was tight-lipped. Not until I got to the compound did the news dribble out. The VC had hit the city full force Wednesday night, August 30. They dropped mortar fire on parts of the city and then sprang nearly 1,200 prisoners from the city jail. Many of these prisoners now rejoined the twelve VC battalions operating in the province.

In a sweep of the area to seek the attackers that morning, Mr. Liu, the chief of district revolutionary development teams, was traveling toward Tu Binh village, east of Quang Ngai in the direction of Junk Base 16. Meanwhile, intelligence was received in Quang Ngai that two VC battalions were in that vicinity and that a heavy ambush was awaiting Liu and his small force.

A small group of American advisers, including Dee, left Quang Ngai at about ten a.m. August 31 and sped toward Tu Binh to warn Liu. Just west of the village they halted their jeeps and hurried by foot to circumvent the ambush.

The small band made contact with Liu near Tu Binh. All were returning through rice paddies and a field of grain when a strong enemy force poured fire their way. "Mr. Tall" and a companion were breaking for fresh cover when a grenade landed between them. The concussion dropped Dee to the ground. When he rose, he was struck by a bullet. With his companion's help, he was able to run another hundred yards toward the jeeps. But he was too weak; he fell and died.

At his burial service in the compound, I cried a little, prayed, and took a few photos for his family, in case I might later have a chance to meet them. Luckily, I did meet them years later. Mrs. Owen was a granite rock, cheerful and inquisitive even under the heavy weight she bore.

On election night itself, in a large theater downtown, I found myself a couple of seats in an uncrowded row in the middle. Other journalists greeted me indifferently. They knew who I was from a couple of trips we had taken together—like the night we were flown to Da Nang, where a few hours before a heavy mortar attack had been launched on our "invulnerable" air base. In the thick darkness, we had toured the damage with torchlights. At one barrack that had taken a direct hit, we arrived just as some soldiers were sweeping out into the dusty street a small wave of red blood from one of the Americans killed that night. His term of service over, he had been scheduled to take a plane home the next morning.

Among the journalists, you could tell the level of status by the way the stars carried themselves, or were deferred to by others. "David's here!" or "There's Gloria, over there." My own status as an amateur was negligible. Still, I did have one small and recent hit. I had published an article on the immense work the Catholic Relief Services of the United States was doing with hospitals, clinics, food supplies, and other necessities. To my surprise, though, the CRS was not "neutral." It was clearly not helping people in Vietcong areas but instead limiting itself, more or less strictly, to the areas of South Vietnamese (and U.S.) presence. Obviously, this was partly for security. As a strong opponent of the Vietcong and a firm supporter of the war to keep South Vietnam independent of the North Vietnamese and the Chinese, I mostly approved of this strategy. Still, it seemed that Catholic relief ought to be as broad as God's love, bringing care even to "the enemy."

That humble article attracted attention back home. The *New York Times* recapitulated it on their front page and wired their offices around the world to look into this in Vietnam and elsewhere. The Catholic Relief Services undertook a broad and deep reconsideration of its tactics in the field around the world. I am saddened by some of the later effects of my article, though. It helped contribute to the sickly atmosphere of "moral equivalence" between contending forces. I strongly believed in the moral superiority of forces fighting for freedom, and I detested the perversely backward use of the term "liberation forces" put forth by Communist cadres of repression around the world.

Yet from an orthodox Catholic point of view, one test of Christian love is the love of one's enemies—not from a human point of view, but from the point of view of a God who loves every single human person, whom he created for that love.

It is best to keep these two moral standards clear and distinct—the natural, human one, and the higher one that Christians are called to, nearly impossible for humans, but possible for those who love with God's own love within them. States are not bound to that supernatural love, but in their private capacities Christians are. The inner energy of CRS does not come from state interests, but from the personal interests of the Christian heart. Or so, against my patriotic views and against my commitment to political liberty, I reasoned.

REPORTERS KEPT FLOWING IN to that downtown theater on election night, milling around and exchanging information: the latest word on the street, conversations they had taken part in. (Most didn't mention the stories they meant to use themselves.) As we all expected, the hour for releasing returns kept being put off well past the announced time. It was perilously close to the Saigon curfew when the first serious returns started coming in. For quite a while Mr. Dzu was running first, then a close second, then first. . . .

With Dzu in the lead for almost an hour, I was the beneficiary of a strange new respect. There were no computers in those days, but some reporters were getting nudged by home offices about my articles on Dzu in the *National Catholic Reporter* ("What the hell is that?"). First, journalists from the *New York Times* sauntered over to me and asked what I knew, followed by *Time*, CBS, and a steady trickle of others. Since my mailed-in article would appear in print long after theirs had, I had no competitive reason not to give them what I knew about Dzu—his strength in the Buddhist areas, his out-of-sight village campaign. Dzu knew what Americans didn't, that in the villages the best medium of mass communication was the Buddhist monk. No one out there had television.

As it turned out, the votes for Dzu began to wane, and in the end Thieu and Ky won—with a plurality but far from a majority. Counting all the votes for the different "peace candidates," Dzu leading among them, some 60 percent voted for peace. Considering all the votes in the army and the swollen government (and their families), the government party got a stinging rebuff. But they had won.

When the reporting of the returns was winding down in the election night theater, and it was clear that Dzu had finished second, it was way past Saigon's nightly curfew. No one was permitted in the streets without a pass. Naturally, there were no taxis or rickshaws to take me home. I hadn't thought about that in advance.

The IVS residence was at least three or four miles away. The streets were empty and still. As I stood there weary and perplexed, a military jeep approached me. It was driven by an officer, by the brass on his shoulder a colonel, in full uniform with a pistol on his belt and an automatic rifle at his feet. He asked me in good English where I needed to go. I wasn't certain from his expression whether he was friendly—I had already met one colonel who, I learned, was working secretly for the Vietcong. When I gave him the address, he offered to take me there. I really didn't trust the mischievous look on his face, but what alternative did I have?

We rode on and on with the night breeze upon our faces, past the frequent streetlights of the city, out where it got darker and darker. He looked down at his automatic weapon and darted me a deliberate smile. We drove quite silently. At one point I didn't recognize where we were. It seemed to me that he had missed the key turn. But he actually did bring me to the IVS house, which was now entirely dark.

My not quite trusted colonel stopped the jeep abruptly at the walkway, thirty paces from the door. As I thanked him and turned to let myself out, I saw his hand reach for his pistol. After I took three steps toward the door, I heard him cock his pistol. I thought: *I'll be damned if I'll let him see an American run.* I kept my steps deliberate. I got my hand on the doorknob, then turned to give a wave, and let myself in. I could hear the jeep turning sharply and loudly, and through the small window I saw his headlights sweep around toward the city. He was probably laughing.

A FEW DAYS LATER I flew back to California. My thoughts, feelings, and impressions were pretty much a jumble. Being in Vietnam had certainly given the term "complex" a new meaning. Going slowly through my Niebuhrian list, I had identified many powers and interests at play in Vietnam. I hadn't seen much, or heard much, about any material interests for the United States—the best things I saw were steadily good weather for two, maybe three, harvests of rice per year, and a very long, beautiful seacoast. I had seen on all sides a passion for fighting until death.

Help the Vietnamese to reunify again, I kept thinking. *There's no other way there will be peace. And badly needed economic progress. But that will take a long, long time.*

On the flight home I felt there was so much heavy work to be done back in America. I was afraid the Chinese and the Soviets might draw many misguided lessons from an American defeat. They might begin pushing in many other places around the world, certain that they had us on the run. In Vietnam I could sense that the war on the ground was going better and better in places such as Quang Ngai, where there were intelligent local leaders like Dwight Owen and their teams. But I doubted if the American people could possibly keep up their patience with the effort so many thousands of miles away from Vietnam's steamy jungles and rocky hills.

The irony of Vietnam: so much heroism, so much goodness, and so many dark jungle paths! John F. Kennedy was correct about the inescapable and precious cause of liberty. He could hardly have been so clear-eyed on just how heavy the burden would be, and how high the price to pay.

8

Bobby Kennedy and
Gene McCarthy

I had already announced in the late spring at Stanford that I would depart at the end of June 1968 for a new position at the experimental college of the State University of New York, located at Old Westbury, Long Island. Not long after that announcement, classes being over, I got a call from John Seigenthaler, famed editor of Nashville's *The Tennessean*. He told me Robert F. Kennedy was coming to San Francisco that night and would like to meet me in person the next day at his hotel. "You know," Mr. Seigenthaler said, "it was your article 'The Secular Saint' that got to him. It was the final prod to his announcement of his candidacy. He knows you're a leader of young people around the country, and he wants to meet you."

Political aides frequently talk like that, so I had no idea how much to discount. I got the main point, though, about being in San Francisco the next day. Besides, that article had appeared in *Motive Magazine*, edited by the sophisticated and delightful B. J. Stiles and published by the Methodist Student Movement in Nashville. So it made sense that Seigenthaler would have seen it and given it to Bobby.

There was one difficulty. Just a few months earlier, candlelight dinners had been held all around California in support of getting my old friend Gene McCarthy on the state ballot for the Democratic primary. I had been a minor leader of that write-in campaign, and I took great pleasure in it, for Gene was my kind of Catholic. We had read most of the same books, especially of what those in the know called the "Modern Catholic Renaissance" of the twentieth century. A brilliant sunburst of Catholic writers had exploded across the darkening skies of that bloody century, a great many of them converts to Roman Catholicism, and some great "close neighbors" such as C. S. Lewis (whose book sales during that period were second only to the Bible) and probably also the greatest poet writing in English, T. S. Eliot. Neither Lewis nor Eliot had joined the Roman Catholic communion, but their minds had certainly plumbed its artistic and intellectual traditions.

I couldn't possibly switch publicly to supporting Kennedy without calling McCarthy first, and that would be a painful conversation. Yet I had already been telling Karen that McCarthy was not pulling the numbers from the working-class Catholic and ethnic districts across the country that he would need to win; he was drawing the suburban vote ("Clean for Gene") much more dynamically. The sudden new idea of supporting Bobby was very tempting to me.

I told Mr. Seigenthaler I would be happy to meet Kennedy, and he gave me the time and place. When I arrived at the hotel lobby the next morning, Seigenthaler, holding a newspaper under his arm, came rushing across the polished floor and led me to the elevator. Bobby was waiting over coffee in his suite.

This was clearly, I saw, a working campaign suite, with rooms off to the left and right. Not much was going on yet. The spring had flown by very fast, with primary after primary coming into view as relentlessly as ducks in a shooting gallery—hit one, miss another, keep firing away. All too late, Kennedy was at last concentrating his attention on Oregon and California. Oregon came up first, in a week or so. But the real prize would be California.

Bobby was in shirtsleeves, a slighter man than I had imagined, and terribly vulnerable, wounded almost, somehow saddened and rote-like, and yet burning with determination. I had already written in an article somewhere that the more the pundits and the experts called Bobby "ruthless," the more I liked him. I had thought his candidacy was inevitable. The ethnic working peoples of the cities were hoping for someone ruthless to come in and crack some heads to get things moving. They knew by experience that this would take a very tough guy.

Bobby began by saying how much he had been moved by my "Secular Saint" piece. "Liked it very much" was his laconic understatement—anything more would have sounded sentimental or flattering and, after all, we were now in the neighborhood of Dashiell Hammett and the taut, tense language of those who had known a tough life and been knocked around.

"Look, I need you. I know your reputation as a leader of the younger generation. Around the country, not just here in California. I'm going to need the young people. I'm going to need every single voter I can get. This state is going to be very tough for me to carry this year. Very tough. We started too late. Well, very late."

Bobby had a way of gazing off into space. Part of him was living somewhere else. Yet the fire of his determination kept bringing him back to the task at hand. It seemed like he poured as much into every working minute as he could, to get it right, but not an extra second more.

"This is all going to end in Chicago—everybody knows," he confided in me as if I knew everything about political campaigns. Truth is, I had never been engaged in one. I had just read a lot about them. I could only hope I nodded sagely. "Mayor Daley's going to decide this one. I know he doesn't think I can win California. 'California,' he says to me, 'is the big one. You win California, I'll see what I can do. Otherwise, don't come to me. Understand?'"

Now, all this is my memory forty-plus years after the fact. The quotations may not be exact, but I am certain they represent the gist and pace of what was said.

"An election these days is really two elections. I have to run one way to win the primaries. I have to run another to win the country. But first I have to get Mayor Daley's help. And that comes down to California."

I had never expected to get to the center of his campaign on this first meeting. He didn't owe me a thing.

"I need your help," he said. "Oregon is next, and that's where you come in. McCarthy's strong up there. But we have some surrogates coming in, and I want you to be among them. I want you to go to Oregon for a week, speak at the universities, generate some news." The room fell silent for a moment, and I noticed that the air conditioner was already running. He took my arm, looking me directly in the eyes. "Can you do it? I'd like that very much."

"I'd . . . I'd love to," I stammered softly. "There's only one thing. I helped Gene McCarthy get his campaign launched here last January. Gene is a friend of mine. I'm convinced I ought to help you, because you can win. But I have to make a call to Gene first. Can I have twenty-four hours?"

He took that pretty straight. "Okay, you call him. Then get back to John here. I really hope you will join us. It is really important that we win California, but first of all Oregon." He nodded farewell, we shook hands, and Seigenthaler led me to the door, handing me a note with his number on it. "Until tomorrow," he said. "Good discussion. Good meeting."

I walked slowly down the soft rug of the hallway to the elevator. As it descended, I thought to myself, *What the heck do I say to Gene?*

When I called Gene later that night, I just put it bluntly in two or three sentences. He was obviously wounded, but he ended the conversation with something like, "Well, Michael, you do what you have to do. But I still think I'm gonna whip him in Oregon and beat him in California. Thanks for calling, anyway."

It cut me to the quick to turn against Gene's candidacy just at the crucial moment. *"Et tu, Brute!"* I am also absolutely positive, now as then, that Gene did not agree with me about how the primary votes up to that point were turning out. I thought he was doing less and less well among the urban ethnics, state by state, and better and better in the cheese-and-Chablis "constituency of conscience" (as it was called at that time).

To my mind, the strategic constituency in the United States of 1968 and thereafter would be those traditionally Democratic precincts in which the vote went as urban ethnics went—all those Catholics and cognate types whose grandparents or parents came from southern and Eastern Europe. Mostly such folks did not speak English when they arrived, and they had to work their way up steadily, the hard way. By 1968 they felt that the Democratic Party was theirs, and now it was being taken from them. Since a great many of their comrades in arms were also Irish, a Kennedy versus McCarthy cut across some tender lines. To my mind, Mayor Daley represented the quintessential urban ethnic (although he was far too partial to the Irish, and tended to respect the others no more than necessary), and I was fairly confident that McCarthy, to Daley's eyes, represented a different part of the Midwest from the part he championed, gloried in, and embodied.

For me something deep was going on in the contest between my old friend Gene and this candidate I hardly knew, Bobby Kennedy. I thought it was very important that Kennedy win the presidency. He was the only man in the country—well, not the only one, but the most *inspired* one—who could bring equal excitement to two diverse audiences at once. The urban ethnics would cheer him on, and so would the blacks who, more and more, were living in the same neighborhoods. That, to my mind, was the greatest cultural hurdle for this nation to jump during those two decades, the sixties and the seventies. (You never heard of a race war back then, did you? That was the dog that didn't bark. There were a lot of people brought along by Bobby Kennedy who worked everywhere, in city after city, to make sure that didn't happen.)

I loved Gene McCarthy. But I loved this particular cause more. Gene understood this cause, too, and thought that he could bring a better cure than Bobby. I saw the lines of class running in a different direction. In any case, I kept recalling Aristotle's line, to bring myself a little comfort: "I love Plato. But truth, better." Here the issue was not truth, but racial healing and class rebalancing. My dream at that time was later fulfilled by the "Reagan Democrats," who picked up the banner Reagan waved: "Work, family, neighborhood, peace, and strength." It helped, I thought, that Reagan was an Irishman, a former Democrat himself, a union man who had learned the ruthlessness of low-level communists as he went about doing his job.

In 1968 we were a long way from that. But as John Lewis and I plodded down the streets of one campus town after another in Oregon, we were in a way dramatizing the very point that was most important to me. John was the civil rights hero from Georgia, one of the founders of the Student Nonviolent Coordinating Committee, who had gotten his head bashed in by angry cops. He had become a kind of martyr-hero; I was the descendant of miners and steel men from a rough town in Pennsylvania—and we were both handing out large blue buttons for Robert Kennedy. (First, we had to learn to pronounce "Oregon" the way its citizens do: The last syllable rhymes with "gun," not "gone." Luckily, someone corrected us early in the game.)

To make a long story short: Bobby Kennedy lost in Oregon, and

Gene McCarthy won. So now the full weight of the 1968 campaign would come down to California. I was fairly confident that Mayor Daley would not be too depressed by Bobby's losing Oregon; that would be like Daley losing the western suburbs outside Chicago—it didn't really matter. It would have been better for Bobby to win Oregon, too, but California, with its huge battalion of Democratic votes at the convention and its commanding electoral vote in the autumn election to come, was the big prize.

WHEN WORD GOT OUT in the spring of 1968 that Karen and I were leaving Stanford, some of the students planned an ambitious going-away party for us, attempting to contact everyone who had been in any of my classes. The leaders reserved a large room in the university dining hall, about half an hour after the main dinner was served. Somehow they had hung lots of crepe paper and a few hand-painted signs; somewhere someone had obtained a large, thickly iced cake, and carbonated cider was served. There was a master of ceremonies, and a mysterious present sat in a large, beribboned box wrapped in white tissue paper, not far from the microphone. Eventually the gift was presented to Karen and me, and we cut the paper. There stood in all its glory a shiny black Stanford captain's chair, "so that we would never forget Stanford." (I have that chair still; a wave of gratitude wells up in me every time I look at it.) The approximately three hundred students who were present clapped, and I was invited to the microphone. I remember a few emotional words but have no idea now what they were. How does one convey one's love and gratitude without becoming maudlin? I opened the floor to questions.

There were a few serious ones, a few brief testimonials, and lots of laughter. Then came the most gripping question of all: Why had I switched to Bobby Kennedy? I knew most of my students were invested in Gene. After all, I had helped them become so, in public meetings outside the classroom. No one suggested that I had been a traitor to Gene, but most were seriously puzzled. I did my best to explain what I have recounted above, but more briefly, and I called attention to how important the upcoming election was going to be. It probably would be the axis upon which the rest of the next ten years would turn.

EARLY ON THE DAY of the California primary, I got a call saying that Bobby had asked whether I would like to fly from San Francisco down to Los Angeles on his private plane to spend the evening with him there. My problem was that I had been away from my wife rather a lot, and we had a young toddler and an infant—Richard was not yet three, and Tanya only seven months. I was deeply appreciative, though. The early predictions that day looked very good for Bobby, and I would have loved to be there. I was powerfully tempted, but I felt I had to say no.

Thus it transpired that, not long after Karen and I had put the children down and turned on the television to get the last returns from Los Angeles, we saw the horror unfold. There was the just-arrived Bobby being escorted into the hotel the back way, with his close aides (I might have been among them) at his side, when suddenly a man stepped forward, his hand up—people shouted; Bobby crumbled. *Oh, my God! My God! No. No.* And everything inside me just went blank.

part two

Ethnicity,
Economics,
and the
Universal Hunger
for Liberty

9

The Old Westbury Experience

As I was finishing up my appointment at Stanford, I had a visit from
Harris Wofford, chief assistant to Sargent Shriver in the founding of
the Peace Corps and former civil rights adviser to John F. Kennedy.
Harris wanted to talk to Karen and me about our joining him on the
founding faculty of the new experimental college of the State University of New York at Old Westbury. He could offer me an appointment as full professor with tenure (he thought), teaching philosophy
and religion—although SUNY had so far not recognized religion as
a legitimate field of study.

The main thing Harris wanted to communicate was the excitement of founding a new university, an experimental college for
SUNY and, in fact, for the whole United States. A university where
all students would be "full partners," and new ways of weaving together learning and action would be explored. Work on the new
curriculum would begin in August. The first faculty and the first
student body (about a hundred students) would assemble on a temporary campus at a famous estate on the north side of Long Island,
near Oyster Bay.

It didn't take us long to decide. Out in California, Karen missed

the thunderous storms and occasional tornadoes, the colorful au-
tumns and white Christmases back east. We both loved Stanford
and had enjoyed our time there. Karen's painting and her big
exhibitions—in San Francisco, most of all—had gone swimmingly.
But now we had two active children. The thought of a whole estate
where they could roam and the warm company of a small faculty,
led by Harris and his beatific wife, Clare, pulled at us quite a bit.

I thought Old Westbury would be interesting because one of the
earliest tensions in my sense of the vocation I was made for was between my desire to become a novelist and philosopher, as well as an
influential political writer. I had become fascinated with the comple-
mentarity of fiction and philosophy, and then with the complemen-
tarity of philosophy, theology, and political influence. It seemed as if
Old Westbury would bring me closer to my inner calling.

I was proud to be asked to take part in the project, and I looked
forward to it eagerly. I had thought I understood the language of the
New Left—its logic, its deeper, inarticulate springs. I had thought it
reflected some of the tumultuous quest—after so much pragmatism,
so much value-neutral pretenses—for conscience, honesty, courage,
and community. The gropings of the student movement of the late
1960s, as I experienced it in my own students at Stanford, reminded
me of Albert Camus's struggles to find a way out of nihilism and
Reinhold Niebuhr's awakening to evil.

I have thought for years about how to describe those first two
years at Old Westbury. Some of the things that happened there were
just too surreal. One example: Many of our students went barefoot,
and others wore flip-flops or very thin sandals. One night in pitch
darkness, on the spacious flint entrance of the main mansion (then
our administration building), someone had painstakingly turned
hundreds and hundreds of thumbtacks sharp-side-up all across the
floor. Anyone stepping inside unawares that night or early the next

morning would have gotten an awful set of prickings, more so if the shock made them jump and keep stepping up and down.

Although for a long time it was hard for me to admit it, many things at Old Westbury were just crazy, rebellious, and anarchic. Yet every deed, when finally brought to light for discussion, was accompanied by justifications taken from classic texts of the modern Left, not least in France: anti-liberal, utopian. When I told people that Old Westbury drove me to the right, they retorted that the tiny college was by no means typical of the Left. True, but everything done there was done in the name of leftist writers: based on equality, systematic suspicion of authority, *hatred* for authority (plus a suppressed but ardent search for it), and contempt for normality and "bourgeois" norms. All of this made me face the full implications of the deep leftist principles, and face them in an overruling left-wing context, without any palliative or other form of reason. In moving leftward at Stanford, I had begun to accept the premises of these principles, seeing them as a kind of salt to give savor to a middle-class campus. With no rightward-pulling balance at Old Westbury, I was sometimes left speechless. A little salt is one thing; all salt is awful.

When we first moved to Old Westbury, our family lived in a modest brick home on campus, surrounded by flower gardens. Karen also had one of several Quonset huts on campus, painted in earth colors, to use as an art studio and for offering lessons to any students who might want instruction.

One day I must have said something that rubbed some students the wrong way. An ugly scrawled note signed by "The Committee" appeared in Karen's studio, quoting me and threatening the children. Such a note could be taken only half seriously; overheated imaginations were hardly unknown on campus. But it was a bit of a worry—and also disgusting.

Maybe a year after I left Old Westbury, I wrote a short story called "The Experimental College at Athensbury." It had been scheduled for publication in *Harper's*, but a new editor opted to bump it in favor of another manuscript of mine, a nonfiction piece on the family. Later "Athensbury" was published in a collection of essays called *Religion as Story* (Harper & Row, 1976). I now include it here, because it tells the essential story of those first few years at Old Westbury more understandably than any other way I can think of.

THE EXPERIMENTAL COLLEGE AT ATHENSBURY

The stars were right. Youth was in ascendance, nay, at zenith. The hour for experimental education struck. Athensbury, long existent in the Master Plan of the State University and the Cosmic Plan of God, was ushered into life.

The two years set aside by the state for planning for the first one thousand students of Athensbury were not really needed. Three of the four great intuitions through which Athensbury would revolutionize higher education in America were already dimly known to its president. *Full partnership to students*—that would capture the Berkeley syndrome. *The whole world as campus*—that would capture political revolutions and relevance. *Each man his own teacher*—that would capture "Do your thing," and lead serious, intense young people from the smorgasbord of electives to independent study in the great tradition.

The administration added the notions of *community* and *person*. "Athensbury," they resolved with liberal righteousness, "will not be a factory. We will not put together another institution; we will build a community. What the world lacks is *community*. No more 'Do not fold, mutilate or spindle.' No more College Board scores or other numbers games. We insist that people be treated as people: all equal, each responsible, each a mature adult." On these principles Athensbury was founded.

The first faculty, all eleven of them, came in August. All were modest, utopia-inclined. Five had PhDs. The others had proven skills: men and women, as it were, of the world. Those without PhDs, among them Jane Parker, who had a master's in comparative literature, deeply resented being classed among the "gifted amateurs," as they were called.

As a faculty, they were a surprise to one another. None of them had ever met before, and their relative inexperience startled them. Each had privately thought he or she wanted to be associated with an experimental college. But each had counted on the others being professionals in that sort of thing. To their dismay, each learned that those enticing phrases that had brought them to Athensbury—"full partnership," "university of the world," "each man his own teacher," "community and person"—were the only phrases any of them knew about experimental education. Nearly all were privately skeptical about the few sentences they did know, but fell back upon the sacred word "experiment." All relished the sweet humility of "not having all the answers."

The first meeting of the new college was, in retrospect, a disaster. This plenary meeting of the faculty was convened to plan a curriculum for the autumn; classes were to begin in six weeks. Several of the faculty and students were sitting on the grass outside the meeting room. It was twenty minutes past the hour when the meeting was to have begun and urgency had not yet bestirred them. The university president, sitting cross-legged, was holding forth.

The academic vice president was hovering over the group.

The president held up his wrist. "Is it time? Sorry I won't be able to stay." His face fell in sincere disappointment. The father of the college would miss his very first faculty meeting. "But it's for a good cause. The Police Investigators Group— PIG—is holding a conference on drugs." He raised his eyebrows. "With *all* the college presidents and deans. Be good to be there, don't you think?"

Two of the girl students nodded.

"Well, take care of my college for me. Wish me luck." With a wave, the president was gone.

The faculty meeting, then, was late in starting. Quite obviously, the full partners had a right to be there too. Twenty-eight minutes past the scheduled hour, students and faculty were still filing in. Miss Parker entered, searched for a seat, hesitated. All the chairs at the table were taken, one of them taken by Susan Ponsonbee's collie, whose tongue was hanging out pathetically in the August heat. Miss Parker sank unwillingly onto the floor in a corner. "We are going to be, quite obviously," she thought, "a very sweet community. Of equals."

That prospect did disturb her a little. It would require of her a little readjusting to feel the full-bodied equal of the boy with the torn khaki shirt and the dirty hair, for example. Through some strange deficiency she'd never despite twelve years of analysis discovered, she could not tolerate the sound of someone loudly chewing gum. The slow grinding of this boy's jaws was, to her ears, deafening.

"The subject for today," Blaise Kendall began. He was the academic vice president, a dear sweet man and, as events were to prove, a well-oiled mariner's compass of direction: place him between four or five conflicting pressures and he would unerringly locate the vector of reconciliation, and he would proceed objectively, patiently, calmly, to explicate its necessities.

"The subject for today," he cleared his throat and smiled sweetly. A large girl, who wore no bra under her sweaty tee shirt, was loudly whispering across the room for a boy with shaggy eyebrows to throw her a cigarette.

"The subject for today is *curriculum*. Very soon now we must talk about governance, evaluation, field programs and"—he gestured inclusively—"a whole host of other problems. But today I thought—"

"Blaise, one minute!" the boy with the shaggy eyebrows, having thrown one damaged cigarette across the room, interrupted with authority. "One damn minute. Is it true that students are full members of this meeting?"

You could hear people sweating in the silence. "No one, I think, has denied it." The beautiful cautiousness of the canons of evidence: Vice President Kendall never affirmed too much.

"Well, I mean, like that sign, man. It said *fac-ulty* meeting?" David "Bull" Connor (that was his name) was very bright, but he had a slight stutter. "I just wanted to be sure you meant we're *all* fac-ulty. I don't wanna start the year gettin' screwed."

"C'mon!" said the one well-dressed boy in the room, with contempt. He was a transfer student from Harvard.

Bull fought to keep on top. "Yeah, well, I know it's goin' to happen. Sure it's gonna happen. We'll get screwed. The whole fuckin' country's getting screwed. I thought maybe here we could get through a day or two before it happened."

One quality Blaise was jealous of was his fairness. "I thank you. But I'm sure"—you could see him ready himself for the effort, like a pole-vaulter about to lift himself above ground level—"I'm sure I know of no one who is trying to—screw you." The word came painfully, and Blaise attempted a silly grin to disguise it. Jane Parker stirred uncomfortably.

A few giggles covered the awkwardness. A girl with rose-tinted glasses beamed with admiration.

"Blaise!" This time it was a tall, pretty girl standing in the back of the room. "How do we know how decisions are being made around here? Who decided how to decide? Like, who called this meeting? Who picked this time? This place? I didn't even find out about it until I went into the john. I still wouldn't know about it if Amy hadn't told me. Are there privileged groups here?" For a pretty girl, she had a mean, snarling lip. "Are some partners here more equal than others? Like getting information others don't get? We haven't even started yet, and already the administration is playing tricks."

The meeting was in disarray. Blaise was trying to say, "Now just a minute, just a minute—there's a lot of work we have to accomplish this morning." But some people were groaning, others looked at the ceiling, and still others buzzed angrily and busily. A critical moment in the credibility of the school had obviously come.

"Blaise . . . Blaise . . ." a calm voice said from the other side of the table.

"Shh! Shh!" the girl with rose-tinted glasses said.

"Professor Pratt, you have the floor," Blaise said.

"Look, it's too hot in here. Why don't we go outside on the lawn and get to know one another a bit. I don't agree with some of the allegations that have been thrown around in here. But it's clear we can't make any headway until we talk about some preliminaries." He laughed slightly. "Like trust."

The crowd pushed out the doorway into the lawn. Unwillingly, Miss Parker had her first sensory experience with Athensbury students: an intense whiff of wet, sweaty straw on the clothes of one of the boys who was sleeping in the tepee.

The meeting on the lawn did not go a whole lot better. Miss Parker felt dismay after telling one boy—it was a shocking explosion, for her—"No, goddamit, I am not your servant!"

"*You're* not special people," the boy had jabbed at the faculty.

His name was Carl Sherman. "You don't know anything about my life or how I want to live it."

At that point Miss Parker was on the verge of saying: "Your life would bore me to tears." The effort to choke it down was her undoing.

"*I'm* a faculty member," the boy asserted. "Equal to you. Even superior, because schools are meant for students. I'm a faculty member: I'm my own teacher. But I'm a student, too. And you people"—he pointed a thin, dirty-nailed finger at all eleven faculty members, one by one—"are functionaries. You help me—only when I need you."

"Then why are we paid, and you're not?" Ralph Portly, the bearded sociologist from Penn, asked gently.

"Because you're functionaries," Carl Sherman replied triumphantly.

Miss Parker exploded. "I am not your functionary. You're crazy if you think my life revolves around you."

"Then why are you here?" the girl with the rose-tinted glasses asked.

Miss Parker really didn't want to lose the girl's rosy beatific glance. She didn't feel at all like trying to justify herself. But she found herself thinking: *How can there be an experiment, unless all our assumptions are examined?*

"Like," she said, "to teach." Instantly, she hated herself for saying "like." She hurried on. "But you're mistaken if you think my life is exhausted by my life with you. Students are only part of my life. I'd be of no use to you, or to myself, if I let you devour me."

"Oh, well," Portly laughed, shrugging merrily but looking at Jane with puckish eyes. "They're only kids."

Kids! Jane thought. *Eels. Ticks.* She could feel them, already, sucking her life away.

After the whole group ate lunch together on the lawn beside the Stable House, the meeting reconvened. "Now that we have gotten to know one another, at least a little," the academic dean began again with a truly charming smile, "perhaps we had better turn to curricular planning?"

"Shall we talk about independent study first?" Blaise asked sweetly. "We have four topics: humanities seminars, social science seminars, field projects, independent study. Shall we begin with the last? Professor Pratt, do you have anything to say?"

"Not really. I mean I didn't know I would be called on. I didn't bring my statement. I have it in my office, just in some notes, if you want me to go get it."

"Professor Pratt is in charge of Independent Study," Blaise explained to the braless girl, who had pulled his arm.

"Can a student do anything she wants for Independent Study?" Bull Connor asked archly. His tall, thin friend, in frayed dungaree shorts and no top, whispered something mischievous to him.

Blaise directed the question to Pratt with a look. "With the consent of his faculty advisor and me," Pratt said.

"You don't trust your own faculty advisors to make solid decisions?" Pettibone asked incredulously. He was the youngest faculty member, a new PhD in political science.

"Trust them, yes. But I have the final responsibility."

The buzzing, blooming confusion of reality exploded.

"Order, order!" Blaise pounded the table, a candle in the dark. "Professor Pratt has the floor."

"I haven't made my whole presentation yet. But I certainly don't intend to be a rubber stamp. I'll use my own head in certifying Independent Study projects."

"We've been fucked over enough in high school," Bull Connor commented. He was twenty-five, had led sit-ins at three different colleges, and was expelled from all three. Athensbury was going to show there was at least one school where such independence of mind was not perceived as a threat.

"Well, I want everybody to know," Pettibone announced, "that as a faculty member I intend to approve of any project any student wants to do."

There was a significant silence. Then Pettibone continued: "You're all mature, adult kids. I intend to treat you as adults. Your project may sound silly to a lot of people and still be important to you. When Columbus sailed west, people laughed at him. 'Fall off the edge of the world.' People always laugh at new ideas. In order to get one percent creativity, you sometimes have to support a lot of ideas that seem wacky. I underline *seem*."

"Suppose someone proposes to lay matches end to end across the Brooklyn Bridge," Pratt began calmly. Jane was pleased to see his cheeks reddening. "I'm not going to approve of that."

"Why not?" Pettibone said. "I would."

"Because it's silly."

"But even in an example like that . . ." Pettibone was inspired and shifted his weight in his chair. "Even in a case like that, a given individual might learn a lot. Would he try to get permission, or just do it as a kind of sit-in? How far will the establishment go in allowing academic freedom? And suppose the kid went to jail. He'd learn a lot about our society."

The whole room was nodding.

"Look," Pratt said slowly. "Everything in the world is educational. But there are some forms of education I intend to support, and others—"

"Who the hell died and left you judge of my education?" a short, heavy girl broke in with indignation.

"So long as I have the responsibility, I intend to exercise it. Making distinctions is one-half the business of education. I'm sorry, but I intend to make distinctions."

"Yes, but not for other people," the girl said. She seemed ready to cry.

"Look, Alfred," Portly addressed Pratt. "In my view we're making too many assumptions. I think Athensbury should select only students who are college material—bright, mature, responsible. Then, give them their degrees the first day they arrive and turn them loose. I'm convinced they'll do better work."

"Well," said the academic dean lamely, "maybe it's just my hang-up. But I still feel as though there has to be some procedure of evaluation."

"Give them their degrees the day they arrive," Portly said emphatically, boxing the issue with his thick hands. "Let them do what they want to. I'm sure it will work. They're all intelligent kids." He summed them up with his eyes, while under his gaze each of the kids grew an inch.

"I don't intend to submit my Independent Study to anybody," Oliver Cretin said slowly and genuinely. "If I did, it wouldn't be independent."

"Wait a minute," Pratt said. "Logically, Independent Study does not imply there won't be any supervision. The work is independent, and the choice of project is largely independent. But I am certainly not going to run an unsupervised, chaotic program."

"Unsupervised does not logically imply chaotic," Pettibone mimicked.

"True, but experience counts for something in the use of logic."

"Aren't we going around in circles?" Professor Pickering asked softly. Everyone strained to hear his voice. "We have to make a decision. Some people want the school to certify whatever anyone wants to do. Others want some definition of standards—perhaps *any* definition, even an entirely revolutionary definition, but some definition of standards. We can't do everything at once, we have to limit ourselves to one form of standards. What'll it be?"

He took a deep breath. "I never saw any group of human beings avoid having standards, even if they try. Never heard of one. Can't imagine one.

"Raised eyebrows, intonations, sympathies—all these tell you what is in bounds, what is out. We're going to have standards, all right, the only thing is, are we going to choose them consciously or just allow them to happen?"

"It's all right for you 'cultivated, perfectly socialized' people to talk standards," Bull Connor said. "I can tell you in advance what they're going to be. You're going to make us over into people who are just like you. Some of us, at least, are saying 'no thanks.'"

"Then it's a little hard to see," Pickering said sadly, "why you have chosen to study with us or—"

"We didn't choose it. We have no choice. The draft, remember? That little war somewhere—where is it now, somebody help me to remember."

Pickering pushed on very softly: "—Or why we have chosen to teach you."

The temperature of the room flowed cold in Pickering's direction.

"The point is," Pickering picked up in a barely audible whisper. His hands were shaking. "We came here for the sake of experimental education. We don't think we're gods or anything, and we don't mean to inflict ourselves upon you. But we can only teach you what we know as success and failure, good or bad, or even mediocre."

"Don't you see the ideology in that?" The tall pretty girl's voice had authentic despair in it. "Can't you understand why we despise you and your society? We're not asking you to teach us. We just want to be left alone. We want some space to educate ourselves."

"Then there's not much point in being a teacher here, is there?" Pickering asked.

"That's childish, Pickering," Portly said calmly. "She's not saying that. She's overstating the case a little. What she means is, these kids are unusually intelligent and mature. I was on the Admissions Committee. I can assure you that these are the very cream off an incredibly good bundle of applications. What they want is a new kind of education. That's what 'experimental' means. They just want a chance."

The crowd was loving it.

"But Roger," Pickering was saying quietly to Portly, "we can't abdicate our own experience and intelligence. Naturally, these kids are bright and mature—outstanding even. But they can't ask us to lie down and play dead. I'm willing to argue with them all they want. But when I think they are wrong I intend to say so. I don't think it's right to give in to their prejudices. They have a right to expect adults to stand and fight."

"I'll stand and fight," Pettibone smiled. "But I'm on their side. I'm probably just young enough and just old enough to see both sides. I hated every minute of graduate school and thought that nine-tenths of it was bullshit. Yes, bullshit." He looked around the room expectantly. "I don't want to inflict on other young people what was inflicted on me. And that's why I'm here."

"Well, I still have my hang-up, I guess," the academic dean laughed. "We certainly haven't decided much but it seems to have been a fruitful discussion."

"I think we've decided," Pettibone said.

"Decided what?" the academic dean asked.

"Well, if I can read the sentiment of this room, the vast majority of us are in favor of *independent* Independent Study. That is, no faculty advisors, no supervision. Except for record keeping."

"You mean everybody just passes, automatically?" the academic dean asked.

"That would be my inclination," Pettibone shrugged. "But I know you have the State to worry about. So I'll compromise. To that extent, I'm a realist. I say that students should evaluate themselves. If they do passing work, they know it. If they don't, they'll be honest about it."

"*Nemo judex in causa sui.*" Pickering barely parted his lips.

"What was that?" Pettibone's eyebrows went up above his smile.

"Never mind. It's useless," Pickering waved.

"Shall we have a vote?" Pettibone encouraged.

"Well, this is a faculty meeting . . ." the dean began.

"I thought we've agreed we're all faculty," the students said.

Someone shouted derisively: "Full partner-ship!" And others joined in: "Full partner-ship!"

"It's a participatory democracy," Pettibone added. "One man—one vote. Isn't that what this college stands for? Isn't that what democracy is?"

"Let's not get into that one now," the academic dean grimaced. "We discuss governance next week."

"Look!" Pratt requested the floor, closing this meeting as he had the last. "I haven't made my presentation yet. Can't we hold voting until we discuss this in an open, full, and formal manner? The informality of this place is getting me down. I don't mind feet up on the table and things—even without shoes—but I think you, Blaise, ought to run meetings a little more tightly. Otherwise, school will begin and we still won't have a curriculum worked out. We need an agenda and we should be forced to stick to it."

Blaise slapped the table with a smile. "And I'll begin right now."

Then he gave his characteristic fade-away laugh. "Meeting adjourned."

After some months, four or five colleagues and I were sick of the indiscipline (not to say peculiar "madness") of the place. We asked to form a separate college, on the Oxford model, to which we would invite faculty and students who loved the classics: ancient, medieval, modern, and twentieth-century. To underline our purposes, we called ours the "Disciplines College." I was elected provost (and was ceremonially reminded of a fictitious twelfth-century provision at Oxford that allowed a provost one free assassination a year). The few of us, students as well as faculty, loved our little Disciplines College.

One real privilege I did have as provost was to bring in outside speakers. Herbert Marcuse was frequently quoted on campus (and also *mis*quoted), so when I happened to meet him on a lecture trip, I invited him. After mingling with the students, he was affronted and disgusted. At his lecture he set aside his prepared notes and instead described the severe Prussian discipline of his own education: the classics he had to master; the languages he had to learn by exercises and constant tests. His theme was that no one had any standing on which to rebel against the past—or dare to call himself a revolutionary—who had not mastered the tradition of the West. This was not at all what the students expected. From then on a chill came over quotations from Marcuse.

The students also idealized and sentimentalized the Vietcong guerrillas in Vietnam. So I invited in Tran Van Dinh, who had fought with the guerrillas against the French before the surrender of 1954. That gave Dinh heroic legendary standing among our students. He told the students how he and his men recruited villagers to join them. They would march in, summon all the men of the village into an open space, and boom out a few words of propaganda about their cause. Then, with submachine guns raised, they would ask for volunteers to step forward. If no one stepped forward, they would shoot one man in the stomach until he collapsed and, when he was on the ground, give him another burst. Then they would ask again for volunteers. Dinh said coldly to the students that he would sometimes have to kill two men and added: "If you are not willing to do that, don't call yourself a revolutionary." Except for a gulp or two, there was silence among *our* revolutionaries.

With these and other lecturers, the Disciplines College served the students well in the college at large. They poured in for the likes of Marcuse, Dinh, Susan Sontag, and W. H. Auden. But once there, they did not get what they wanted.

The reader can see why I was going back deeper and deeper to the roots at Old Westbury—that is to say, departing from utopia and returning to the classics. I was being hurried on my way to becoming—I shouldn't even say the word—"conservative." Only my own anticapitalism and residual commitment to the Democratic Party slowed my utter downfall right then and there.

10

With Sargent Shriver in
Thirty-Nine States

One day early in the summer of 1970, I was reading the *New York Times* at the breakfast table in our home in Bayville, Long Island, when I saw a story about Sargent Shriver opening a new office in Washington to begin a national campaign to help elect Democrats to Congress. Mr. Shriver had just returned from a triumphal tour as U.S. ambassador to France, and now, early in the days of Nixon and Agnew, he was eager, the story implied, to join the battle for the future direction of this country. "Sounds like fun to me," I told my wife over coffee, nudging the paper over to her. Refilling my cup, I headed upstairs to my third-floor study for another day of writing— I was working on a college textbook (*Ascent of the Mountain, Flight of the Dove*, Harper & Row, 1971) for the new courses in religious studies then burgeoning on secular campuses around the nation. It was not three hours later that the phone rang. It was Sarge, inviting me to come down to Washington to write for him.

When I caught up to Shriver the next morning at Timberlawn, his sylvan home just off Rockville Pike from downtown Washington, I learned that he had been reading *The Experience of Nothingness* (Harper & Row, 1970) during his last days in France. He read some of it aloud to me right there and then asked me if I would be willing to come and write for him in this exciting new campaign. We would be on the road all summer right through Election Day. My family could come and live at Timberlawn in the pool house, so that we would not be separated for too long. I would need to take a semester's leave of absence from the university in the fall. I said yes.

When I was introduced to Eunice a little later that day, she smiled, welcomed me, and said Sarge would be tough on me. "Give you five dollars if you're still here on Election Day," she said, tossing her hair in the way parochial school girls used to do (and probably still do). Her look was full of mischief and fun. It was a dare. There was no way I was going to lose that bet.

It was a most marvelous adventure, those five months. Along with Sarge and me, there were people working in the office on K Street; there were advance teams; there was a press secretary and sometimes an old-time Kennedy (or Stevenson or Humphrey or Johnson) hand, for advice and company and schmoozing. We toured thirty-nine states and conducted close to a hundred campaigns. Sarge almost killed himself by taking a dare in South Dakota and allowing a bunch of the Democrats there to seat him on one side of a big inner tube near the shore of the local lake, with a rope tied to its other side, the rope then strung out about thirty feet to a big power boat headed outward. When the men at the controls—with drinks in their hands—roared off at high speed, I was sure Sarge was going to lose both his legs in the force of the boat's wake, and he sure took some rough bouncing. But he came back all smiles, and only a little white in the gills.

I also remember campaigning for Ron Dellums (I believe it was his rookie year) in Oakland, and I remember Dellums (or maybe the local mayor) telling Sarge in front of the crowd that Oakland was so tough that even the muggers walked in twos. We also put in a stop for another freshman, this time for the California State Assembly, John Vasconcellos (who stays in touch with me to this day), and met in Sacramento with Jerry Brown. We baked our lips in the desert at 110 degrees in Palm Springs, deplaning from a four-seat Cessna flown briskly by a woman pilot who wore a white jumpsuit with a flying tiger emblem on her buckle; she had been trained to fly bombers cross-country during World War II. We did Vegas, Albuquerque, Toledo—anywhere anybody wanted a headliner for a chicken (or salmon) dinner fund-raiser. Movie stars and athletes joined us at almost every stop. There were always Peace Corps veterans, or Job Corps veterans, or Upward Bound leaders. An army of Shriver people was everywhere.

Eunice's little joke aside, Sarge and I had great fun. He liked to have index cards block printed with felt-tip pens, three or four cards on each of the six or seven themes he was hitting on the campaign. The main facts, a story or two to illustrate, a funny line or two, a throat tightener, a punchy ending, or a lead-in to the next sequence. He would vary these sequences, depending on the crowd or the occasion—or even his mood. He thought that a good speech ought to move an audience through several different moods, from hilarity and delight through sadness and serious reflection and resolve and inspiration. He liked to keep things fresh. Every day he would hand me new clippings with facts or stories to "work in." He always wanted a touch of "class," by which he meant a quote from a theologian, philosopher, or classic figure. He wanted the aura of the Catholic tradition, not so the unattuned would notice it, but so the people who knew would pick up on it and reverberate to it. In this he reminded me a bit of Gene McCarthy, who had brought the same light Catholic touch to his national campaign. Both McCarthy and Shriver were Catholics not only by birth but intellectually and knowledgeably, and both thought the Catholic tradition shed an intellectual light on American perplexities that nothing else rivaled. Both knew they could do this while the Kennedy brothers couldn't.

I LEARNED EARLY ON that Shriver always hired someone like me—Colman McCarthy, Mark Shields, a legion of others—to play just this role. He also wanted someone to talk to on the airplane about Teilhard de Chardin (the Jesuit paleontologist), Dorothy Day, Mother Teresa, Thérèse of Lisieux, Peter Maurin, G. K. Chesterton, Danilo Dolci, the Worker-Priests of France, and Cardinal Suhard. Shriver loved the vein of Catholic thought that wanted to "reconstruct the social order," "put the yeast of the gospel in the world," "feed the hungry, comfort the afflicted"—generally, that is, to make a difference in the world. He thought of the Catholic faith as a culture-changing force, a shaper of civilizations, an inspirer of great works, a builder of great institutions that bring help of all kinds to the needy in all dimensions of need. Thinking about the future, with so many human needs unmet, propelled him on with a truly driving passion and an amazing energy.

Some people thought this passion was a Kennedy thing. Shriver had a certain nobility of soul regarding the Kennedys, and I never heard a negative word cross his lips. But I know *he* knew it was a Shriver thing. Shriver had a sense of himself as an aristocrat, needing vindication by nobody else. His family had helped to launch Maryland on the side of independence, had fought on both sides of the Civil War (all Maryland was like that, riven down through family after family), and served gallantly in every American war. Long before he got involved with the Kennedys, he had excelled in prep school (in fact, he bested Jack Kennedy there by far), in the Experiment in International Living (which took him to Europe every summer until 1939—he was on the last ship to leave France the day the war broke out), at Yale College, at Yale Law School, in the navy, at *Newsweek*. He excelled in everything he ever tried to do. He had joined the navy after Yale and emerged as a war hero (with a Purple Heart) from a decisive but very bloody battle off Guadalcanal. He was from the beginning handsome, dashing, athletic, self-confident, full of fun and zest, a magnet for the girls, a terrific dancer, a restless thinker, and a man with an instinct for the truly grand and an acute sense of destiny. Well before he met the Kennedys he was preparing himself for high ambitions, certainly a governorship or Senate seat, or . . . something bigger still. Neither overly proud nor vain, Sarge knew from his own inner voices that whatever great things he could imagine, he would have to push on to grander ones. Why not? His faith wanted him to, his family expected it, he had been granted great opportunities to prepare for such things, and his inner energy and expectations longed for them.

Most people have forgotten, if they ever knew, that Sarge was *almost* Lyndon Johnson's choice for vice president in 1964, instead of Hubert Humphrey. Johnson really liked and admired Sarge, and knew he could be his salesman on the Hill—and also a hedge against the ambitions of Bobby Kennedy. He entrusted Sarge with the War on Poverty, which, as much as it is mocked today, gave scores of thousands of African Americans entry into professional careers and dramatically altered the political position of African Americans in the United States. Symbolism should not be mocked, either. "Care!" and "Give a damn!" and other slogans really did change the national ethos for the better, even if many unintended consequences sent crime and out-of-wedlock birthrates steadily upward. In race relations, for all the mistakes made afterward, no one dreams of going back to where we were pre-1963. Sarge helped to turn the country around.

Because of his late start in the 1972 race for the vice presidency, Shriver's cause was almost hopeless. But Mickey Kantor, Mark Shields, Doris Kearns, and a host of really talented volunteers turned out to join the happy warrior, and I was among this lively group. Presidential candidate McGovern assigned us the task of winning back the Catholic ethnic vote that Nixon had so knowingly cut into in 1968. (Pat Buchanan had invited me into the White House in 1969 to sketch the lay of the land.) We saw a lot of Philadelphia, Pittsburgh, Youngstown, Cleveland, Toledo, Detroit, Chicago, Milwaukee, occasionally St. Louis, and then around and back again. Toward the end, the crowds were huge and enthusiastic. It seems unbelievable to say this, but we actually began to feel that the press *must* be wrong—we were going to win. What we failed to pick up was what the crowds were telling us: They just weren't going to be able to vote for us; they were sorry about that; we shouldn't take it personally. Something like that. We got beat pretty soundly.

Two slogans early on had gone out from the McGovern campaign: "Amnesty, Acid, and Abortion" and "Women, Blacks, and the Young." These slogans did not help us on the factory floors in our cities. On one occasion, one of our advance persons on a factory floor was wearing a see-through blouse, a miniskirt, high boots, and a big red abortion button. Workers were turning away from Mr. Shriver, not meeting his eyes, and I saw one hold his anger face-to-face and then spit on the ground after Mr. Shriver passed—this was in a factory in Joliet, Illinois, from which, in a really close election, we could have gotten, maybe, 114 percent of the vote. It wasn't Sarge's fault—far from it. But this sort of experience of the new Democratic Party that year, not really any longer respecting its own base, was enough to make a neoconservative out of me, and in fact it pushed me to take a major step in that direction.

Most people also forget that Sarge ran for president in 1976.

Once again, as in 1970 and 1972, Teddy Kennedy and his professionals didn't rally round. Just before the crucial Massachusetts primary, after he sat down from a rousing St. Patrick's Day talk at a big luncheon in Boston, Teddy got a sharp rebuke from Eunice, because not once had Teddy even mentioned Sarge's name, or urged the faithful to help him. Sarge was there fighting for his political life—he was out campaigning nonstop, which was why Sarge was not present. We knew already in 1970 and 1972 that Teddy and his guys were carping about Sarge's speeches—once Sarge even threw in a mention of Teilhard de Chardin just to torment them a little. Sarge kept doing things his way, and even today a number of his best lines keep getting picked up, like his "Culture of Life, Culture of Death" speech.

After 1976 Shriver turned his attention back to all his beloved charities and activities in public life, including (in his law work) all sorts of activities to link civil society in Russia to the outside world. (On one trip to Russia, his young son, whom he had taken on this trip, chased a ball down the hall, opened a door, and found Russian agents inside monitoring tape recording devices that were picking up everything the Shrivers did.) Sarge also kept up his support for all the institutions he had helped get started. Many of the institutions he founded are still operating, and even thriving, fifty years later. Not only the Peace Corps, but also Upward Bound, Head Start, the less successful Job Corps, and not a few initiatives of the much mocked but still goal-setting War on Poverty. It is astonishing how many of these programs anticipated later writings on civil society. Sarge *designed* them to nourish flying buttresses *outside* of government, involving many "mediating structures" (most notably, black churches and other urban churches, big business, and the world of celebrities). One of his central preoccupations was *civil society:* all those institutions and associations that thrive in between the great state and the lonely individual. Much that Shriver had a hand in creating contained significant elements of "compassionate conservatism." Okay, there was a lot of big government liberalism, too—but with an arresting number of conservative elements.

Sarge could understand liberal Republicans; many of his Yalie friends were such. He could see the tony similarity in the good spirits that certain Republicans and certain Democrats share, which lead them to believe that *they* are not ideological. People like Reagan, now, *they* are beyond the pale. Yet for Shriver, this was not a matter of social class but something much deeper. For Mr. Shriver, his politics (his ancestors helped found the Maryland Democratic Party) was quite akin to his religion. Not the same thing; he would never confuse the two. But on some parallel track, his politics was quite equally a thing of faith—not a religious faith but a political faith, tenacious and deeply rooted in the sinew of his soul. Those outside that faith, poor souls, seemed to him woefully afflicted. Sarge experienced them as strangers, odd fish, and felt sad for them. In a political campaign, he would lambaste them with zest. Face-to-face, one-on-one, he would try to charm them and do his best to try to understand them, as if they were another species. He could even extend to some of them his trust—trust, but always verified.

Among political leaders I have known at least a little, Shriver reminds me most, for his easy affability and love of laughter, of Ronald Reagan. They were happy warriors both. And I think of both of them as, quite deeply, good men.

In fact, I used to wonder over many years what would happen if Sarge would, like the Gipper, come to see the flaws in the Democratic Party's way of construing many issues, such as taxes, poverty, crime, welfare, and abortion, and so become a conservative. There were many aspects about his life that could have led him in this direction and, in truth, on economic policy his business experience never did allow him to sound like Tip O'Neill. For example, in

1970 and 1972 I was much to Shriver's left on such matters—not more conservative than he, but an academic lefty—and more than once he rebuked me, or wordlessly struck out lines I had written for him. On abortion, he and Eunice were always out of accord with their party—but not ready to break from it, or even to insist on their voices being heard in its public platforms. I always expected Sarge to have more sympathy than he ever actually showed with those former liberals who had been "mugged by reality" (aka the neoconservatives). I even thought—but only as a passing fancy on my part—that he might join them. The truth is, he really was a big "D" Democrat (a party man) all the way. That wasn't just a Kennedy thing; that was him.

SARGE'S POLITICAL LIFE HELPS to bring to life a critical span of American history from 1960 until about 1976: the revivifying excitement of "Camelot," the Peace Corps, the magnificent arc of the almost miraculous leadership of Martin Luther King into the largest leap upward for American Negroes (as the word was then) since the Emancipation Proclamation. It was the rise of "pay any price, bear any burden, meet any hardship, support any friend, oppose any foe" of the first inaugural of JFK down into the crushing disgrace of the fall of the U.S. embassy in Saigon in 1975. It was the hope of youth and newness, interrupted by the bloody assassination of a young president, and then, of his brother Bobby in 1968. It was the rise of the blacks (the new name), women, and the young. It was the assertion of the longtime base of the Democratic Party in the northern tier from Massachusetts to Minnesota and Iowa and Missouri—"ethnic" immigrants (largely Catholic and Jewish, but also Scandinavian Lutherans and French Huguenots) who were the backbone of the cities: policemen, firemen, insurance agents, clergy, and nuns.

The Democratic Party was in turbulence. It was being remade. Never before buoyed by the "Negro" vote, that vote was now intensely loyal to it. "Women" were clamoring for leadership in the party—but here "women" (silently) meant both "college-educated" and "liberal." A new class divide was emerging: the college-educated from the high-school educated; the new middle-class professional workers from those with more menial jobs and more vulnerable positions.

A long *Commentary* article of mine noting Reinhold Niebuhr's death in 1971 was at last published during the 1972 campaign. Its point was how Niebuhr had broken away from the anti-war, disarmament, and (in some cases) pacifist Christians, whose ranks had swollen from 1914 through 1941. He had also broken away from the high moralists (who were without irony) and heartfelt sentimentalists, and also from the hard utopians on the left (for their cruelty) and from the soft ones (for their blindness and naïveté). I called my celebration of Niebuhr "Needing Niebuhr Again." Forty years later, editor Norman Podhoretz commented to me, "I certainly remember 'Needing Neibuhr Again' as one of the seminal pieces of the period." My experiences with the glitterati of the new class showed me how badly we did need him again.

Mr. Shriver lived through all of the social and political shifts of the seventies gracefully; he had more than a small hand in bringing them about and symbolizing them. He was a man from an important, tailored-suit business profession who turned to politics to do good, bring hope, get his hands dirty in the field, sleep on thatched mats in nations where almost everyone did, and bring good cheer wherever he went.

To understand some of this turmoil close up, you have to gain some experiences down on the ground of real American small towns in South Dakota and ethnic neighborhoods in New Hampshire and

Baltimore and Detroit and Chicago. You have to go to the rough industrial neighborhoods of eastern Ohio—Youngstown, Akron, Cleveland, and Toledo—and, of course, you have to make at least one stop in Hollywood and on university campuses and in country clubs. Without Mr. Shriver bringing me on, I would never have had the privilege of seeing America up close and one-on-one for so many months, both in 1970 and then again in 1972 (and even a touch in 1976). It was no surprise to me that George McGovern, not on the first try, called Sarge to be his running mate in 1972. In fact, I had already written most of Sarge's acceptance speech before McGovern even announced his official choice. Political logic demanded it. I showed up at Sarge's home at Timberlawn without even being invited. With Sarge, I knew one didn't wait to be asked. He didn't like to be indebted to volunteers, and he acted as if it was sheerly amazing of you to come to help him of your own volition. It turned out he had a whole gaggle of Kennedy speechwriters coming in.

The next day, going over all the drafts presented by the half a dozen writers, Sarge chose the draft he liked best. He handed it to me to go over. He didn't even ask me until after he had given the talk, with much success, whether I had written it. He had thought so, but he wasn't sure.

If you want to get a feel for what Sarge said on that occasion in Washington, D.C., here is a portion of the text. The whole thing was barely a thousand words, by design quite brief and to the point. The event was held in the ballroom of a Washington hotel, and it was nationally televised as if it were the second act of the Democratic National Convention.

> My fellow Americans, I am filled with gratitude and joy— gratitude to George McGovern for selecting me and to the Democratic Party for nominating me—joy for this new

chance to serve my country. I accept the nomination of this great party. I pledge myself to your service.

I am not embarrassed to be George McGovern's seventh choice for Vice President. We Democrats may be short of money. We're not short of talent. Ted Kennedy, Ed Muskie, Hubert Humphrey, Abe Ribicoff, Tom Eagleton—what a galaxy of stars. Pity Mr. Nixon—his first and only choice was Spiro Agnew.

Tonight, George McGovern has given another new example. John Kennedy's victory ended discrimination against Catholics. Lyndon Johnson's victory ended discrimination against Southerners. And now George McGovern has proved there is no discrimination against in-laws.

The Democratic Party is the party of life. It has been the party of my family in Maryland since 1796, when Thomas Jefferson started it. It renews itself with every generation. It seeks new people. It is the party of Franklin Roosevelt's concern for the depressed and the weak, of Harry Truman's toughness. It is the party of John Kennedy's courage and Lyndon Johnson's desire to help people as poor as he had been. It is the party of Eugene McCarthy's witness in cold New Hampshire, and of Robert Kennedy's desire "to tame the savageness of man."

It is the party of Mayor Daley and Shirley Chisholm, of Averell Harriman and Philip Murray, of Hubert Humphrey and Cesar Chavez, and of Ted Kennedy and Ed Muskie. It is the party of immigrants, of diversity, of hope.

"The United States is not merely a nation," Walt Whitman said, "but a teeming nation of nations." George McGovern and I will give a voice to all the teeming nations of America. We will build again the coalition Robert Kennedy dreamed of—of Poles, Jews, Italians, Irish, of Blacks and Latinos, of farmers and workers—the party of the streets, the neighborhoods. The party dedicated to children and families.

Unless all move together, white and black, poor, middle class and rich, we do not move at all. There must be fairness for each, or else there is fairness for none. But are we fair to all? Where is justice missing today in America? It's missing mostly in the life and circumstances of the working man and woman of America, white and black. We used to look on massive unemployment only as a problem of the ghetto. But now it appears in Youngstown, as well as Watts; in the steel mills of Buffalo and the aerospace industry of California; and the textile mills of Lowell and South Carolina.

Three months from today, Americans will choose between jobs and unemployment, between peace and four more years of war, between special treatment for corporate interests and general neglect of the public interest, between equal justice for all versus special justice for some.

The people will choose not merely between two men or two parties, but between national greatness and national decline.

Americans have been numbed by years of useless war, the savage bombing of Vietnam, by the cruel, unusual prosecution of technological war in a simple land. We will not feel clean until we rid our souls of this obsession. But the war is not our only sickness. The best-fed nation in the world suffers famine of the spirit. We have a sense of something lost, something missing.

Now we mount a wider stage, with new and greater

responsibility in a harder world than we have ever known. But "someday," as the philosopher told us, "after mastering the winds, the waves, the tides and gravity, we shall harness for God the energies of love, and then, for the second time in the history of the world, man will have discovered fire."

11

The New Ethnicity

During the long summer of 1971, I was struggling to write the first edition of *The Rise of the Unmeltable Ethnics.* The world has changed a great deal since then, yet some of the goals I set out to promote in that book did come to pass. My subtitle was *The New Political Force of the Seventies,* and ethnicity surely was. In fact, the word "ethnic" (used of white ethnic Catholics, especially the relatively unknown ones from Eastern and southern Europe) entered public speech during 1971–72. Further, by their voting power the newly identified "ethnics" reached out and grabbed the attention of politicians as seldom before. Candidates as diverse as Senator Howard Metzenbaum of Ohio and Governor Mario Cuomo of New York told me how useful that book was for them in thinking through their campaigns.

In those years, reporters slowly began to pay unaccustomed attention to ethnic voters and to the leaders who were rising from their ranks, such as Richard Celeste and George V. Voinovich in Ohio, Dennis DeConcini in Arizona, Peter Domenici in New Mexico, and Barbara Mikulski in Maryland. In 1974 President Gerald Ford initiated an Office of Ethnic Affairs at the White House under Ukrainian-American Myron Kuropas. Jimmy Carter opened his September 1976 campaign by celebrating "family days" in the white ethnic neighborhoods of Newark and Pittsburgh. In 1980 I was both surprised and pleased when the sunny Californian Ronald Reagan showed an unerring instinct in speaking the language of those who, after his two unrivaled landslides, came to be called "Reagan Democrats," and also when he chose as his campaign slogan symbols that could have been taken directly from the last pages of my book: "Work, family, neighborhood, peace, strength."

In fact, I learned much later, Reagan's strategist Dick Wirthlin picked up that slogan from an article of mine addressed as a challenge to *both* Democrats and Republicans. Wirthlin tested these terms in his polling, and they rang the bell, so he recommended them to the future president. Like many other ethnics (if I may so include him), Ronald Reagan had started his political life as a labor-oriented Democrat and then, feeling more and more abandoned by the cultural left of his party, became increasingly conservative. Much of the rest of the country, including that other stout pillar of the Roosevelt coalition, southern and western evangelicals, began to do likewise. Reagan had the historical instinct to cast this "revolution" as a *re* plus *volvere* (a revolving back) to this nation's founding principles. He portrayed a new/old progressive vision—not a socialist or statist vision, but one based on the American tradition of limited government and self-rule, personal initiative and hard work. It inspired many of us, and it infuriated the cultural left.

The publication of *The Rise of the Unmeltable Ethnics* in 1972 marked my declaration of independence from the cultural left—at that time the preeminent force watching over what couldn't be said in American culture and what could. I was still writing as a man of the anticapitalist left, but I was, in truth, departing from left-wing orthodoxy by singling out cultural issues (rather than economic issues) as the primary neuralgic point in American life (as well as in the life of many other countries). I was defending—no, trying to inspire political and cultural self-consciousness in—those whom the elites liked to picture as paunchy fascists in undershirts, bigoted and unwashed. I was repelled by the unworthy prejudices of the cultural left. At a time when the "liberation" of the swinging singles was being celebrated, I thought intellectuals ought to be stressing the importance of family (even the psychological differences between "family people" and those who find the unencumbered self a more fundamental reality). They ought to be admiring the latent strengths of traditional values and ethnic neighborhoods (even ethnic suburbs). To say the least, these ideas were premature. At the time they were regarded as reactionary.

Secretly, of course, I wanted very badly in those days to be accepted by the cultural left, the gatekeepers all aspiring young writers must please if they are to be allowed into the national dialogue. I wanted to be seen as offering a necessary and helpful corrective to mistakes being made in progressive politics, mistakes that were alienating the Democratic Party from its base and even from its traditional tacit commitments. Naïvely, I thought this difficult analytic effort would be greeted with gratitude. I was thrilled when the *New York Times Book Review* called my publisher and said that my book was scheduled for a front-page lead review in two weeks. The great American gateway to literary fame! But when the scheduled issue arrived, my book was not on the first page. It was buried halfway through the magazine. And it was obvious why: It was a devastatingly bad review. Expecting to be exhilarated, I was crushed. Not only did that review not help my reputation; but the reviewer accused me of spreading hate (the insult our elites hurl when they are being unmasked). Really tough to take.

I did not then know the fury of the Left when it marks someone as beyond the pale of acceptability. I had never before understood how secular excommunication works—how effectively one can be banished from the innocent banter of old circles of trust, how even old friends change the flow and tone of a conversation when one approaches, signaling with a certain chill that one's presence is no longer desired. All this is a good thing to go through when one is young. One needs the toughness later.

I had noted some years earlier that people on the left increasingly lived in one culture, people on the right in another. This process only got worse in the 1980s and 1990s, and in the twenty-first century the old closeness still deteriorates. Certain exceptions are made for persons of proven social graces. A few on each side are allowed, on certain polite conditions, to penetrate the circles of the other. A few mischievous persons, knowing exactly where the limits are, could always light fuses by saying with feigned innocence in a left-wing crowd something kind about Reagan, the religious right, Jesse Helms, or pro-life demonstrators—or, at a right-wing table, something about Teddy Kennedy, Tip O'Neill, feminists, and how this country is taxed too little.

In the circles of the Left during this period, guests from the Right felt like social climbers admitted to the inner sancta of this culture's movers and shakers. In the circles of the Right, guests from the Left usually felt as though they were slumming. Reagan, with his Hollywood glamour, changed that a bit, but not much. The contempt for him at the heights was wonderful to behold. Not that this really mattered. Clare Boothe Luce once explained that a movie star who became president had an occupational advantage: Early in his career, a B-actor like Reagan had learned the difference between the box office and the critics, and, being secure that the public was with him, could cheerfully be very kind to the press and to professors.

The fall of 1971 was already the run-up to the presidential election of 1972. I had promised myself in 1968 that, because of his disgusting appearance at Stanford, I could not support Humphrey in that election, so I would give a whole year to defeating Richard Nixon. Accordingly, I asked for a leave of absence from Old Westbury to join the fray. I started visiting primary states with candidates, and by late autumn I got a temporary job helping out the famous speechwriter Bob Shrum in his work on the staff of Senator Edmund Muskie. I got to fly on the campaign plane with the senator for a trip or two, but mostly I worked in the office. I didn't do well writing speeches for him. The senator had a wholly different manner of speaking and a sharply different set of interests and perspectives from my friend Sarge Shriver.

In 1972 Muskie failed to catch fire and lost in the end to Senator George McGovern of South Dakota, a thoroughly decent and approachable midwesterner, and a moral idealist. Once he won, McGovern asked me to join his campaign and help out in the big Catholic ethnic cities of the Northeast and the Midwest. I did write for him one op-ed and one big speech on the Vietnam War, which he gave at a Catholic high school in Chicago. His campaign chief and others high on the staff did not want McGovern to speak at a Catholic school at all. They feared that Catholic boys and young men might be very pro-war. They didn't want a huge anti-McGovern scene on TV.

I explained to the nominee that allowing their sons to go to Vietnam was the most difficult moral choice many Catholic ethnic voters had ever made. They still believed in their country and in serving the flag. They didn't like that particular war, but they sure couldn't stand any candidate, including McGovern, calling it *immoral*. They weren't evil, and they couldn't stand hearing themselves and their sons called immoral. That accusation slapped their faces and undermined the heroic sacrifice of their sons. Their sons, not being in college, were serving in disproportionate numbers in Vietnam, and that didn't feel fair, either.

The speech draft I gave McGovern did not call the war immoral, as he had been doing elsewhere. Instead, it noted how many young men went into that war for highly admirable moral reasons. It implied that there were good reasons for the rest of us to see corrupt and immoral behavior in the government of Vietnam, but we should not even hint of evil in the arduous, bloody service of those brave young men and women who risked being wounded, losing a leg to a land mine, and death. It explained that this is why McGovern wanted the war to end soon, so they could come home, job well done!

When Frank Mankiewicz, the campaign manager, saw the draft of the speech McGovern was about to give the next morning, he flew out to Chicago to try to stop it. McGovern insisted on giving it. As they heard it roll out line by line, the students at the Catholic boys' high school were attentive and approving, and so were the adults in the auditorium. At the end, the students and faculty clapped and cheered, some students even standing on their seats whistling and shouting so loudly that the brother who was principal of the school took the floor. Quieting the audience, the brother thanked the senator and said that since the whole school was so excited, he was going to declare the rest of the day off. More wild hooting and cheering ensued. Talk about triumphs—so much for the stereotype of the warmongering, hawkish, uncritical Catholic ethnics.

The candidate was a terrific man, and he understood many things that key supporters and staff in the field did not. Some of their behavior was shocking and disturbing to the ethnic and religious audiences they were trying to win over. They seemed to have no idea about the sensibilities they were offending. They were out of their element, totally ignorant of people who had been the most faithful and reliable Democratic voters for at least forty years. By the end of it all, I found it hard to throw my shoulder to their wheel—except that Senator McGovern was so decent and loyal I could not desert him.

Even more heroic in my mind—almost saintly—was Sarge Shriver, that model of a man, to whose vice presidential campaign team I was transferred as chief speechwriter. As we had done in 1970, our campaign plane sometimes hit three cities in one day, with a major speech and some minor meetings at each. We were assigned to all the ethnic garden spots—the working-class areas of Philadelphia, Scranton, Pittsburgh, Cleveland, Akron, Toledo, Chicago, Milwaukee, Duluth, and back again.

Toward the end, our crowds were so enthusiastic I actually fell under the illusion that the press was getting this wrong; we were going to win. What I didn't realize was that many in these crowds were coming out of loyalty, and letting us know that they didn't mean to be disloyal, even if they were actually going to vote against us on Election Day. They cheered us, but with a bit of nostalgia.

In a word, what we saw day after day verified the main theses of *The Rise of the Unmeltable Ethnics,* and played them out in vivid and unforgettable color before our eyes. I was beginning to see how the Democratic Party was riding two different horses—one racing in the direction of the welfare culture and the glittering culture of Shirley MacLaine; Peter, Paul and Mary; Mike Nichols and Elaine May; and others in the Hollywood and literary elites. Meanwhile, the other bridle was desperately trying to hold together the main portions of the great Rooseveltian coalition, especially the small-town, rural, and suburban evangelicals (who were becoming more educated and affluent and professional every year) and the white urban ethnics (ditto).

The Democratic Party—and the labor unions—needed to learn to deal with the cultural threats that were overwhelming just plain Americans of many different ethnic streams. Their main concern was no longer merely economic. They did not want *their* kids taking acid. They did not want *their* daughters sleeping around, or having abortions. They did not want *their* sons fleeing to Canada or Sweden to avoid serving their country. The Democrats and the unions needed to shore up and comfort their longest, most loyal base. And they were losing touch with how to do that.

WHEN ELITES IN THE universities tried to put their heads around ethnicity, they couldn't help twisting it into a mushy "multiculturalism," which from a different hostile direction—and hostile it was—aimed to undermine the traditions and values and symbols dear to the immigrants who poured into America from about 1880 to 1950. Left-wing Democrats, more and more empowered in the party, couldn't keep themselves from mocking the ancient Jewish/Christian culture that those Statue-of-Liberty peoples had so long cherished.

The United States long ago became a planetary culture, with people coming here from all over the world. Yet during the 1970s and 1980s, more *legal* immigrants came to the United States, *not counting the illegal ones,* than in any other decade of our history—except two. Through immigration during the 1970s and 1980s (in large part Latino), the United States added a new population equivalent to that of Switzerland, Sweden, Denmark, and Norway combined. Nearly all these newcomers soon found jobs; some forty million new jobs were created during the 1980s and 1990s, and by the end of it a higher proportion of American adults was gainfully employed than at any earlier time in our history.

Furthermore, most of these new immigrants were nonwhite. Their rapid success proved two points to most of the American public: the United States is still a haven for people capable of hard work and enterprise, regardless of color. And the new immigrants—as long as they stayed off welfare—resembled the old in their strong family life, spirit of enterprise, and love for their new land. They were exceptional in one way, though: They succeeded, even *more* quickly than the old immigrants, often in one generation.

"Multiculturalists," however, sometimes used the new immigration to diminish our own national traditions by forecasting a third-world composition for our future population. These forecasts of future diversity were then used to justify a "multiculturalism" that borrows the logic of relativism in order to assault the tradition of the *Unum*. But that *Unum* is as much a part of our nation's heritage as the *E Pluribus*. No university worth its salt announces itself as, for instance, "The Pluriversity of Michigan." Rare are the nations on earth that hold at once to both the *unum* and the *plures*. Yet that is the glory of this "land of immigrants." We are many peoples; we are at the same time one people.

That was the premise of *The Rise of the Unmeltable Ethnics*. I called the new version of this old principle "the new ethnicity." I pointed out that most of those who wanted to identify with their cultural roots in older generations had a *choice* about doing so. Some chose simply to become "American" and to forget the past. Some chose to become more aware of their rootedness and plumb its meaning.

Today's "multiculturalism" has only a loose relationship to truth. It aims at bolstering "self-esteem" (as if self-esteem could be helped by anything but truth), and practices a flagrant disregard of fact. It undermines canons of evidence and rational standards by dismissing these as Eurocentric. It pretends to be "nonjudgmental," but the one thing about which it *is* judgmental to the point of intolerance is any appeal to rational evidence. It pretends to rest upon "cultural relativism." It recognizes no transcultural standards for judging cultures as more or less adequate—the support of institutions of liberty and the development of free men and free women, for example. Undercutting its pretense of relativism, multiculturalism is aggressively hostile to certain cultures, chiefly our own, with our Jewish and Christian vision of the one and the many, the different peoples of the one Creator held to the same transcendent standards.

The new ethnicity teaches us a certain humility before the truth. Each of us is born from the womb of a single woman into a particular segment of human experience, at a time, in a place, within a language and a particular set of cultural symbols, beliefs, rites, gestures, emotional patterns, and a not universal sensibility. Each of us is limited, singular, concrete. We are, none of us, Universal Man or Woman. On the other hand, by virtue of our unlimited drive to inquire, to seek understanding, and to expand our capacity for sympathy, we are each potentially open to the universality of our species. We can become self-critical, not only of our individual selves but also of the limits and faults of our own communities and nations. We can learn from others, adopt new and better (or worse) ways, and grow in our capacity for appropriating cultural riches from our own past traditions and also from traditions outside our own.

My father, for example, with no more than a sixth-grade education but a lifetime habit of reading history and culture, never ceased to instruct his children to be grateful that our family had come under the sway of English political and civil institutions and the riches of the English language, even as he wanted us also to cherish our Catholic and Central European heritage. He considered us lucky to have both these gifts, as well as other gifts such as the opportunity to draw as much benefit as we could from the rich cultural diversity surrounding us in America. He encouraged us, too, to travel and to read, as if the whole world belonged to us—as, in a way, it does.

Writing *The Rise of the Unmeltable Ethnics* in that difficult summer of 1971 was the beginning of my own inner voyage "home," to discover the true, down-to-earth nature of this country and the system of which my family was now a part, as well as America's not yet crystal-clear place in human destiny.

In 1971–72, my mind was in a fruitful turmoil regarding my left-wing tendencies. I had begun to notice the appearance of *two* lefts—one that included my whole family and what it represented, and the other a "new" left, based on a suddenly emerging "constituency of conscience," no longer rooted among people who worked with their hands and backs. Instead, secure in its own affluence (and in its own suburbs), this new left was now expressing a more refined "morality." It was a rather more utopian morality: More interested in "peace." More interested in "sensitivity." More interested in its own "moral purity," which marked it as superior to past political classes. The New Left was no longer of the old left—which was patently more vulgar, unsophisticated, and unrefined. "Left" now meant "morally superior."

In Italy the Communist theoretician Antonio Gramsci had already noted that the Communists had made less progress among "proletarian" working stiffs than among journalists, artists, and other cultural classes. Socialists were less and less entrapped in the grubbiness of economic issues, and more and more interested in morals, culture, and sensibilities. Some of the great industrialists of Italy had informal understandings with the government. The government subsidized certain industries, while the Communist unions held back the number of strikes and maintained the industrial peace.

This new class structure was bringing to birth a new politics, in the Communist as in the Western world. A new right was waiting to be born, rooted less in union strength than in a new grasp of the usefulness of competition and creativity and invention—and a new realism about how things actually work.

Curiously, even in the 1970s (and maybe even the 1960s), writers with Democratic sympathies thought Republican "moderates" were

Republicans who voted with Democrats. They were blind to how far out on the extremes of the cultural and moral fronts their own positions now extended. They thought "conservatives" were those who were moving left, but more slowly. They had full confidence that history was inexorably leading everyone leftward. It never occurred to them that, in the eyes of a growing majority of the public, those on the left were now extremists.

12

1972, Working with the Very Decent George McGovern

An important year in the rightward turn of my political thinking was 1972. True to my promises to myself in 1968, I was determined to devote the autumn of 1971 and most of 1972 to work to defeat Richard Nixon for the presidency. My biggest opportunity came when I was involved with Senator Ed Muskie's campaign for six weeks, when Bob Shrum was my mentor. He had already begun winning a national reputation as one of the best speechwriters in the business. Bob was especially good at creating frequent punchy lines whose sharpness made it almost impossible for the audience not to break out into applause. His lines could be mordant or outright funny, or passionate; they could lay down a dare, or ridicule a line used by the opposition, or merely throw down a huge chunk of red meat that the audience could sink its ravenous teeth into. Bob was skilled at writing for highly partisan, highly motivated crowds— labor union conventions, for example, or conventions of Democratic Party members hungry for a win.

Yet Shrum could also create more patriotic and soaring melodies. From a relatively poor immigrant labor background himself, he combined a bit of the cynicism often found among Americans at the bottom of the social ladder with a deep, misty love for this country, conceived in a progressive, labor union way—acquisitive politics as an almost religious vision of the kingdom of gold out there just over the horizon. In Shrum I also sensed a visceral hatred of the opposition—of Republicans, of the country club set, of all who laid down the rules for style and worth and entry. How he wanted to bring them down!

Shrum and I were not kindred spirits. But I had hardly any idea of how to make a political speech, and I am eternally grateful to Shrum for how much he taught me in a short space of time. The essays in journals I had written until then can be imagined as quiet arguments between friends, or among a small group in a parlor over cigars and perhaps a spot of brandy. Subtlety and wit, sly insinuation, and, in the sweet amicability of the hour, an occasional lightning-fast exposition of the most important point are the highest arts in such essays. But these elements are virtually useless for a public political occasion, which calls for a stage, an expectant room filled with high passion, and a hunger for the next concrete steps and marching orders.

A political speech also calls for half a dozen other elements: moments of laughter; a biting stretch of tart mockery that smacks the other side dead on (the malignant presence of the other side must always be felt in the room); one or two heart-grabbing episodes that move hearts toward pity and even soft tears; the awakening of the rousing force of anger and its consequent raw determination to go out, wear one's shoes out, and WIN!

Along its spine, the political speech must also have sequences of staccato applause lines, designed to bring the crowd into fervent complicity with every word. The best of these lines must be saved for the up-on-your-feet finale.

I never got to be very good at speechwriting. But I did learn to appreciate the craft of it from Shrum. Aside from these lessons, I also was able to observe a campaign from the inside, traveling by plane or bus. I had covered the campaign of 1968 week by week for Long Island's *Newsday,* and in 1964 I had even written from a distance about the folks I knew in Johnstown and McKeesport and their reaction to the Goldwater campaign. Neither they nor I were much attracted to Goldwater—our family traditions were too Democrat for that—but we were already beginning to feel that our Democratic Party was being torn apart, pulled one way by its local, labor, mayoral part and in the opposite direction by its increasingly national media, Hollywood part. The strains of the culture war were already beginning to eat away at our innards . . . and our brains.

For the second semester of the 1971–72 school year I had to get back to campus. But I managed to fly out for primary weekends to observe and write about a lot of the major campaign events. I thoroughly enjoyed meeting the working press by air and bus, talking and arguing and exchanging tidbits along the way. I especially remember asking some of the women journalists about abortion. They surprised me by saying an abortion was like having an appendix removed, and not very different from losing tissue in menstruation. What was aborted was simply part of their own bodies, a discardable part. I didn't see how that could be correct, but these were conversations, not arguments. *Roe v. Wade* had not been decided. We didn't yet have the genetic science to know about the unique, individual DNA of the child from its conception, which only came to light years later. Nor did we have the prenatal sonograms of the growing child in the womb from the very early weeks. Looking back on those conversations now, they seem like they happened a very long time ago.

When Muskie lost out in the primaries, I was invited to join the McGovern campaign. There are two things I have always kept in the back of my head about George McGovern. First, this is a fellow who flew thirty-five bombing missions over the shrapnel-filled skies of Central Europe in World War II. A lot of those pilots never made it back to England. A pilot needed nerves of steel to take the bouncing in the air and the flashes of new antiaircraft fire going off all around him while still keeping on course, in order to drop his bombs on the appointed target for the night, and then fight his way back home again.

The other thing is that McGovern later attended seminary and worked for a time as a student Methodist minister; he was a gentle and a kind man, with a slowly awakening passion to serve his country once again in public service. "The Prairie Populist," I called him, reminding myself of how many times since William Jennings Bryan—and Thomas Jefferson—"the sons of the soil" had arisen to bring back the country through often unpopular but brave leadership.

But the scene from his campaign that I still love best was his maiden experience in Madison Square Garden, at a huge, superglitzy event called "An Evening with McGovern at the Garden," headlined by movie stars and other celebrities up the gazoo.

McGovern protested that night that he was as square, old-fashioned, and staid in his morality as any Middle American, and that both his enemies and the media unfairly caricatured him as a creature of the counterculture, imprinting him with the three scarlet As: abortion, amnesty, and acid. Early, however, perhaps out of short-term necessity, his campaign identified itself with the college youth culture, with the music, appearance, and speech of "the movement"—the vocabulary and symbols that, not always unwittingly, excluded many traditional Democrats. The trauma and hard-edged desperation of urban working people, blacks as well as whites, never reached the center of his campaign. McGovern appeared as "the man with the white hat," a relative innocent from the prairies, whose style was "tender." These images did not touch the harsh conflicts people actually felt.

McGovern spoke of being "different" from other politicians. He made unnecessarily high moral commitments. Political realities again and again made him back down. He was then subject to charges of hypocrisy. A political leader can generate passionate moral energy without any appeal to his own moral purity; John and Robert Kennedy, for example, did not campaign under the banners of purity, honesty, and superior moral character. Means in politics are inevitably mixed, and less than pure.

Perhaps this main public event of his virtually uncontested primary campaign in New York State served as well as any other symbol to illuminate how McGovern unwittingly separated himself from millions of traditional Democrats. The event foreshadowed the exclusion of the Daley slate from the Democratic National Convention in Miami later that year, which clinched McGovern's character in the public mind. (If Mayor Daley wasn't a good enough Democrat for George McGovern, then who was? If purity tests were to be established, many wanted to be counted out.) If McGovern had wanted Daley in the convention, he could have kept him; McGovern refused to intervene.

It was a celebration of moral purity in Madison Square Garden on June 14, with the purpose of raising funds for the McGovern campaign. June 14 was Flag Day, but there were no flags onstage. No flags surrounded the Garden; high up, forlorn, the huge Garden flag waved alone.

Trying to tune his guitar, Art Garfunkel teasingly demanded that the crowd be silent: "Can't you see we're sensitive!" ("Sensitive" was the key word of "the movement.") Like medieval jesters, with threadbare jeans and some fuzzy blond hair shining in the light, Simon and Garfunkel offered songs of the vulnerable, the compassionate, the idealistic, without edges and toughness or the bite of economic reality. Songs of those who scarcely recognized that they were middle class, loved wine with dinner, loved a place to go in summer, loved cheese and fruit, and did not love blast furnaces and mines and assembly lines.

No Lawrence Welk. No Johnny Cash. No Benny Goodman. The music, as at most McGovern rallies, celebrated the resurrection of the youth culture. The most public campaign event in New York State was not chosen with the *New York Daily News* in view, but *Variety* and *Rolling Stone*.

Nostalgia. A last gathering of the decade that had been the sixties. But also bravado. When the aging Peter, Paul and Mary took the stage, baldheaded Peter told the crowd that the campaign picture of McGovern, shirtsleeves rolled up, "is the best picture since, you know, Kennedy." And he boasted: "I'm not going to move toward the center. The center is moving toward us!" There were raucous cheers.

Elaine May and Mike Nichols hit the tone exactly. "After so many years of being a liberal, after so many years of losing," Elaine began, "it's nice to know we're about to break a perfect record." After the laughter: "At first I was skeptical. But now, more and more, I'm beginning to have the feeling he could do it. Yet as a liberal, and as a Jew, it seems to me wrong just to coast. I need to keep alive a tiny, burning flame of doubt."

Elaine and Mike, playing liberals, said they didn't "understand, exactly, McGovern's economic policy." But they did know that policy was motivated by "idealism and harsh, pragmatic realism," that it was "tough but tender." "Now what is it again?" It was so hard to keep the right thoughts straight.

Hubert Humphrey, Elaine confessed, was "great in '48." Mike was dry: "I don't think Hubert Humphrey ever was what he was."

"Part of the Democratic Party," Elaine pieced out, "is the Democratic Party machine. The other part is the Democratic Party." Cheers.

Approaching the event's crescendo, the entire cast gathered onstage, flashing peace signs, for a three-minute ovation. Then a great chant went up: "We want McGovern!"

George and tiny Eleanor, radiant with the success of their first evening at the Garden, finally appeared. McGovern's midwestern twang was touchingly attractive, making people feel ecumenical and large, as though through him they had a tie with that dark, sprawling beast they knew as "Middle America."

"It is a wonderful night of coming together," McGovern said. "Not only for so many of you." The performers ducked and nodded while applause gathered. "But also, after many weeks of separation, tonight will be a wonderful coming together for Eleanor and me." The crowd cheered, a growing naughty edge upon billowing laughter. In his hayseed voice, McGovern replied: "I'm just not used to this New York sophistication."

McGovern told them how he loved "this country, enough to hold it to a higher standard, away from the killing, death, and destruction now going on in Southeast Asia." "I love this land and cherish its future. I want to set about making this country a great, decent, and good land . . . to be a bridge from war to peace . . . a bridge across the generation gap . . . a bridge across the gaps in justice in this country. . . . As the prophet wrote: 'Therefore, choose life . . . be on the side of blessing, not cursing . . . on the side of hope, health, life. And peace for ourselves and peoples all around the globe.'"

"Each of us," he concluded, in a message to be heard again at the convention in Miami and throughout the autumn, "is a child of a great and free people. We must match our decisions and performance to this nation's ideals so that future generations will love the great and good land you and I have made it, . . . a people who truly care about each other."

Six weeks later, on a triumphal night in Miami, at 3:00 a.m., George McGovern was nominated by the Democratic Party as its candidate for the presidency. No Democratic Party officials had been with him on the stage in New York. Many were absent or disgruntled by Miami. Yet against impossibly high odds, this decent, tender man, at the culmination of years of effort and organization, had seized the presidential nomination. He would spend the autumn trying bleakly to reunify the party's factions.

"Come home, America!" McGovern proclaimed. But his vision didn't look like home to a majority of Americans. The movement of which he was a symbol failed to represent the country.

When he finally retired from Washington politics, George McGovern and Eleanor settled in New England to take over the running of a country inn. It was a humble thing to do, straight out of his character. The experience even made him surprisingly critical of federal regulation and high taxes. Doing just the paperwork required an immense waste of time, and the costs and fees he was required to pay were enough to put his inn on the line for closure year after year. He had never felt government regulation and taxes from *that* side, he said.

One of the greatest joys of my life is having retained the friendship of such a good, brave, and true man all my life. More than once the senator agreed to read and commend a book of mine, and he did so with pleasure and aplomb; he helped me out quite a lot. What an extraordinarily decent man. What a down-to-earth man.

One day, two months after the election, I caught George on morning radio. The interviewer asked him about his memories of the campaign.

"Ever since I was a little boy, I wanted to run for president in the worst way. So I did."

How could you not love the guy?

13

Any Serious Christian
Must Be a Socialist

It was easy to grow up anticapitalist in my hometown. The great Bethlehem Steel Mills winding along the banks of the Conemaugh River at the foot of the green valley represented a huge amount of capital from out of state. The owners lived back east in Philadelphia, and even the local managers did not live down in the shadows along the valley floor with the workers, but rather on Westmont hill, the green and sunny hilltop with its beautiful golf course and country club some six hundred feet above the city.

Work in the steel mill was extremely hot, dirty—and dangerous. Overhead hung a huge vat of molten white steel, into which steel was steadily poured from a thick, tilted funnel still higher up. The men working on the ramps up there were in constant, searing heat. Once when my uncle was on duty (he later rose in the ranks to become a foreman), a man high above him on the scaffolding lost his footing, tried desperately to save himself, but tumbled into the molten vat. My uncle told me two things, reluctantly, about that day. Afterward not a sign of the man remained in the white-hot steel. Even his bones had melted. The second thing he could not get out of his memory was the heavy odor in the air. That part of the mill smelled for an instant like roast chicken.

Uncle Johnnie had walked into the mill with that man every day for three years and more, had gone to church with him year after year, and tossed back many a beer with him at the Slovak hall. Johnnie was particularly fond of the departed man's teenage boys.

Every Johnstowner knew the story of the Pittsburgh tycoons who had built their yacht club on the broad, blue lake created by a huge earthen dam. Remarkably, not everybody blamed the rich when that thick dam burst its seams. But a few did, with keen bitterness. The dam gave way on the last day of May of 1889, under an immense weight of water gathered behind it from almost three weeks of incessant rain, occasionally in cloudbursts dropping six or more inches each time. The devastation to the city down below in the narrow valley fourteen miles away was the worst peacetime disaster in the early history of the United States.

No one growing up in Johnstown could evade the steep contrast between the rich and everybody else, the brawny and battered workers most of all. Of course, in their homelands in Europe the contrast had been even more marked. And the aristocrats of the Austro-Hungarian Empire had far more power over the lives of those under them than did the industrialists of Pennsylvania over the steelworkers.

Nonetheless, Johnstown prepared my imagination well for a later reading of Marx, the muckrakers, and union firebrands. It prepared me to think that the Democrats were for people like us, while the Republicans were for those who had starch in their collars, those up on the hill—the managerial class, some doctors, some lawyers, large store owners, an undertaker or two of the better class, a few teachers from the local high school. Owners, investors, people like that.

Well, my father had begun to get a handle on that. Although he seldom (maybe never) earned more than $10,000 in one year, after the end of World War II my father began buying run-down houses on the hill sloping up out of the valley at the lower end of Menoher Boulevard, a slum inhabited by poor folks, many of them blacks. He would take out a mortgage for $4,000 or less, keeping his eye out for smart, ambitious tenants who wanted to better their condition. In them he recognized his own parents and his neighbors where he had grown up on Virginia Avenue, the sharply steep street cut into the opposite face of the same hillside, one of the poorest streets in the city. He struck a deal with his tenants. He would buy paint and other supplies if they would agree to choose improvements they wanted to make and would perform the labor themselves. He made good friends with all his tenants, checking in on them often, sharing a beer or coffee with them, telling stories—oh, how my father loved to recount stories with a moral, real stories about events he had witnessed! He also loved to give advice to young people, and to teach. And tell jokes.

With the rent he received, my father covered his mortgage, with a bit left over to put back into beautifying the houses. In that way he achieved two things. He had unusually steady, happy, proud tenants, and he slightly increased the capital value of his homes. He tried to persuade some tenants to buy their homes for themselves. For most, that was beyond their comfort level. Meanwhile, when it came time to put his own five children through college, he was able to sell a property here or there—or, where the mortgages were all but paid off, use the income from the rent.

One thing my father always told me: "Michael, never envy the rich. They lead such unhappy lives. Their marriages often fall apart. Many of their children are rebellious and resentful. You think riches prevent unhappiness? Seldom do. The rich have no excuse for not being happy. And yet many are unhappy." He taught me to feel sorry for the rich, and to pray for them.

Sometime after my years in the seminary in Rome and Washington, while in graduate school at Harvard, I had come to see that my inventory of knowledge was pretty empty of economics, sociology, and political science—not to mention practical experience. To be sure, Reinhold Niebuhr had given me a congenial starting point into political analysis. I had studied Catholic social thought and glimpsed its depths and richness. Two really good courses with Robert N. Bellah at Harvard had taught me that I had a lot more to learn. Most of all, there was a yawning gap in my empirical knowledge.

But I also needed to read Troeltsch, Durkheim, Weber, Schumpeter, and Tawney to learn their methods and most important findings. Not to mention Talcott Parsons, David Riesman, and leading public economists from Friedman to Heller, Hayek to Galbraith. I had an awful lot to catch up on.

To push me along in this line, during 1966 and 1967 I taught three-week sessions in Cuernavaca, Mexico, alongside Richard John Neuhaus, the activist Lutheran pastor (and later Catholic priest) in New York, and Peter Berger of the New School. Neuhaus taught me how to think more concretely about our urban and racial problems. Master sociologist that he was, Peter was just then studying materials seldom noticed in religious circles: the astonishingly rapid successes of capitalism in Southeast Asia. He was also beginning to take on two deeper questions of equality and poverty: (1) Empirically, how much equality does socialism actually achieve? (2) Empirically, is socialism better for the poor?

Berger had begun to collect all the arguments *against* capitalism that he could find. His ultimate aim was to reduce these arguments to sociologically testable propositions. Some years later, in 1986, he did so in *The Capitalist Revolution: Fifty Propositions About Prosperity, Equality, and Liberty.*

Peter taught me to frame my thinking around empirical evidence. I saw that in my leftist years I had framed my thinking around "visions" and "dreams," as in Irving Howe's famous line: "Socialism is the name of our dream." Berger led me to think of the unfairness of this comparison. Those on the left presented a glorious, pinkish dream of a new dawn, and they held that dream up against capitalist realities, such as the tawdry smokestacks and factories of capitalism. (I thought of the mean streets of Cambria City, the mill district in Johnstown.) On one scale, the grim actualities of our families' beginnings; on the other, the untested dream of a socialist paradise.

What if we reversed this too easy comparison? Weigh the actual bloody and polluted industries of the socialist paradise, its countryside hospitals without running water and two patients to a bed, against the dream of democracy *cum* capitalism: "liberty and equality for all," together with the ultimate dream of capitalism, to break the chains of almost universal poverty and raise every single woman and man on earth into broadly spread affluence. In other words, compare dreams to dreams, realities to realities. Bring these arguments down to earth.

As I pondered these things, one stubborn fact awakened inner rebellion. I was glad, really glad, that my grandfathers on both sides had picked the United States for their immigration. Others in their villages chose Argentina, Germany, Australia, Italy, Brazil, or Ghana. We were so lucky to have come to the United States. And why? At the humblest level it was the relative openness of the economic system. In America a man could make something new of himself. One could rise from the bottom and go as far toward the top as talent and confidence took one. Where else in the world could one reap so many rewards, even from less arduous work than before?

For the poor of the world, the United States was the country with the best record (by far) in helping them rise out of poverty. But *why*? Why was capitalism better for the poor than socialism? Why did socialism keep failing? Or, forgetting about socialism, what was it in capitalism that I still did not understand?

It was easier for me to decide against socialism than in favor of capitalism. I could not get the plight of my family in Slovakia out of my sense of reality. But then I thought: *Suppose real, existing socialism of the Soviet type is just a poor example?* Then I asked myself, *Where is one socialist system that does work?* I looked in vain at Cuba, China, Albania, and even among the Basques—the favorite of all my Catholic socialist friends. I didn't particularly admire Sweden either, and, besides, the part of it that worked and paid for the rest was the capitalist part, in which the Swedes were unusually hardworking and imaginative. (All my American friends who detested multinational corporations, I noted, drove Volvos.) Swedish newspapers are capitalist, and free speech survives. Not everything was yet under government control. And they are good inventors, the Swedes.

They were good inventors much like Karen's Norwegian grandfather and his brother, the two Swensons, who secured nearly fifty patents between them, including for high-quality lightning rods, the extension ladder, the hay binder, and the most famous of all: the "machine that cleared the West" (the Gold Medal winner at the St. Louis World's Fair in 1904). This was the "grubbing machine," a device for taking out tree stumps with only a special chain that tightened like a vise below the ground. It was operated by a workhorse plodding slowly around and around the stump until the vise cut the stump free. Until the powerful Caterpillar bulldozers came along, the grubbing machine took out scores of thousands of stumps across the western United States.

In short, my first thought was: *Socialism is a pretty good idea; it's just that we haven't found a way to make it work yet.* Then I couldn't help thinking: *But after scores of attempts around the world to make it work, all of which failed, maybe there's something wrong with the basic idea.* Margaret Thatcher would later famously put it: "The problem with socialism is that eventually you run out of other people's money." Socialism, I was beginning to infer, is not creative, not wealth producing. It is wealth consuming (it consumes the wealth of others); it is parasitical.

These insights nudged me toward another nest of puzzles. Isn't capitalism based on self-interest? That sounds like selfishness and greed, and it seems verified when economists concentrate all their attention on the "bottom line." How crass does one have to get?

I can remember looking over page after page of the *Wall Street Journal* and feeling sorry for its readers, who had to spend the substance of their lives worried about the prices of tin, copper, corn, lumber (you name it)—and buried all day long under the problems of breakfast cereals, auto parts, underwear, aluminum pans, cellophane wrapping, flashlight batteries, paper mills, waste management, and other dirty jobs, with almost no daily uplift. How tedious, how soul emptying, how deadening to human aspiration and feeling, to be up to one's armpits in things, things, things!

Of course, I had been brought up and educated in the liberal and fine arts. Fine cutlery, linen tablecloths, soaring poetry, delicious irony, the vivid taste for inquiry, experiences of high and exquisite beauty, noble sentiments, heartrending experiences of wracking tragedy. My associations with commerce and the things of commerce (and more darkly, steel mills and soot-billowing factories) were of things cruel, brutal, philistine, bourgeois, vulgar, crass, belonging to the inferior kingdom of means, not the kingdom of ends in themselves.

It eventually became clear to me that inventors and discoverers in many fields of business were over and over proving to be benefactors of the human race. Not only were their inventions and steady improvements making my own daily life easier and (in some but not all dimensions) of better quality, but they were also inspiring huge bursts of philanthropy, particularly in the areas of medicine and pharmaceuticals. Better eye care, dental services, hygienic products, vaccinations, and "miracle cures" were saving lives in almost every family known to me. Older people who a generation earlier would have been dead were still living, and in many ways living better.

Bangladesh (introduced to us by my brother Dick) was an apt example. The population of that "poorest of all nations" in 1951 had been just under 42 million and was growing at such a rate that by 1991 it would exceed 100 million. To many, these numbers appeared to be tragic population growth, but to the villagers of Bangladesh, these numbers represented grandparents, uncles, aunts, and children still living; a generation or so earlier an awful number of these people would have been lost to infant mortality or death at a very early age. Mothers in Bangladesh were not having more and more children. Rather, newborns had a better chance of surviving childhood, and the life expectancy of adults had greatly improved. They rejoiced in that.

Thomas Malthus, a dour nineteenth-century preacher, imagined mass starvation as a result of growing longevity. In an essay that meant a lot to me as I was moving toward my affirmation of capitalism, the careful historian Gertrude Himmelfarb showed how Adam Smith's optimism (and emphasis on creativity) triumphed over the dismal pessimism of the Malthusians. Where Malthus saw universal starvation amid wars among the desperate, Smith saw the birth of a world of universal affluence. As the brilliant Julian Simon would put it later, the human mind is the "ultimate resource," the residence of the sort of inventive genius that changes the whole trajectory of what counts as a resource (electricity for lamps), and what eventually counts as a relic (whale oil)—the power of a horse's back versus the horsepower of a gasoline-propelled piston engine.

But what about the market? If markets are "unrestrained," won't individuals take wild advantage of the lack of rules and supervision and give way to their darker angels? This nut took me considerably longer to crack. I didn't even know how to think about the problem. Then little things kept occurring to me—or should I say, being thrust upon me by more advanced thinkers.

My long-held suspicions about markets were focused on potential disorder and arbitrariness. Uncritically, I imagined that there could not be order without an order*er*. To my mind, order was a form of intelligence imposed from above. Abraham Lincoln taught me differently. He signed into law the Homestead Act of 1862 in order to put land in the hands of as many different families as possible, partly in order to prevent the building up of large plantations (inviting slaves), partly in order to put daily practical decisions under a myriad of independent minds. There is more practical brainpower in the thousands of families whose livelihood depends on good decisions than in the smartest hundred government planners. Water flows differently on every patch of forty acres in Iowa; the sun strikes the fields differently—variances enough to make some seeds more fertile here than there. Those closest to the action have much higher probabilities of bringing the best results out of their particular piece of land.

That is not to say that each family could not benefit from scientific advice about every aspect of farming. To meet this vital need, Lincoln also insisted that each new territory establish a land grant college in agriculture and mining to develop the knowledge that improves farm husbandry, fertility, and yield, as well as techniques of planting, plowing, weeding, and harvesting. Wealth comes from intellect. The improvement of the yield from one seed is equivalent to making a unique gift to each farming family, to the wealth of the territory, and to the wealth of the nation. Wealth wells up from below, from better intelligence ordered to practical action, as an adjunct of (and condition for) speculative intellect. The cause of the wealth of nations is practical intellect—*caput,* the old noggin.

Friedrich Hayek taught me an equally simple point about order. He taught me to recall my own amateur hiking in the Alps, particularly in walking up the more accessible peaks. I noticed the pathways marked out by centuries of hikers, experimenting with the most efficient ways to climb up (and the yet more difficult art of striding down, guarding against strain on the hamstrings). Sometimes one sees two paths, one more arduous yet direct, the other more leisurely and energy preserving. No one commanded these paths; no one planned them. The practical knowledge of hikers down many centuries had settled upon them, and they worked very well. There are many forms of highly workable order flowing from practical people learning by experience—others' as well as their own.

Another insight came to me from Max Weber. I loved his recovery of the ancient motto: "City air breathes free." Towns tended to grow up around markets, and these markets were run according to customary and slowly evolving rules. To take possession of a booth in the marketplace, a farmer or merchant had to pay a fee and meet certain rules. Measures of weight and size were required to be "true." Many other rules governed wastage, daily hours, and time limits on space.

As a lover of freedom and contingency in baseball, the unpredictable "breaks" in football, the blowing hot and cold of shooters in basketball, I do not find it hard to believe that law and rules are necessary conditions for liberty of action—and yet there are marvelous emergent orders within the uncommanded fluidities of team movements and free adjustments by individuals.

As a great game of basketball can be ruined by over-refereeing and overly literal application of the game's rules, so also markets must be well ordered but not stupidly overregulated. Currently, the statutes of commercial law governing markets and products in the United States run to shelves and shelves of volumes. Forgetting about the individual states, federal regulations alone fill well over 150,000 pages. In this context, it is untruthful to call markets in the United States unregulated and untrammeled.

Still, I have always felt instinctively troubled by a "pure" free-market approach. I could never become a libertarian. A human being is a lot more than dollars and cents, much more than choices regarding goods and services. Human beings live by habits of mind and spirit, and even economic activity depends on the power of these habits. Virtues depend on the culture, on what parents instill in youngsters and what the national media reinforce. Culture comes before economics. The great Nobel Prize–winning economist James Buchanan once told me that he was trying to find a way to measure the effects of the good personal habits of the Japanese on that nation's wealth. An odd question: What are good intellectual and spiritual habits worth? But quite illuminating.

I BECAME MORE AND more disgusted with myself for being taken in too much by the government spending of the new Keynesian liberalism (as everybody called it). Pre-1930, three Ages of Liberalism had been concerned with taking power *away* from government—from kings first, then from barons, and then by checking and balancing all state institutions—through a division into rival powers. I still appreciate the fourth Liberalism, the New Deal, and I recognize that governments can sometimes harness state powers in order to do good. Governments can sometimes provide positive humanitarian relief to the suffering and the needy. I still believe that, in times of recession, governments should spend some limited amount to stimulate demand—and yes, for a while live with deficits. Ours is an imperfect world. After all, it was good for me to own my home as early as possible by borrowing money for a mortgage.

You can see here the beginnings of my full-blown theory that a good society is composed of three interrelated systems: cultural, political, and economic, each depending on the others; each checked and balanced by the others.

But so imperfect is this world that even virtuous, idealistic, humanitarian attempts by government "often gang awry." There is a right way and a wrong way for government to get involved in humanitarian attempts to better the human condition. One wrong way is for government—especially a distant, impersonal federal government—too easily to become a tyrant, too easily to become inefficient, meddling, bureaucratizing, corrupting, enervating. Even Franklin Delano Roosevelt recognized this truth. Though usually thought of as the founder of the welfare state in America, FDR very early recognized a grave danger our nation had better avoid.

Roosevelt warned Congress in 1935, as no Democrat after Lyndon Johnson could have written: "The lessons of history, confirmed by the evidence immediately before me, show conclusively that continued dependence upon relief induces a spiritual and moral disintegration to the national fiber. To dole out relief . . . is to administer a narcotic, a subtle destroyer of the human spirit."

I was led by such markers to compare closely the Lyndon Johnson programs for welfare spending against the Roosevelt programs. Roosevelt was steadily true to his own warning. His weakness lay, I eventually came to think, in feeding the habit of deficit spending. (But this is to get ahead of the story a bit. For more on this, see the discussion of *The New Consensus on Family and Welfare* in chapter 20.) The great break toward the welfare state happened *after* FDR, in the too hasty thinking of the Great Society of Lyndon Johnson. With all good intentions and many real accomplishments—improving the condition of the elderly, for example, and bringing attention to the economic needs of blacks—the Great Society lost sight of each person's actual need for personal responsibility, each recipient's human need to give as well as to receive, and other checks and balances against the sapping of national character.

I recalled Jonathan Swift's fable, telling how, by fastening thin silken cords painstakingly one by one, the Lilliputians slowly imprisoned Gulliver. As Tocqueville wrote:

> Over men stands an immense, protective power which is alone responsible for securing their enjoyment and watching over their fate. That power is absolute, thoughtful of detail, orderly, provident, and gentle. . . . It provides for their security, foresees and supplies their necessities, facilitates their pleasures, manages their principal concerns, directs their industry, makes rules for their testaments, and divides their inheritances. Why should it not entirely relieve them from the trouble of thinking and all the cares of living? . . . It does not break men's will, but softens, bends, and guides it; it seldom enjoins, but often inhibits, action; it does not destroy anything, but prevents much being born.

The modern welfare state takes motherly care of the individual in almost every detail of life. All it asks in return is the surrender of personal responsibility. Gain security and be minutely cared for. Set aside your passion for liberty—choose equality. In the name of compassion, submit to authoritarian bureaucracy. Suspicions stirred in me that to be a modern liberal is to be led slowly into authoritarian ways. ·

Perhaps the single passage that most deeply stirred this line of thought in me was part of an extemporaneous talk in April of 1976 by an exasperated William E. Simon Sr., Secretary of the Treasury under President Ford, before an ill-attended, unserious, listless, and futile session before Congress. In those years the nation was writhing under inflation, an oil crisis, and a crushing economic slowdown. Instead of being able to work on such radical problems over the course of his usual sixteen-hour days, during his tenure the Treasury secretary was summoned by Congress to testify at more than fifty such torture sessions. On these occasions bored senators and congressmen asked questions written by members of their staffs, did not listen to the answers, and evinced very little interest in getting to the truth of things. Secretary Simon on this particular day had had enough, and he showed why he had earned his reputation for no-nonsense toughness and his Beltway nickname, "William the Terrible." In his fiery book *A Time for Truth* (1980), he recorded how in these very dark and dangerous economic times, no one in Washington, of either party, was willing to face the truth.

The fundamental problem, the secretary declaimed, was not excessive spending. It was not a lack of regulation, or even too much regulation. It was not deficits. No, the fundamental problem was that their own lust for power had led governments around the world, here as well as in Europe, to claim "humanitarian concern" as a cover for their own self-aggrandizement. The human good they actually did, as opposed to the human good they claimed to be doing, fell far short of being worth the constantly diminishing daily liberties that Americans (and others around the world) were suffering.

Here is a substantial passage from those April 1976 remarks before Congress:

> What is our free enterprise system? Isn't free enterprise related to human freedom, to political and social freedom?

God Almighty, our forefathers understood that. The millions of immigrants who came to participate in the American dream understood it. When we see this monstrous growth of government, we must realize that it is not a matter of narrow economic issues. What is at stake is equity, social stability in the United States of America. What is at stake is the fundamental freedom in one of the last, and greatest, democracies in the world. . . .

You asked, Mr. Chairman, about the consequences of deficits. But we all know what they are. . . . In the case of the federal government, we can print money to pay for our folly for a time. But we will just continue to debase our currency, and then we'll have financial collapse. That is the road we are on today. That is the direction in which the "humanitarians" are leading us.

But there is nothing "humanitarian" about the collapse of a great industrial civilization. There is nothing "humanitarian" about the panic, the chaos, the riots, the starvation, the deaths that will ensue. There is nothing "humanitarian" about the dictatorship that must inevitably take over as terrified people cry out for leadership.

There is nothing "humanitarian" about the loss of freedom. That is why we must be concerned about the cancerous growth of government and its steady devouring of our citizens' productive energies. That is why we must be concerned about deficits and balancing the budget. The issue is not bookkeeping. It is not accounting. The issue is the liberty of the American people.

The concluding words of this extemporaneous blast were these: "Mr. Chairman, I am leaving office next January. I am going home to New Jersey a very frightened man."

As I say, I resist libertarianism, but Simon's book sang in my ears, even though I did not accept its philosophy as my own. A philosophy of free enterprise alone, then as now, struck me as too narrow. But never had I encountered so coherent and cogent an argument for the libertarian point of view.

By about 1976 or 1977 I was ready to "come out of the closet" as a capitalist. I had been thinking about socialism for many years, having been brought up to be anticapitalist and to align myself most closely with such democratic socialist writers as Michael Harrington, the editors of *Dissent* magazine, and others of the social democratic left. One could clearly sympathize with socialist ideals in academic theological circles without drawing any attention to oneself. However, if one were to call oneself a "capitalist," one would encounter manifest hostility—as one still does even today in circles of religious intellectuals. The more I thought about it, the more I realized that I could not be, even though I wanted to be, a socialist. The first piece I wrote in this vein was "A Closet Capitalist Confesses" (*Washington Post*, March 14, 1976). Here is a portion of that piece:

> I first realized I was a capitalist when all my friends began publicly declaring that they were socialists. How I wished I could be as left as they. Night after night I tried to persuade myself of the coherence of their logic; I did my best to go straight. I held up in the privacy of my room pictures of every socialist land known to me: North Korea, Albania, Czechoslovakia (land of my grandparents), and even Sweden. Nothing worked.
>
> When I quizzed my socialist intellectual friends, I found

they didn't like socialist countries, either. They all said to me: "We want socialism, but not like eastern Europe." I said: "Cuba?" No suggestion won their assent. They didn't want to be identified with China (except that the streets seemed clean). Nor with Tanzania. They loved the *idea* of socialism. "But what is it about this particular idea you like?" I asked. "Government control? Will we have a Pentagon of heavy industry?" Not exactly. Nor did they think my other suggestion witty, that under socialism everything would function like the Post Office. When they began to speak of "planning," I asked, who would police the planners?

Practical discussions seemed beside the point. Finally I realized that socialism is not a political proposal, not an economic plan. Socialism is the residue of Judeo-Christian faith, without religion. It is a belief in the goodness of the human race and paradise on earth.

That's when I discovered I believe in sin. I'm for capitalism, modified and made intelligent and public-spirited, because it makes the world free for sinners. It allows human beings to do pretty much what they will. Socialism is a system built on belief in human goodness, so it never works. Capitalism is a system built on belief in human selfishness; given checks and balances, it is nearly always a smashing, scandalous success.

It's presumptuous to believe that God is on any human's side. But God did make human beings free. Free to sin. There is an innate tendency in socialism toward authoritarianism. Left to themselves all human beings won't be good; most must be converted. Capitalism, accepting human sinfulness, rubs sinner against sinner, making even dry wood yield a spark of grace.

In a later piece cautiously called "An Underpraised and Under-valued System," I characterized capitalism as the lesser of two evils:

> To announce support of democratic capitalism it is not nec-essary to hold that paradise has thereby, or will someday, be reached. It is not necessary to assert that democratic capital-ism is a good system. It is certainly not a Christian system, nor a highly humanistic one. It is in some ways an evil, cor-rupt, inefficient, wasteful, and ugly system. One need only assert that it is better than any known alternative.
>
> Socialism, meanwhile, no longer has the status of a dream or an ideal. It has been realized in something like fourscore regimes. Comparing like to like—actualities to actualities, dreams to dreams—it is not clear to me that democratic capitalism is inferior (in performance *or* in dream) to social-ism. The defense, "Democratic socialism has never yet been fully tried," sounds like a classical apologetic for Christian-ity. Mind grasps it, doubt remains. Socialism is inherently authoritarian. Its emphasis upon democracy is inconsistent with its impulse to plan and to restrict.

Around this time I took part in a conference on capitalism and the-ology at Notre Dame, where the central question for discussion was "Can a Christian work for a corporation?" I gave a talk praising capitalism as the least bad system. The audience fell silent. At a uni-versity one simply does not praise capitalism, for the word connotes selfishness, self-interest, greed, evil. Afterward the large group of participants walked over to the dining area by the underground pas-sage below the Hesburgh Center. Everyone seemed too stunned to speak with me. Even at the table at which I (randomly) sat down, no one wanted to bring up what had just been said. I think they meant no ill, but they simply did not know how to begin, or what to say. It was the most awkward lunch I have ever experienced. My public affirmation of capitalism left me temporarily without a base, and without a sure sense of the future. I had not realized how much my own ideas about the future were affected by the socialist ideal. I had been taught to think that democracy is noble, but that the capitalist part of our system is inferior and would gradually be replaced by something more ideal. Even though some of us did not quite dare to name our dream "socialism," we had thought about capitalism only within a socialist framework. When I rejected socialism, how was I to imagine the future?

My literary guide on this point was Irving Kristol. He himself was examining the then heretical idea that, with all its faults, the American experiment might surprisingly be, after all, this world's "last best hope." Wryly, Kristol wrote that as a Jew he was said to belong to "the chosen people"; and now as an American he might have been "twice chosen."

I began reading steadily about the American experiment. My favorite guide was Alexis de Tocqueville, whose *Democracy in America* I ended up reading in three translations.

14

The Election of 1976

The year 1976 was the two hundredth anniversary of the Declaration of Independence, and during the week of July 4 the "tall masts" from around the world sailed in line, scores of lovely full-sailed craft, from New York Harbor up the Hudson River from the Statue of Liberty. With soaring hearts, Karen and I watched from a huge picture window overlooking the Hudson in the glorious uptown condo of friends from the Kennedy campaign of 1968, Peter Edelman and his wife, Marian Wright Edelman, as the stately tall ships passed by silently, one by one.

That night around the Statue of Liberty, military jets roared just overhead in wingtip formation, with their sudden earsplitting sounds of jubilation, and the subsequent ceremonial firing of great gun salutes. For the whole country, the night's fireworks around Lady Liberty in the soft, dusky dark—and their multicolored reflections off the windows of the soaring skyscrapers of Manhattan—burned into happy memory.

Through friends in the Ford White House Karen and I received prime tickets on a U.S. Navy vessel in the harbor for us and our three children. The unbelievably beautiful and haunting events of the evening and the glow in our children's eyes were unforgettable.

By July 4, of course, for all practical purposes the presidential candidates from both parties had been selected, if not yet formally nominated by their respective conventions. But for Karen and me, the election campaign had begun in the summer of 1975 and, in a sense, at the end of the election campaign of 1972. Even then I had told Sarge Shriver that I was ready to help him out if he decided to run for the presidency four years later. Before making that decision Sarge waited and pondered for a very long time. Something Clare Boothe Luce told him helped him make up his mind. Sarge had been thinking of running for governor of Maryland, his home and the home of his ancestors going back before the War of Independence. He was dreading four years of fixing roads and building new highways. "A man gets only one line on his tombstone," Clare told him. "What do you want your line to be?"

Meanwhile, my friend Jim Wall, an editor at *The Christian Century* in Chicago and longtime supporter of Jimmy Carter, phoned me in the late summer of 1975 with a heads-up that he had given his friend, the governor of Georgia, a copy of *The Rise of the Unmeltable Ethnics,* and told him that on his first visit to New York he should spend a day with me talking about the Catholic vote (and the "ethnics"—who were soon enough to become the "Reagan Democrats"). So that's how I met the governor and his "boy genius" aides, Jody Powell and Hamilton Jordan.

With his clipped naval commander's voice and palpable approachability and sincerity, Carter was businesslike in his presentation, not too folksy (which in New York would have been off-putting), and not too Christian (the group I saw him address was heavily Jewish), but candid about his roots as a peanut farmer, a Sunday school teacher, and a reformist governor with a remarkable, quiet, somehow moving appeal. At one point, he promised, "I will never tell a lie to you," a line that made me cringe but which went down—past some skepticism—very well. It drew a subtle, understated contrast with the still vivid memory of the disgraced Richard Nixon.

Afterward, I warned Carter against that line, telling of my experiences in the McGovern campaign. McGovern too had promised not to lie, and I had observed some astute reporters on the press bus marking down every occasion on which McGovern was even a little evasive, as well as a couple of times when he told white lies. Once he made an excuse for taking a day off: "to be away from campaigning." In fact, he slipped away for a couple of unannounced hours with Lyndon Johnson. The fact of that secret meeting came out not many days later.

On another occasion—I forget the issue—McGovern said something else that was less than true, and that same astute reporter wired it in to his editors as another lie. His worried editors, well aware of the reputation McGovern had built up as a straight shooter and its importance to his campaign, queried their man in the field sharply. The reporter got out his little notebook and recited the precedents. His accusation appeared in print. I warned Jimmy against saying he'd never tell a lie, because reporters would only take it as a challenge. There are always times when a president (or a candidate) cannot properly tell the whole truth and a little fudging is necessary; it's a fact of daily life, so don't tempt fate. As near as I could tell, that riff seemed to disappear from reports of Jimmy's speeches for a week or two. Then it reappeared. I began to worry.

The day after that event with Governor Carter on his first campaign visit to the Big City, I wrote a brief article for *The Christian Century* recording how it went. I said that this long shot candidate might be "the Baptist John Kennedy" and surprise everyone by how well he might do in the race. I reported accurately the good impression Carter had made in Manhattan in front of a quite skeptical audience. For nearly a year this was the only article (however nationally insignificant) suggesting that Carter might be a surprise winner the next year. It went out in all the Carter press kits for many months.

For my own part, I told Carter himself how impressed I had been, but said I had promised already to support Sarge, so I would not be free to endorse anyone else until Sarge decided not to run.

Many months into the campaign I started to note that the governor seemed very elusive on matters of international affairs and military preparedness, and especially silent about the ever widening activities and influence of the Soviet Union. This really troubled me, after the United States had so ignominiously withdrawn from Vietnam. Since I had severely criticized the way we fought that war and then worked for its ending, I had privately taken on myself an obligation not to contribute to U.S. disarmament, and to be alert for predictable aggression by the USSR and maybe even China—lest such powers misread the U.S. withdrawal from Vietnam as irresolution. Their obvious strategy then would be to stir up rebellion in several widely separated places around the world. Those of us who supported ending the particular adventure in Vietnam would have an obligation to strengthen the American spine during such a difficult period.

I reluctantly decided by April of that year that, from fear of foreign policy weakness, I just could not support Jimmy Carter, even though he was doing very well in the primaries and even though Sarge was not running. By chance, my break with Carter occurred in North Carolina, where I was attending a weeklong seminar of select journalists. I didn't really belong with Sander Vanocur of television fame, Gloria Emerson, the great reporter on the Vietnam War, and other veterans. But I think the people who ran the program also liked to include one rookie each year—and I had just begun my twice-weekly syndicated column for the *Washington Star*.

In fact, on one Sunday it happened that both the *Star* and the *Washington Post* ran full-length articles of mine on the new phenomenon of the year: evangelical voters. The first article was on the importance of the evangelical vote in the United States (including who the evangelicals *were*—a subject rarely covered in those days, in even the best university educations). The second was on the new personal style, rooted in his evangelical tradition, Jimmy Carter was bringing to presidential elections. The *Star* had already scheduled its article for its Sunday magazine. The *Post* later accepted the second article and immediately sent it to press (without informing me of its abrupt scheduling). When both appeared as lead articles on the same day, I was a bit embarrassed, but terribly proud, too.

Let me try to express in a fresh way a couple of the points I made in those two articles. There are far more "born-again" evangelicals in the United States than public journalism then dreamed of—at least 30 million and, depending on the definition, maybe something above 60 million. Further, it is the great strength of the evangelical tradition that it speaks directly to the individual heart, the need for moral conversion in one's personal life, and the personal decision to bond to Our Lord and Savior, Jesus Christ. Its corresponding weakness is that it is relatively inarticulate about social institutions. Its one truly crucial contribution to American social thought is its historically very strong grasp of the workings of voluntary associations and their importance to a larger society. It is not so good about supplying principles for less personal social institutions or public policy, both political and economic. I did not say so then, but it has turned out that after the Carter years, evangelical thinkers would borrow more and more such principles from Catholic social thought, including subsidiarity, the common good, social justice, and the (admittedly treacherous) concept of "sinful structures."

As Reinhold Niebuhr pointed out in *Moral Man and Immoral Society*, there is a major difference between morality in individual life and morality in larger institutional frameworks. For example, a socially evil tyrant who is quite cruel in torturing "enemies" in public life can be very kind, considerate, and tender to nieces and nephews and other intimate loved ones in his family life, and affectionate and gentle even with family pets. On the opposite side, having to take up a public role often obliges a man to reach for a moral objectivity and equanimity that he has not fully developed in his private life.

For myself, I discovered when over the next few years I served overseas (three times) as short-term ambassador of the president of the United States, there is a great difference between saying in public what *I* think or feel and committing the whole United States for future years. One needs to learn the sharp difference between one's personal feelings and the binding social commitments of the entire nation. It is not that I then disagreed with the positions taken by my government, but to a remarkable extent the president and the Department of State allowed me to set in place arguments and policies of my own devising, although I took great care to get them officially approved in advance.

As a Roman Catholic, it was easy for me to distinguish, so to speak, my "liturgical" role, which was often of a nobler and more demanding moral discipline than I habitually live up to in my personal life. I used to admire the way President Reagan and House Speaker Tip O'Neill would fight like irreconcilable tigers on the public stage then meet in private afterward for a cheerful session of coffee and swapping funny stories.

Toward the end of his life, in *Man's Nature and His Communities*, Niebuhr came to see that, contrary to his earlier view of "immoral society," in his public role a man sometimes has to be nobler than in his private roles. It is not one's individual heart that is so engaged; one needs to stand up taller to play one's public role nobly and well, with a certain detachment from one's own feelings. For instance, the ambassador of the Soviet Union might be a very humane and sensitive man, but the relations between the two powers, the one he represents and the one I represent, must be played out on a larger stage than that of private personalities. The ambassador of an allied nation might be a lying SOB, but the warm cooperation between our two nations in times of crisis is far more important than one's private feelings. Power relationships endure, while personalities briefly come onstage and soon depart.

In this way, I predicted, as president, Carter would be sorely tempted to reduce relationships between nations to matters of individual hearts learning to love each other. His public manner would be warm, personal, and peaceful. Even in speeches to large audiences, Carter would lean toward speaking to individual hearts. By contrast, public reasonings for and against institutional policies would seem to him impersonal and distancing. It is the difference, so to speak, between an Episcopalian and a Baptist style. No wonder that by far the larger number of presidents in American history, especially successful presidents, have been of Episcopalian upbringing. Baptists do enthusiasm better, while a cooler, less personal style characterizes the Anglican-Episcopalian temper.

DURING THE WEEK AFTER my pieces ran in the *Post* and the *Star,* I learned that Jimmy Carter was going to address a crowd at a nearby motel, so I decided to go. The Pennsylvania primary was coming up, and I was resolved to help out Senator Scoop Jackson, now that Sarge had been driven out of the race. Two of my best friends, Ben Wattenberg and Penn Kemble, were already helping out in the Jackson campaign. We were part of a group formed after the 1972 election called the Coalition for a Democratic Majority, and Senators Daniel Patrick Moynihan, Hubert Humphrey, and Scoop Jackson were our leaders, along with future House majority leader Tom Foley of Washington State. Some people called us the "hawks" of the Democratic Party. Military strength in the United States was the best (in fact, the only) guarantee of peace, we thought. We also were the party of human rights and *their* best guarantor, the form of government accurately called the democratic republic. Carter, I had begun to fear, had set his mind on wooing the more liberal Democrats of California and the Northeast; he figured the more conservative Democrats would end up with him anyway.

After Carter's talk in the conference ballroom—a good, warm talk as usual—I tentatively waited for the candidate to walk up the aisle, shaking hands, until he got to me near the back. We greeted each other warmly, and then I told him I was sorry, but after Sarge's exit from the race, I would not be able to work for him after all. "Who will you support?" he asked me. "Scoop Jackson," I replied. The governor stepped backward as if taking a blow. Then he summoned up grace and wished me well. I could see that in Carter's eyes, Jackson was way too close to the unions and too much of a hawk for a southerner longing for the support of the northern liberals. (Later, after his election to the presidency, a popular joke captured his predicament: With one foot planted in his base, Georgia, because of the Kennedy liberals Carter had to keep his other foot planted in Massachusetts. Which explains the pain he felt right about the area of the District of Columbia.)

Walking behind Governor Carter, Jody Powell and Ham Jordan stopped at my row and asked me why the governor had stepped back at what I had said. I told them I was going to support Scoop Jackson. Jody Powell tossed his head back, saying: "Ah, he doesn't give a shit!" That let me glimpse a contrast between the candidate's supermoralism and a two-facedness at the center of the Carter team. It also showed political inexperience—no matter what one's pique, one must hold back, never knowing when you might want a voter's support at later stages of the campaign.

After Carter beat Scoop Jackson in Pennsylvania and later in Michigan (where my sister Mary Ann was co-chairman of his underdog state campaign), the nomination was his. Not even these two highly unionized states could resist the appeal of Carter's quiet demeanor and his naval commander's mental precision. Even his Sunday school candor seemed restful after the trauma of the Nixon years.

Working that spring with Senator Jackson also taught me a great deal. How I admired him! I was proud to tour with him in Pennsylvania and to prepare his remarks for my hometown of Johnstown. I remember him saying (I don't think it was a cliché then, although it certainly is nowadays) that he had only three priorities: "Jobs. Jobs. And jobs!" Johnstown at that time had 18 percent unemployment, partly visible in its shuttered steel mills, but it also boasted the lowest crime rate of any other city its size in America. That showed something about the character of the people there—as did the great sports arena of the War Memorial, with all its memorabilia of great Johnstown athletes and coaches of national fame.

Readers may remember seeing the inside of the Memorial Arena in the movie *Slap Shot*. Many of our neighbors and friends had bit parts in the crowd scenes of that film. About a dozen Johnstowners even agreed to have their bare butts filmed, pressed out the windows of a passing bus (supporters of the visiting team, no doubt). The fee for this work was small, but it was at least a paying job. I also enjoyed telling the senator about the giant home run Babe Ruth once hit in the red-brick Point Stadium, over the wall and the scoreboard in right field, 407 feet from home plate. According to my father, who saw it, the ball was still rising as it disappeared into the darkness beyond the wall.

As I've mentioned, my wife, Karen, was from a partly Norwegian family in northern Iowa, so when the senator told me his own family was Norwegian, the explanation for something in his behavior really clicked. Senator Jackson was at times amazingly reticent and short syllabled. He didn't like fancy speech. This reminded me of how, when we stayed in Iowa for a few weeks every summer, I found I had to speak more slowly and deliberately—people there didn't trust fast-talkers from the East. A mixed marriage in Karen's hometown (population 2,000 when everybody was home) was when a Norwegian Lutheran married a German Lutheran, or a German Catholic married an Irish Catholic. During election seasons, I found, it was safer to talk about the corn, the heat, and the rhubarb. Everybody already knew what everybody else in town thought, and it was no use breaking up a happy dinner table. People had to get along all winter. Well, anyway, like these Iowans, Scoop kept his eye on the ball and kept things brief. To many reporters, he seemed relatively inarticulate and even colorless. Scoop liked it that way, and I liked him for it.

Scoop was the country's greatest champion of worldwide human rights. Prisoners in the Gulag later said that they banged on the pipes (their only means of communication) when they heard of his straight talk—unvarnished and quiet, but tough—about the Soviet leadership. Throughout the Gulag, he was maybe the most famous American. He was particularly watchful over the Jews in the Soviet Union who wanted to emigrate—the "refuseniks"—and the outspoken protestors against daily acts of Soviet repression. In later years he was watchful over Sakharov, and Sharansky, and many another lonely hero. I loved being with him.

Later that summer, at the time of the Democratic Convention, Scoop telephoned me from his Manhattan hotel and invited me to dinner. He had received a heads-up call that he was one of the two finalists for Jimmy Carter's vice presidential pick. He wanted me to stand by to help with his public remarks in case the call came down to him. The call never came. The nod went to Senator Mondale of Minnesota instead (another Norwegian). Mondale was much more beloved on the left, and I thought the choice was a mistake. Not that Mondale was not a very good man—he was. But Carter had already won the support of the Left, and he could better have united a divided party, both left and right, if he had chosen Jackson. Or so, in my amateur way, I imagined.

Later in the campaign, Carter asked for Jackson's public support in the national race. Jackson was quick to reply that his price would be a strong commitment by Carter to an international human rights platform during his presidency. Carter concurred. Although he seldom talked human rights during his campaign—the term does not show up in the index of reporters' later books on his campaign—Carter did fulfill this pledge by some strong words after his presidency began and by setting up a human rights office in the State Department. There was, however, a lot left to be desired in the Carter approach to human rights. It was so utopian, and it neglected the great political and military powers that were most systematically stamping on human rights. His method gave way too much attention to fine words and not nearly enough to powerful realities. As vice president Jackson would never have allowed that, and the Jacksonites became very strong critics of what Carter meant by human rights. Jeane Kirkpatrick was their leader, among many others, like the young Josh Muravchik, who was just getting his PhD with a thesis on the subject at Georgetown. Jackson stood with them. He wasn't much moved by swings of opinion in such matters. He stuck to basics, like a rock—entirely midwestern Norwegian of him.

15

The Economic Debates
of the Carter Years

In 1977 a world-class think tank on economic and social thought, the American Enterprise Institute in Washington, D.C., invited me to join its team of scholars. I accepted eagerly, pending only Karen's approval. Karen really wanted to live in either New York or Washington, since both had artistic communities, and when we paid an exploratory visit to D.C., she speedily found artist friends.

At AEI I felt like a lucky graduate student soaking up learning from the stars above. I gladly took a pay cut in the move. AEI specifically wanted a theologian, to add a humanistic perspective to their programs, alongside their existing major emphases on economics and foreign policy. AEI president William Baroody Sr. had Lebanese roots and well knew that in his ancestral land the dividing line (the "killing line") was not politics or ethnicity or language, but religion. He thought the West was much too ignorant about religion. There were no theologians in any other think tank in Washington. He would have the first.

In my own theological circles, by contrast, the very words "Enterprise Institute" conclusively branded me as right-wing, a sellout to corporate America. But AEI in fact was eager to expand its existing cohort of active Democrats: Ben Wattenberg, Norm Ornstein, Tom Mann, Jeane Kirkpatrick, and others.

I got to AEI just in time to secure a front-row seat at the great economic debates of the next three years. Those debates were the most extensive, grandest public arguments about economics in my lifetime. A big idea born at AEI just before I arrived concerned supply-side economics. The supply-side theory is often attributed to Jude Wanniski (*The Way the World Works*), but Irving Kristol was also very near the center of it. From his perch at *The Public Interest* and then at AEI, Irving was Congressman Jack Kemp's mentor (Irving was mentor to most of us), and through Jack the idea gained political currency.

Supply-siders stress two points, one affecting income taxes, the other affecting investment taxes (capital gains taxes). First, reducing tax rates on income puts more money in people's hands, and many will spend it, thereby increasing demand. But some will invest it, even a lot of it. Second, if you cut capital gains taxes—taxes on such important activities as investment in invention, discovery, new products and services—markets that didn't even exist before will come into being.

Inventions such as personal computers, cell phones, fiber optics, copy machines, gene therapy, and many others awaken people's appetites (and newly discovered needs) for new and different goods. Sometimes, as in the case of robotics, inventions mean not only new products but also new kinds of automated methods of production. Mechanical auto parts came to be replaced with electronic ones that are cleaner, smaller, lighter, and of vastly greater ability and efficiency; they also make the diagnosis of problems under the hood much easier. Cuts in certain tax rates can revolutionize economic life, supply-siders claimed, and actual results bore them out. The idea of strengthening the supply side through lowering taxes in job-creating investments is simple enough and immensely fruitful.

Jack Kemp used to remind his audiences that the supply-side argument was put on the agenda by a Democrat, John F. Kennedy. That jogged my memory, and I recalled President Kennedy's surprising tax cuts back in the early 1960s. Kennedy's stated purpose was to boost incentives—incentives for investment and entrepreneurial activity. A later colleague of mine at AEI, Steven F. Hayward, cited Kennedy's actual words: "It is a paradoxical truth that tax *rates* are too high today and tax *revenues* are too low, and the soundest way to raise the revenues in the long run is to cut the rates now. . . . The purpose of cutting taxes now is not to incur a budget deficit, but to achieve the more prosperous, expanding economy that can bring a budget surplus" (emphasis mine). That bit of jujitsu seemed to me wonderfully counterintuitive—"lower to raise"? Once it clicked in my mind, the policy made perfect common sense.

The main point is that investors want to risk more money on creative ideas when faced with tempting incentives. It's the same with entrepreneurs, who are willing to risk their savings to start new businesses, but only when the incentives are promising. They are less willing when the economic sky is dark and foreboding. Under propitious conditions when tax rates are lowered, more jobs are created. Further, this circulation generates new tax revenues over and over with each new change of hands. Economists may find me wrong in these musings, but that is how I reasoned it through. In those days I especially appreciated help from columnists such as Warren Brookes, at that time an unusually good teacher who brought practical light to many of us who were neophytes. Lower tax rates tease money out of bank vaults, where it sits uninvested and unused. Lower tax rates awaken "animal spirits"—keen-eyed spirits, eager to invest in new businesses in order to bring new technologies to market and create new jobs. Economic growth brings into the Treasury gushers of new revenue. Low tax rates equal higher new revenues. Maybe I am only an amateur, but the logic makes sense to me.

In 1979 Jack Kemp and Vin Weber invited me to a meeting of Young Republicans at Camp Ihduhapi in Loretto, Minnesota. As the day unfolded, I learned quickly that Jack was an extraordinarily gifted teacher. He stated the issues more clearly than I had ever heard. The questions from the young people in attendance were also extremely helpful, for many of them asked just what I needed to learn, too.

Congressman Kemp's congressional district was in a heavily Democratic area of Buffalo. Of course, Jack had been a quarterback for the Buffalo Bills, leading the team in the 1960s to three consecutive Eastern Division titles and two straight AFL championships. Jack had also been a leader of the AFL players union. At one of his campaign appearances, the Bills' former center, a diehard Democrat who agreed to speak for Jack only out of friendship but not really wanting to endorse a Republican, stood up after dinner to say a word of limited endorsement. "All I can say is that I spent nine years bending over in front of Jack Kemp. This is a man you can trust." The deliciously loud laughter that followed was worth its weight in gold.

Back when I was writing speeches for George McGovern during the summer of 1972, one of the young "brains" on the McGovern team had proposed an economic program whereby every American with an earned income over $15,000 per year would give back $1,000 in taxes, and every person earning below that would receive $1,000. They called it "Demogrants." I hated that idea. I knew my father's story, and how he had sacrificed, skimped, and saved to put every one of his five children through college, precisely so they could earn more than he ever had.

On this point Jack Kemp told an illuminating story, which I'll paraphrase here. "I am not a green-eyeshade Republican!" he would say. "I believe in incentives. I trust you with your own money. If you do hard, sweaty work in the mills your whole life so your kids can go to college, do you want the government to take a big chunk of it, just to give it to people who maybe did not sacrifice as much as you have? Is that fair? Is that what you want? It's not what I want.

"I want a government that trusts you—and your kids—to spend your money better than the government can. If your kids can keep more money in their own pockets, they will start businesses, and that means they won't have to do the sweaty work that you did all your life. And they will send their kids to college without skimping on nice things for the Mrs. as much as you did.

"I'm for tax *cuts,* not for higher rates. I'm for letting you keep your own money, to spend better than government can."

Jack explained how his garbage man once stopped him at the curb to tell him, "You keep fighting this Demogrant shit! I don't want the rules changin' just as my kids start to get ahead. I don't mind hard work, but I don't want my kids doin' what I'm doin'. I want better jobs for them, using their brains, not their backs. I ain't voted Republican ever, but I'm with ya', Jack. Give 'em hell!"

These new economic ideas were percolating in my head during the Carter years. Two primary issues in play at AEI during that time made my economic thinking even more concrete. The first was AEI's project on regulation, and the second was the fight to cut capital gains taxes. AEI led the way in both these battles, with surprising success.

My new friend Murray Weidenbaum of Washington University in St. Louis was the father of AEI's project on the costs of regulation. His idea was to find ways of measuring just how expensive regulation is, and to propose that every government program with new regulations should be required to prepare a statement in advance of these regulatory costs, in terms of both time and money. This new requirement would balance the already required environmental impact statements.

The tally of annual regulatory costs Murray's team came up with was staggering but also stood up to reason. And the beauty of it was that any who objected to this particular system of national measure were free to improve it on their own. As experience dictated, it could become more exact with every passing year.

Miracle of miracles, on the very first day of its release both the *New York Times* and the *Washington Post* endorsed Murray's measure with enthusiastic editorials. Very quickly, Senator Ted Kennedy endorsed deregulation of the trucking industry. (I knew at least one Massachusetts trucker who may have called the senator, for I had heard him say angrily that he was about to lose his business because of stupid regulations.)

The epic fight for cuts in capital gains taxes, so vital for coaxing new venture capital out of safe, tax-avoiding investments, such as municipal bonds, and into investment in companies with new inventions was a little more complex. It was exciting for someone as new to Washington as I was to watch this battle rage, and I was surprised to find myself cheering for the underdog. The hero's name was the slightly portly, non-imposing congressman from Wisconsin, Representative William Steiger. Steiger understood the crucial role of sound incentives to lure capital out from hiding. The trouble was that almost no one else understood—or cared. Not labor. Not corporate leaders, who thought they had more urgent matters to confront in the business-depressing Carter years, with the soon to be infamous "misery index" (inflation plus unemployment). But the venerable Bill Baroody, our boss at AEI, backed the idea to the hilt.

When Mr. Baroody introduced me to Congressman Steiger, I was surprised how young Steiger was and how midwestern plain. He was not physically imposing, which is all the more to his credit, because he had courage, tenacity, and skill. In a House that was overwhelmingly Democratic, the Republican Steiger had managed to round up nineteen votes (all fourteen Republicans, plus five Democrats) out of the thirty-seven on the Ways and Means Committee: a majority. People began to notice. That committee was the primary mover and shaker on tax policy in the House, and in our system the House is charged by the Constitution with originating tax policy. If a man grabs a majority in that key committee, the minds and hearts of the House eventually come along—most of the time.

Those nineteen votes stayed strong all through 1978, despite vicious attacks launched in the name of "fairness," a term Jimmy Carter had begun using politically. In and of itself, that term did not tend to resonate among a large share of rank-and-file Democrats. A study commissioned by the Democratic Party discovered that a majority of voters heard "fairness" as "higher taxes for me."

But President Carter had also hit upon two gangbuster images on the stump: the "three-martini lunch" and the "twenty-one taxpayers" who were millionaires but showed not a cent of income tax liability. Joe Six-Pack did not have the leisure or the cash to take three-martini lunches (chances are he didn't drink martinis anyway), but what really galled him were millionaires not paying any income tax at all. And the strange three-martini lunch made the twenty-one millionaires look even more distant from the ordinary guy and gal. For two years President Carter and his allies—chiefly, future majority leader George Mitchell in the Democratic-dominated Senate— held off the growing sentiment in favor of the capital gains tax cuts.

Bill Steiger's counterarguments to the Democrats were these: President Carter himself was just then publicly confessing his government's own helplessness. The old Democratic-Keynesian playbook read: Use higher government spending, even if it fans some inflation, in order to increase demand and thereby cause job growth.

This time, however, that policy was causing "stagflation," a new word for the toxic combination of a stagnant jobs market plus inflation at the rate of 9 to 10 percent for more than a year at a time. (In three years, fixed incomes lost a third of their total value; millions of seniors on fixed incomes tumbled below poverty levels.) The president himself described the sullen miasma over the country as a "malaise," the causes and cures of which his "brights" seemed really not to understand. The whole country seemed to be begging for a new economic vision. Congressman Steiger was providing just that, or at least one main dynamic engine of it.

The key to this vision lay in two historical precedents with well-established facts. To Democrats, one was less troubling, but the other really did get to them. Less troubling was Treasury Secretary Andrew Mellon's dramatically low tax rates in the 1920s, which ignited that decade into a roar. The more troubling one was President Kennedy's unexpected and successful cuts in capital gains rates, so short a time ago as the still vivid 1960s. Evidence notwithstanding, well-known Democratic economist Walter Heller and others bitterly attacked Steiger's reasoning (and Jack Kemp's also) as illusory.

But Steiger's people countered with a very damaging statement from Heller himself, made only a few years earlier. Based on his own studies, Heller had clearly demonstrated that the surge of revenues from Kennedy's cuts in rates not only had paid for themselves down the years but had helped produce a Treasury surplus. That was a fact; Heller testified to it. His case against the supply-siders sagged.

One by one, the pillars of the Democratic case were crumbling, and more and more Democrats in the House and Senate were joining Steiger's troops. In December 1978 his amendment passed, and President Carter silently signed it into law. The humble Steiger Amendment was the launchpad for the Reagan boom of new tech companies in the 1980s, companies founded on little more than a patent and a fresh wad of venture capital. New companies sprouted up, and they soon came to dominate the country's business land-scape (Microsoft, Intel, Genentech, Compaq, Recognition Equip-ment, for instance), and in their startlingly rapid growth elbowed aside old blue-chip standbys. The ranks of the rich multiplied from investments in these risky new ventures, tax revenues poured in, and the number of the employed in America set historically new records.

AEI does not deserve too much credit for Steiger's amazing vic-tory, for Herb Stein and a few of our other most storied economists continued to mock the supply-siders and push budgetary discipline, pain, and austerity. The tried-and-true "GOP School of Dentistry" ("it's not good for you unless it hurts") was still fighting to regain control of the party.

Both Weidenbaum's heavy lifting on the costs of regulation and the Steiger fight were central parts of my education in the role of ideas in a capitalist economy. The creative ideas of a few can change the fortunes of an entire nation—and even the world. During the Reagan administration, the United States added to its own GDP an amount equivalent to the GDP of the prospering West German Republic. American GDP grew larger by a whole one-third of what it had been at the end of the Carter term. The numbers of the em-ployed hit historic highs. The median income (that is, the point at which half the income-earning population earns more, and half less) jumped by thousands of dollars. The average incomes of the poor rose, as did the number of those who escaped from poverty. The numbers and proportion of black households (especially of blacks living together as married couples) that earned enough to rise above the median income swelled significantly.

In a way, in the 1990s the Clinton administration made this revolution bipartisan. Clinton stole the clothes of Reaganomics (dis-guising this by raising tax rates very little). Where Reagan set in place conditions for the creation of 16 million jobs, Clinton did even better: nearly 23 million jobs. To get along with the majority of Republicans in the House, Clinton agreed to lower the capital gains tax rate from 28 percent to 20 percent. In a short amount of time, he doubled the actual revenues from that tax. The Treasury got more revenues; the nation got more jobs.

Far better for the nation to bring both parties into the secret for economic dynamism and job creation. Kennedy-to-Reagan-to-Clinton was a powerful double play combo.

What a time to be alive!

16

On Ronald Reagan

Karen and I lived in California in 1966 when Ronald Reagan surprised a host of people by being elected governor—and then turned out to be both more dominant than anyone expected and as affable as any governor had ever been. He killed his critics with friendly merriment.

I was still an ardent Democrat at the time, so by no means was I in favor of Reagan's election. But I did learn to admire the way he refused to be put down by anyone—from TV newsmen to Berkeley professors. He always had better answers than they expected, and quicker humor. He also had a knack for remembering the first steps in any argument, the ones that most of us have forgotten by the time we are past forty. They are so basic that most ordinary people in California saw their importance at once, but those with college educations had long since lost them down the memory hole. It went something like this: "Government is like kids. *Both* spend too much money. When kids spend too much, you cut their allowance. It's time to cut government's allowance."

Once the governor was attending a meeting of the Board of Regents at Berkeley, and while he was inside, some students saw his limo idling in the driveway. They gathered nearby, hoping to ambush Reagan. As the governor ambled down the walk, they moved in with hand-painted signs and shouts. Reagan's security detail shepherded him into the limo and got the door closed. But then the crowd surged against the car shouting and holding placards up against its back window, as close to the governor's face as possible.

Amused, Reagan studied the messages: "We are the future." "1960s, love them or leave them." When some of the more athletic students began to rock the gubernatorial limousine, others began chanting: "We are the future!" TV cameras caught what followed. The governor lifted his yellow legal pad to the window, with letters printed large in his own hand. Held up toward the cameras, his reply read: "I'm selling my bonds!" Then, with a wave from the governor, the limo started easing its way slowly through the crowd.

I never saw the governor lose an exchange with intellectuals. In fact, after his terms in office were up, the governor was booked for a debate with Bobby Kennedy at Yale. My eastern friends, thinking of Reagan as a B-movie star, were waiting for this with glee. I warned them that Ronald Reagan was going to win that debate. By common consensus afterward, that's just what he did. He did it by rapier humor and statements so basic that the former attorney general could not quite remember the simple ripostes. At moments, Bobby seemed tongue-tied with exasperation. In the way Reagan always tried to end things, the two joined in a smiling handshake and a half embrace. Bobby looked quite disgusted with himself, as many had before, and many more would in the years to come.

During the campaign of 1980, I learned a few other tidbits about Reagan. My friend and eminent colleague at the American Enterprise Institute Jeane Kirkpatrick had published a stunning article, "Dictatorships and Double Standards," in the November 1979 issue of *Commentary*. Not long after, candidate Ronald Reagan invited her to California for a conversation. She told me afterward that Reagan was the most secure man in the presence of a woman that she had ever met. She was impressed with his grasp of the exact nature of totalitarianism, as well as of the intricacies of arms control. Jeane was a tough critic and a skilled reader of people. She had not expected to be as deeply impressed with Reagan. She spoke of him with a note of pleased surprise that stuck in my memory.

When Carter and Reagan ended up being the two nominees, the rival campaigns heated up in earnest. I noted one split among my Republican AEI colleagues, and another among the activist Democrats. The Republican "elder statesmen" among the economists—distinguished men who had served in high governmental posts under previous administrations—had little regard for the strong "supply-siders" in our midst, the younger Turks who were close to Irving Kristol and Jack Kemp. (Jude Wanniski, whom I mentioned earlier, spelled out the main insight of supply-side economics at one of our brown-bag lunches.) Irving Kristol too had been a godfather for the youth rebellion. Relations inside AEI were cordial and yet a bit frosty in those days. Early on in the campaign, Herb Stein, former chairman of the Council of Economic Advisers under Presidents Nixon and Ford, and with long years of government service before that, began traveling to California at Reagan's request. I noted that each time this happened, Reagan stopped speaking about growth, investment, lower taxes—the supply side—and tried to emphasize balancing the budget. Each time he did this, the governor seemed listless and his poll numbers dipped.

But Irving Kristol's great friend and protégé in the Congress, Jack Kemp, was also called to advise Reagan on a regular basis, and each time Kemp visited one could see Reagan's spirit soar, and his numbers would begin inching up again. Kemp had the effect of freeing

Reagan to be himself. Reagan was no "green-eyeshade Republican," to use Kemp's phrase, no member of the GOP School of Dentistry.

Before describing further the economic argument that stirred the country during the summer of 1980, I want to mention two events. Karen and I were attending a dinner buffet around the pool at Max Kampelman's home in Northwest D.C. It was a dinner for the Coalition for a Democratic Majority (CDM). There were about eighty of us meeting in the ample living room, when Max telephoned that he was delayed on the tarmac at LaGuardia but should get to the party some ninety minutes later. Senator Moynihan got the meeting started off in Max's stead.

"The question is," Moynihan began in that commanding but light voice of his, "should CDM endorse the Democratic nominee this year?" It was a startling question for our group, most of whom had earlier thought of themselves as the labor left of the Democratic Party. "Just out of curiosity," the senator slowly and coyly drawled, "a show of hands. How many in this room are thinking of voting for Ronald Reagan?" We all got a stunning revelation: First one, then two more, then slowly but steadily nearly every hand in the room went up. It was a drawn-out vote, as some hesitated, and most surprised even themselves in declaring where they stood. "My, my," the senator observed with the familiar bob of his chin. "I am quite surprised—and yet, somehow not surprised. That's why I asked."

Most of us looked around at our friends across the room. We hadn't known. We thought we were each alone.

Secondly, in about mid-October, my son Rich's school, Gonzaga, the Jesuit high school on North Capitol Street that had been for more than a generation the alma mater of famous Democratic sons, sponsored its usual mock election. Rich reported that, to everyone's astonishment, Ronald Reagan had defeated Jimmy Carter handily. No one could remember anything like it. I inferred, maybe wrongly, that was what the young Gonzaga boys were imbibing in their homes—but evidence too flimsy to put in anything I was writing at the time. In the days before the election, the polls reported Carter with a small but serious lead. But Gonzaga's mock election did embolden me to offer my candid opinion when, on the day before the election, in a lecture to a national railway association, an executive asked me for a prediction on the morrow's election. I knew it was too late for whatever I said to appear in the press, but I still hesitated. "Well, I haven't been prepared to write it, but I think that tomorrow Reagan is going to win, and he may win very big. There are signs that Carter's support among Democrats is awfully weak." The conference met my remarks with disbelief.

I myself was not sure that my hunch was correct, and I was glad I hadn't put it in writing. The next day's totals showed Reagan winning 51 percent of the popular vote and carrying forty-four states, to Carter's 41 percent and six states plus the District of Columbia (Independent candidate John Anderson took more than 6 percent of the popular vote). A shocking outcome, considering Reagan's reputation as a B-actor (made much of by the media), his age, and the power of a sitting president with large Democratic majorities in the country.

Over the next few days, the commentators made much of the huge economic debate going on around the country. There had been more debate about basic economics that autumn than at any time in my lifetime (I was too young to have understood Franklin Delano Roosevelt in the 1930s and '40s). There were other issues, too—Carter's perceived weakness in foreign policy, notably with regard to Iran. But most of all, pundits recalled the clinching line of Reagan's debate with Carter. Looking full into the camera, he summed up the entire situation, asking the country: "Are you better off now than you were four years ago?"

I didn't yet know enough about economics to be sure who was

right in that economic argument or to adjudicate between my opposing colleagues at AEI, although I was slowly tilting toward the supply side, and much against Carter's high interest rates. After Karen's and my experiences in buying one home and selling another during the Carter years, I sympathized with the supply-siders. They stressed cutting taxes, updating regulations, and promoting job growth through the creation of new small businesses and new technologies all across the land. By contrast, the Republican establishment called for spending cuts and balanced budgets. The Democratic demand-siders held to the classic Democratic Party prescription: In a recession, raise government spending in order to boost demand. I became fascinated with the great economic experiment being born in the bosom of the Republican Party—that is, rejecting *both* the Dems' School of More Spending and the GOP School of Dentistry.

Now, to that real-world example from our family's experience just before 1980: My wife and I purchased a new home in Washington in 1978, and we were painfully aware of two things. We had watched interest rates rise irrepressibly higher through the 1970s, and we had experienced the high inflation of the Carter years. We watched these two chilling forces crimp our elderly parents, while it threw into poverty some three million seniors who were on fixed incomes. Karen and I were also caught in these pincers—high interest rates and high inflation—by our need to pay for a home in Washington. We had just sold our home in Syracuse, about a block from campus, for about one-third the amount that we had to pay for a home in the District of Columbia. The home in Syracuse was a much better house—bigger, more spacious and brighter, and entirely remodeled under Karen's skillful eye and hand. The new home in Washington, at three times the cost, was smaller, boasted less airiness and light, and had had no updating since about 1935. It was just plain dingy. Still, Karen's eye judged it promising.

If we kept sheer price in mind, in comparison with the price we could get from selling our home in Syracuse, it would have been irrational to buy in Washington. But Karen recognized one feature of our federal government's hometown. Where there are many government workers, somehow the government takes care to keep their salaries rising with inflation. When the rest of the country experiences severe recession, prosperity clings to government and its proximity. Karen figured our new home would hold its value, even at the outrageous price we paid for it. There are only so many lots and so many homes in the tiny District of Columbia. Fixed supply, rising demand.

But the "misery index" of the Carter years was burned indelibly into our minds. Unprecedented inflation (over 13 percent by 1979), plus very high unemployment (7 percent), plus interest rates that had jumped from the original 5 percent of the mortgage on our home in Syracuse to about 10 percent when we bought in D.C. in 1978, and up to 15 percent by the end of 1980. Taking out a mortgage at 15 percent is a fearful burden in a way that the 5 percent mortgage we had assumed just a few years earlier was not.

Eleven days after Reagan's inauguration, the first Karen and I had ever attended (cold but exhilarating because of Reagan's lovely inaugural address), I found myself, totally unexpectedly, in Geneva as the president's ambassador to the UN Commission on Human Rights (see details in the following chapter). We did well enough in Geneva for the president to send me back in 1982.

Because it sheds a nifty light on Ronald Reagan up close, I want to tell a story about Karen and the president. While I was off in Geneva the second time, Karen was invited to the White House for a dinner honoring Polish Americans, and including a private pre-view of a new film about Reagan and the Communist crackdown on the labor union Solidarity in Poland. As the new guests com-mingled, awaiting the entrance of the president, she chatted amiably with Cardinal Krol, Congressman Dan Rostenkowski, and many others, who were quite gracious to her—the only woman in the room. Then, abruptly the door opened and in walked the president.

At this point, most of the men turned their backs on Karen, crowding her to the rear. The president immediately espied her and, his eyes lighting up, summoned her forward. Parting the waves, he escorted her to sit beside him at the table.

After grace had been said and all were seated, to break the ice Karen turned to the president and said, "I notice they don't call it Reaganomics anymore. Interest rates are way down from when we bought our house." Just then she felt a really sharp pain on her shin. She added something else about inflation coming down, and she got another sharp kick. This time she could see from his red face that it was Congressman Rostenkowski across the table, trying to get her to stop. The president beamed. He took her opening words as a great way to start the evening.

Shortly afterward, when I returned from Geneva, Karen told me about the event. Her eyes were still radiant about it. The president had been so "gal-*lant*," she exclaimed, taking her arm and seating her beside him. She had really loved it.

On my return, I was able to give the president a short briefing on Geneva at the White House. When we stood alone for a mo-ment, I took the opportunity to thank him for entertaining Karen so gracefully that evening. He remembered her and the occasion immediately.

"She said you were 'gal-*lant*,'" I added. "But *I* think you just have your eye out for the prettiest girl in the room." He flashed back his trademark grin, "You got it, buddy!" and, as men do, struck his fist into the side of my arm.

Gotta love the guy, I thought.

After Karen's death, our dear friend Mary Eberstadt wrote a tribute to her in which she noted that Karen ran the best conservative salon in Washington. My young friend studying for the Paulist priesthood, Robert Sirico, later the founder and head of the Acton Institute, was there for at least a dozen of these dinners, often cooking with Karen, and he has recalled a number of other regular guests, including Bill Bennett, Jack and Joanne Kemp, Charles and Robyn Krauthammer, Mort Kondracke, Ben Wattenberg, Bob and Mary Ellen Bork, George and Joan Weigel, Irving and Bea Kristol, Midge Decter, Norman Podhoretz, Elliott Abrams, and Henry Hyde. Also, John McLaughlin (the ex-Jesuit speechwriter for Nixon), Pat and Shelley Buchanan, Sonny Abramson, Walter and Irene Berns, and the great sociologist Robert Nisbet.

Clare Boothe Luce—perhaps our favorite guest—loved to come to dinner at our house. When Clare was down for some reason or another, her secretary (who lived in our parish) telephoned Karen to suggest inviting Clare to dinner. Sometimes Karen planned special parties for Clare. Karen was so unpretentious and down-home that Clare was able to unwind and have a great time—leading the conversation, parrying objections, telling stories, and enjoying (compared to her usual fare) simple food.

Once Karen even served Dove bars for dessert, and Clare was delighted, so Karen was able to do it more often. For her own "Last Supper"—before her declining health forced her into seclusion—Clare invited Karen, me, and our daughter Tanya (who was then at Stanford) to join her closest family members. (Clare's daughter had died at Stanford in an auto crash at just about Tanya's age, and Tanya had been baptized in the Palo Alto church that Clare had built in her honor.) That night Clare served Dove bars; the whole menu had been chosen in memory of one of Karen's menus for her. (Sylvia Jukes Morris, the wife of Reagan's unhappy biographer and a journalist herself, wrote a mocking article about this "odd" menu, without ever comprehending the quiet compliment that Clare was paying Karen.) Karen and I were so deeply touched that it was an evening too precious ever to forget.

On an earlier occasion, Clare decided to have Karen and me over as her guests when she was having a small dinner for President and Nancy Reagan in her apartment high up in the Watergate condos. George Will was there, along with the director of the FBI, William Webster. In the background were the Secret Service, charged with protecting the president and the First Lady. The dinner was in November 1985, just before the Reagans were to fly to Geneva for the president's first meeting with Mikhail Gorbachev. I remember two things about the conversation at that table. First, the president's high (and, it then seemed to me, innocent) hopes about the meeting. He spoke of meeting Mr. Gorbachev "eye-to-eye, as one grandfather to another," and putting before Gorbachev the proposition that, between the two of them, they had the power to alter for the better the life that their grandchildren would face. George Will and I caught each other's eyes just then, and we both glanced heavenward.

In my experience working with the Soviets at the Commission on Human Rights and in Moscow for several days (for a planning session), I saw that they did not act out their personal feelings or thoughts. They acted according to the "Program," however good-humoredly and ironically one or two of them did so. I had made it a point to spend time with each man in their delegation personally— out for coffee or a meal, or exchanging stories in the hallways by ourselves. They could chat and laugh, and even crack subtle jokes at the Soviet Union's expense. Still I had observed a certain deadly serious cutoff point where they became impenetrable, and I feared our president wasn't aware of this way the Soviets operated.

I resolved after that dinner to pray for the president every day—that he would not be too trusting of Gorbachev. It just goes to show how little insight I had into Reagan's experience with Communists in the United States, as well as his own insight into the double inner life of Soviet officials. I also had too little insight into the guile of President Reagan himself; he was much more sophisticated than I was.

One tool Reagan especially believed in was the power of ideas, and his ideas were deeper, more basic, and more fundamental than those of his complacent critics. He believed in telling the truth without camouflage and using the logic inherent in a certain family of terms. For instance, when he himself inserted into a 1983 speech the vivid phrase "evil empire," he had a long-range logic in mind. Nine times, officials who were given advance drafts of his speech struck the phrase. Nine times, Reagan put it back in. On delivery, he said the phrase exactly where he had intended to say it, even though it had once more been removed. Academic experts, editorialists, and those praised as wise and serious men expressed horror at a claim that they considered so exaggerated, naïve, and taboo. But there was one thing Reagan knew that they didn't. The term "evil" has a logic of its own.

In Soviet propaganda and internal self-delusion, Western terms about morality were deemed "bourgeois self-deceptions." The only true morality was to press forward history's directive: the only thing morally good was to advance the cause of socialism; the only evil was to retard or to oppose socialism, history's darling. Reagan knew he was inserting another logic into that mythic structure. Inevitably, Gorbachev would be asked by a journalist whether he agreed with Reagan that the Soviet empire was an evil empire. That question now became slippery. Gorbachev would of course laugh and say "No!" But sooner or later a journalist would ask: "But what about Stalin's purges in the 1930s? Don't you agree that they were evil? Even Khrushchev admitted that." Well, of course, Gorbachev would be driven to say: Well, yes, some things were evil, but socialism no longer endorses those actions. All of a sudden socialism in itself was no longer the only criterion of morality. There was a criterion of morality outside socialism. Necessarily, an inexorable dialectic would be introduced into Soviet life: Well, was *this* moral? What about *that*? Despite itself, the Soviet propaganda regime would become drenched in the worldview and speech traditions of the West. The intellectual unwinding would have been begun.

Reagan understood simple things like that.

SOME TIME AFTER THE Gorbachev meeting in Geneva, Richard Perle came to my office at AEI. (He was a top adviser on nuclear weapons to the Defense Department and had been deputed to accompany the president to Geneva.) He told me a funny story about Raisa Gorbachev, Mikhail's wife, and Nancy Reagan. The two attended many events around Geneva together and spent a lot of time talking in their limo—well, *Raisa* talked. It seems that Raisa, with her university degree, assumed that she was much more learned than Nancy and took to lecturing Nancy incessantly about "reality" as the Soviets saw it, in hackneyed ideological terms. Richard said it drove Nancy crazy. She just couldn't stand it.

I surprised Richard by interjecting, "An answer to my prayers! Not in the way I imagined, but an answer to my prayers." I told him the story of the dinner at Clare's. "Not to worry," he told me, "the president knows what he's doing."

I also remember embarrassing myself a number of times at Clare's dinner. At one point, when the conversation turned to Ireland, I said a few words about having lectured there some while earlier—how I encountered the leftward radicalization of many in Ireland's political class, and how that had surprised and troubled me. Since the Reagans were also to visit Ireland, Mrs. Reagan became noticeably uncomfortable as I spoke—as if she wanted everything to go peacefully there, with no ideological outbreaks, no flare-ups. I did my best to drop the subject and retreat. I saw that Nancy dreaded conflict and was not on the same page at all with some of her husband's more controversial thrusts. She was trying to protect him. With Nancy, I learned, be gentle; she alarms easily. George Will, a regular dinner companion of hers, did not make my mistake. He knew better.

Toward the end, during coffee and smoking time, Clare invited the ladies into the other room, to allow the men to talk alone. At this point I took up a line that my father-in-law in Iowa had taught me: about how he came back home to a small town with his law degree and practically starved for the first few months until—and the president broke in—"until another lawyer moved into town, and from then on they both prospered. W. C. Fields, 1948." Well, I'm actually not sure he said "W. C. Fields," but he did name a famous comedian and the year of the scene. I had been about to tell a story the president might appreciate, but I didn't know enough to know how old a story it was. The president had a vast store of funny stories, I inferred; maybe he even had them numbered, accessible in any circumstance in which they might be needed.

Not very long after that, the lights in Clare's condo went dark. The Secret Service sprang into action; with flashlights they took President and Mrs. Reagan by their arms, leading them into the hall and down the emergency stairs, as quickly as their feet could carry them. Director Webster, meanwhile, told the rest of us to wait quietly. He peeked through the curtains, which had been drawn to protect the president from observation. We had seen the anxiety in the faces of the Secret Service as they hustled the president out of the room. No one had any idea what was happening or what might follow. "The whole building is dark," Mr. Webster reported. A harmless accident? Or a prelude to something worse?

After a few moments Mr. Webster and one agent who had stayed with us led us out to the stairwell and, armed with flashlights shining in front of our feet, led us down the stairs as briskly as we could walk. I don't remember the number of floors, but there were at least nine or ten. The turning of turns on the breathless descent— everyone hoping not to miss a step—took a while. By the time we got down to the main floor and into the fresh October air, the president's limo had careened away. As I recall, just as we looked up, the lights in the building sprang back on.

Our dinner had effectively ended. We must have gone back to retrieve outer garb and purses, thank Clare warmly, and reminisce briefly about the evening. Quite stunning it had been.

I loved the Reagan presidency. You could feel the whole aircraft carrier executing a broad turn on the ocean, moving the nation in a badly needed direction. That slow turn would bring the nation out at a wholly different point from the trajectory on which Carter had put us. Reagan's coattails pulled (as I recall) ten new Republican senators into the Senate. In the few blocks around our house in Northwest D.C., in every direction, about a dozen families slowly left town as their sinecures with Democratic senators ended. I had never realized before what a new presidency meant in terms of families and friends moving in, moving out—by the thousands.

Our children's first vivid memories of a president were shaped by Reagan. I was glad of that; it made up for all my years of working for the advancement of the Left. I did hope, however, that they would learn also to sympathize with the Left, so as to see the country as a nation with two wings, not just one. Down the years they have done just exactly that.

A last point: How on earth did I deserve to be plucked out of the air immediately as Reagan's personal ambassador? I would become the first Reaganaut in all of Europe to give public speeches and articulate public policies in his name. My fellow UN ambassadors from other nations and their staffs were visibly very curious. It was almost as if they expected me to arrive in cowboy boots, with six-guns on my hips.

The press in Europe was seldom kind to Reagan during his eight years as president. They interpreted nearly everything in the worst possible (and highly adversarial) light. Reagan was about to launch a worldwide move toward human rights and democracy, and they refused to see it. On my first two days in Europe a cynical article about me in the British *Guardian* said that my instructions were to roll back all efforts on human rights and democracy. In truth I had been directed to do just the opposite.

I later found out that there had been, indeed, objectors in the White House to my appointment. I was not a Republican, and my published record indicated I was clearly a man of the Left. The one thing on my side, someone told me, was that *Commonweal* had asked me to write their one piece making an argument for Reagan, to go with their pro-Carter piece. No one else wanted to do it for them. I did not endorse Reagan, but I made a decent argument on his behalf. The adviser who knew the terrain on which I was fighting pointed out this article to the president's appointment circle. It turned out to be enough.

Besides, I had been writing since 1970 that the Irish, Italian, and Slavic Catholic immigrants who were an important force in large northeastern and midwestern cities and a crucial pillar of the Democratic majority were being shunted aside in the party by new, unproven constituencies led by the Hollywood glitterati. I held that Catholic ethnics were now the central battleground in presidential elections. Catholics, I wrote, vote regularly (and often, and for many Democratic city "machines")—sometimes even from the grave. Further, in presidential and senatorial elections, Catholics (especially the churchgoing among them) tended to swing from party to party by as many as five or six points either way. This swing tips almost all big elections. Reagan's men had spotted this, nourished it with attention, made Catholics feel welcome, and thus brought into being the "Reagan Democrats" who propelled his huge new majorities. My Democrats had lost this group, while Ronald Reagan spoke directly to them, like a favorite uncle. He was one of them, among the very first Republicans to step past the GOP School of Dentistry and the campaign receptions where no alcohol was served, breaking the Democratic monopoly on fun and the Republican monopoly on austerity.

When Nixon was preparing for a debate, his publicists would show him under a night lamp working on a yellow pad. When JFK was doing his prep, he had his men put out photos of him walking with his kids on the beach, or playing touch football with his staff. Reagan brought the Republicans a largely Catholic love of fun. Protestants tended to represent themselves as ruled by a work ethic, while Catholics emphasized play, fun, and family warmth.

To sum up what I learned just before and during the Reagan administration: First, economics is often counterintuitive. It would seem that the common good would be improved by a government supervising the economy from the top down, just as common ownership of property would produce a higher common good than private property. But real experience since the time of Aristotle, Cicero, and Thomas Aquinas has shown that social ownership in practice reduces personal incentives and personal responsibility and induces a common lassitude. A professor I had met in Russia in 1991, who had known only socialism, voiced sharp, sarcastic thrusts about the

Soviet system: "The trouble with socialism is, *who* will stay up all night to take care of the sick cow?" and "Without incentives, you pretend to work and they pretend to pay you."

The irony is that one best raises the level of the common good of all, not through common ownership and top-down control, but by building into the system many incentives for personal industry, invention, and extra hard work. Punishments depress activity. Praise and incentives excite it.

part three

Culture
Trumps
Politics
and
Economics

17

The Amateur Ambassador

On the day after Inauguration Day 1981, I was enjoying our normal lunch in the AEI lunchroom when Jeane Kirkpatrick walked in. I rose to greet her and congratulate her on her new job. She didn't let go of my hand and said urgently: "I was hoping to see you today, Michael. I need you. We have to have a new ambassador in Geneva for the opening of the UN Commission on Human Rights. My first thought was you. We need you to go put forth our theory of human rights and democracy. I've heard you do it, many times. You're the right one."

"Jeane, I'm no lawyer. I know nothing about human rights *law*. I don't know the case law. I don't understand the legal jargon the UN uses. All those resolutions. All those treaties."

"That's exactly why I want you. We don't want the lawyer stuff. We want a whole new outlook. No one else can do it just now."

"Besides, I've got lectures lined up, and Rich is having the turbulent high school years, and Karen won't be at all happy."

"All I can say, Michael, is that I need you. It's part of my new job—the first thing I have to do."

"How long can you give me to think about it?"

"Not later than tomorrow noon. Today would be best."

"When would I have to be in Geneva?"

"Eight days from tomorrow at the latest. Don't worry; we'll get your travel orders, diplomatic passport, temporary approval from the Congress; you won't have to do any of that. We'll want you for at least a day of briefing and visiting with top congressional leaders, so that they get a look-see."

"Could you get me one minute with the president? I'd like to have at least one sentence I can say came directly from him."

"I'll try. No promises."

Well, a week later I was standing at the Oval Office door with the president and one of his aides for my scheduled minute. "Michael, Jeane tells me you'll do a great job. I just want to say: Nearly all Americans came to this country to protect human rights. So this country can never turn away from human rights. Condone no human rights abuse. None."

There, I had my sentence. I prized it, and I recalled it nearly every day. It was exactly the order I wanted to hear, clear but complete: "Condone no human rights abuse." What a very useful piece of presidential instruction! I had it right from the top. I had all the protection I needed.

In those hectic eight days, I learned a bit about the cross-pressures on my new assignment. It made no difference that I was a registered and active Democrat. The Democrats under Congressman David Bonior of Michigan were already announcing to the press even before Reagan took office that the administration would abandon human rights. I read a story to the same effect in the European press on my flight to Geneva the night before the Commission's formal opening. The briefing book prepared for *the Carter team* was in my lap (there had been no time for a Reagan rewrite)—it was now my briefing book, the *Reagan* briefing book. In its conclusions, it was still 98 percent Carter. Carter's final determinations, after all, were always more guarded and moderate (watched over by Scoop Jackson and Hubert Humphrey) than his own rhetoric in attacking America's friends. For an example, consult the aforementioned article by Jeane Kirkpatrick, "Dictatorships and Double Standards."

In the meantime, the new secretary of state, General Alexander Haig, had announced that all foreign policy decisions would be put on hold for two or three months while the administration conducted a top to bottom review. "That's just great!" I thought with bitter irony. So now I would have to face sixty or more votes over the next six weeks, and be required to give speeches on darn near every one of them. Was I supposed to make it up as I went along? Jeane and a few others (I learned later) were hoping that I would. They wanted a new furrow cut for them.

In addition, shortly after I took to the air, Secretary Haig announced that a theological colleague of mine, Ernest Lefever, whose admiring commentaries on Reinhold Niebuhr I had read as a student, had been nominated to serve as Assistant Secretary of State for Human Rights and Humanitarian Affairs. Niebuhr was the cold-eyed realist in the left-of-center ideological force Americans for Democratic Action, and Ernie prided himself on being a "realist," too, rather than a "sentimentalist." But so had Henry Kissinger. I didn't want to follow the Kissinger route of the 1970s (not allowing President Ford to meet with Aleksander Solzhenitsyn in Washington, for instance, and during the campaign of 1976 urging Ford to insist that Poland at that time was "free"). While I cherished Ernie's colleagueship, I wanted to cut my own path quite clear of his. Putatively, I should have reported to him once he was sworn in. But he never was, his nomination killed off in one of those ritual killings the opposition party always exacts from among a president's first nominees. At least one nominee has to die, just to show the new president who is really boss in Washington.

My main reading on the nonstop flight from Washington to Geneva was that three-inch-thick briefing book, composed of guidance on every issue due to come up on the agenda at the UNCHR, together with the positions written for the Carter administration to express after its assumed re-election. As I finished reading it, I arrived at two conclusions. The first was that the Reagan administration (based on what I knew about it from listening to the president, Jeane, and some others in their orbit) intended to do something very different from Carter—different certainly in philosophy and in frankness. The Reaganauts would not accept the ideology implicit in the statements prepared for the ambassador under the Carter administration. That good man was Jerry Shestack, a left-wing lawyer I had met in the Shriver campaign. In fact, I had gone up to Philadelphia to spend a few hours with him, just to learn what I could about what went on at the UNCHR and how to conduct myself. Jerry no doubt feared that the step down from himself to me (he was a lifetime expert, I an amateur) was going to be painfully steep.

Jerry frequently went beyond his written instructions, he told me, and pressed the envelope, speaking only for himself (as he would openly announce). Then, having distinguished his position from the administration's, he would vote as he had been instructed. He thought it his duty to be "cutting-edge," and he thoroughly enjoyed playing that role to the left. He told me that our allies really appreciated it. Being more "moral" than his president earned him a glow of glory among his international peers. He was going to miss the job.

As I studied the huge white binder, my second conclusion was that my new instructions from Washington would not, after all, be that far different from those written for the Carter administration, except for on about half a dozen issues (I was counting). Still, my way of arguing for just about everything would have to be almost entirely different from the Carter way, let alone from Jerry's way. The American history on human rights was nothing to be ashamed of; it was, in fact, a high mark to take pride in. To make this point to the rest of the world, one would have to put the arguments in their proper philosophical/historical context, a little like Tocqueville's approach. So my written arguments would have to be rather thoroughly reshaped. Where we took the Carter path, we would do so on quite new grounds. Our allies, though, could count on the fact that our course would show the consistency expected of a great nation— except on a very few matters—very few, but very important.

The State Department was in turmoil over the thorough review of all foreign policy issues, such that the desk officers assigned to communicate to me could not offer much light. They said I already had the white binder—for the rest, I would have to swim alone. I was pretty certain that I knew how the philosophical compass was set in the mind of Ambassador Kirkpatrick, with whom on certain conundrums (Argentina, for example) I kept in occasional back-channel touch. And how the compass was set in the mind of the president, whose outlook I had begun to absorb from my Stanford days, when he was first elected governor of California.

WHEN I ARRIVED IN Geneva late in the gray end of January morning, the State Department chief of staff met me and told me that I was invited to dinner that night with the leaders of the WEOG (Western European and Others Group) at the home of the ambassador from Norway. When we learned that my baggage had been mislaid in Washington and could not arrive until the next day, I said: "I'll need a razor and a new shirt, if I'm to look presentable. Will this jacket do? It's all I have."

He left me at the rather opulent Swiss hotel where several other delegations and ours were housed, promising to return with shirt and razor after I had had a few hours' sleep. He told me that the Europeans were eager to look me over—they had never met a Reaganaut before. They would be relieved that I did not wear cowboy boots or carry pearl-handled pistols. I smiled a little wanly about what awaited me at dinner.

Once the suitably ambassadorial dinner had been served to the dozen or so of us across the candlelight from one another, followed by fresh wine and dessert, I expected all eyes to turn to me. There was hesitant silence as the plates were cleared, and then all eyes did fix on me. The Norwegian ambassador kindly welcomed me and said they all looked forward to what I had to say.

I don't remember many details about the evening. I do remember beginning with one anecdote and moving along with another. When first being welcomed, I looked around the table and said I felt like this was part of an ancient religious ritual, at which friends eat a good meal and then burn one live offering. And tonight I was the live offering. They laughed, but in too much agreement.

Then I said that I had just read through the thick briefing book prepared by the State Department for what it expected to be the second Carter term, and that those around the table could report to their chanceries that they should expect the United States to be consistent on more than ninety percent of the positions taken a year earlier. A great nation is like a huge aircraft carrier, I said; it must change direction very slowly. Many other agreements and relationships depend on consistency, too. Of course, even a small change in the beginning, I warned, can mean a vastly different terminus across the ocean.

Second, they could expect me to speak quite differently from my predecessor. I would speak exactly as I voted. But I would give a much fuller justification for my nation's positions and their rationale. In particular, I would stress the role of building up the institutions of civil society as the only reliable way to put some practical substance under words about human rights around the world. I roughly quoted Madison that "parchment barriers" do not protect human rights, but only the active associations and civic institutions of the American people. In recent years, U.S. civil rights groups had proven how true that was, by at last organizing, marching, and demanding respect for the rights long ago declared in words but too long treated as a dead letter, without active pressure behind them.

We went back and forth for more than an hour, and I remember the evening as quite pleasant—except for one moment, when someone said that he feared the Americans did not understand the Russians and imagined them to be a greater threat than the Europeans knew they were. Americans lack long European experience, he said. I tend to agree with that, I replied. But twice before in this century we have had to shed a lot of American blood because Europeans failed to understand their own experience and underestimated an enemy. I tried to say this matter-of-factly, without any sting. The line of thought was dropped.

Some weeks later the Norwegian ambassador sought me out at the end of a session. "I want to thank you for what you said at the dinner that first night in our embassy," he said. "I reported it to our foreign office, and when the whole session worked out that way, I was congratulated for my accurate forecasting."

BUT LEST THE READER think I performed wholly professionally during that session, I truly felt out of my element, as green as green can be. For instance, at one crucial juncture in the deliberations I gave an interview to a seemingly friendly woman reporter from a Zurich paper. It turned out that she was rather cynical about Reagan's intentions and the purposes of our delegation. I had made the rookie mistake of not keeping a staff member with me as witness and not having the interview tape-recorded. I then made a bad mistake, and she made a worse one. I repeated to her President Reagan's injunction, "Do not condone any human rights abuse," and then, to buttress my point that the work of the Commission was going well, I reminded her of what I thought she already knew, how that very morning the Commission had voted to send a special reporter to look into a serious human rights abuse behind the Iron Curtain. This was a very serious action (in UN vision). It was the *only* recognition of human rights abuses voted upon in the thirty-seven years of the UNCHR. A great historical moment, I said. That proved that the work of the UNHCR had down-to-earth practical value and was not all hot air.

As I was walking back from the UN hall to the embassy after lunch the next day, a young Russian aide stopped me and said: "You will be back for the afternoon session, won't you?" When I said I might not be, since I had to write my remarks for the morrow, he said with a malicious grin, "You better be. There's going to be some fireworks you shouldn't miss." I continued on my way, wondering what he could have meant by that. It worried me so much that I took the matter to the U.S. Permanent Representative to the United Nations in Geneva, Ambassador Gerald Helman. Gerry told friends later that he felt like the street sweeper who walks behind the circus parades, picking up after me all through the six-week session. He didn't mean that too cruelly, because he was very kind and helpful to me—as he was in this case. He couldn't figure out what the young Russian meant, either, and suggested that he go with me to the late afternoon session.

Good thing we showed up! The Soviet delegation had built up the most marvelous head of steam. They were holding aloft a headline from a Zurich tabloid screaming, "DO NOT CONDEMN ANY HUMAN RIGHTS ABUSE: Ronald Reagan." The Soviet ambassador made much of the hypocrisy this headline exposed in the fine words used by (looking now with disdain over toward me) the distinguished ambassador of the United States. But it is even worse, he went on. The cynical U.S. ambassador has violated the secrecy of this chamber by revealing to the press the exact vote of yesterday's unjust resolution against Poland. The Soviet Union and her allies demand that this violation be punished by rescinding that vote entirely, and wiping it from the record.

Fireworks indeed. Ambassador Helman looked at me. Rather weakly I said, "I told the reporter *'condone,'* not 'condemn.'" But I had left myself no way of proving that. It made me sick to my stomach to think that, by telling the young reporter of the exact vote, I might have ruined the greatest achievement of this session. "I didn't know the actual vote was *secret,*" I said. "The press was talking at lunch about the discussions that morning as if everybody knew everything." To myself I was thinking, *Why wasn't I instructed about what I should not say?* My reply to myself was: *It was your business to find that out at the beginning.*

The Brazilian chairman looked disconcerted only for a little while. He was an experienced professional with a visible touch of white hair and an avuncular voice. Calmly he ruled that the Commission would adjourn for the day, while he made his own inquiry into what had happened. The subject would be taken up again the next day. I had a most miserable night.

Early the next day, having slept very little, I showed up with Ambassador Helman in the antechamber used by the chairman before and after the meetings of the Commission. Without waiting I told him I had made a terrible mistake. I did not know that the *arguments* of the morning could be discussed with the press, but that the *exact vote* was a highly privileged secret (in effect, a kind of secret ballot). I should have known, but I did not. My motive had been to show how genuine and serious the work of our Commission is, and how much new ground we could break, and by quite a strong vote. As for that awful headline about "do not condemn," the poor young journalist had not grasped the English word "condone."

We left the chairman to his own thoughts and took our seats, still among the first to arrive for the Commission meeting. Twenty minutes or so later, after the morning session began, the chairman announced his ruling. The American ambassador was at fault yesterday, he began, but he is not a regular at these complicated Geneva meetings. He came to my quarters and explained his fault, and what he had been trying to do. He said he did not understand the rule, and having weighed the evidence, I have to make a ruling here that I believe him. It will not happen again. Therefore, I rule that the original vote of this Commission shall stand. The official reporter will go to Poland during this year as planned.

A FEW DAYS LATER, help arrived. The blue cavalry came over the hill. My great colleague in these battles, the distinguished Washington attorney Richard Schifter, had not been able to arrive during the opening days, so Jeane Kirkpatrick had suggested that I be the official ambassador, while Richard would offer me lawyerly support. His assistance would be an enormous comfort to me, doubly so now, and we were named co-ambassadors. Richard was famous as a negotiator in difficult and important matters. He ate up controversy as if it were dessert. He was perfectly at home in what I took to be the "warfare" of a fairly cynical form of politics. He used to tell me that he could always tell when the tension was getting to me. "The back of your neck gets red," he said, "and your hands clench."

"And *you* are as cool as a man by the pool in his own backyard," I said, recalling his well-kept home not far from Jeane Kirkpatrick's. He laughed: "This is what I do for a living. You mustn't ever let it get to you." He suggested, though, that he liked the fact that I cared about it enough to get so tense.

Richard told me a story that I really loved as we walked along back streets, and it figured quite closely in a tough battle we had to fight with the Soviets the next year. It concerned his acquaintance with Jeane Kirkpatrick, whom he had come to know in the 1950s as a fellow supporter of Hubert Humphrey. "I was the Democratic precinct chairman in our part of Montgomery County. The Kirkpatricks lived in my precinct. During the presidential election in 1960, I made it a point to visit many voters in my precinct, and I also got reports from precinct workers. I would then calculate how the precinct was likely to vote. I calculated that the vote would be very close.

"On election night, it turned out that my calculations had been quite accurate; I was only three votes off. I subsequently had a conversation with Jeane about that calculation, and she mentioned that her husband, Kirk [his nickname], had voted for Nixon. I had put Kirk in the Kennedy column, but Jeane explained that Kirk was worried about Kennedy's foreign policy positions. If I had gotten that one right, I would have been only one vote off." Kirk's switch counted twice, an unexpected gain for Nixon and an unexpected loss for Kennedy.

Now I understood what Jeane had meant when she said she was sending along a young Mayor Daley to keep watch over the voting in our session. It turned out Richard's voting skills were vital. The following year, on the last of the "working days," we had a big vote coming up. The official reporter on Poland (voted upon at the previous session) had brought in his scheduled document, and after discussion a motion to censure the Socialist Republic of Poland was put in play.

A rebuke had never been given to a nation behind the Iron Curtain during the preceding thirty-seven sessions. The Soviets had always taken care to protect the agenda by scattering red meat far from its own borders: It always dragged out as many days as possible with horrific and disgusting attacks upon Israel, one of the most noble democracies and respecters of human rights—not only in its region but in the world. Then followed another week or more on

South Africa; next, as long as possible on Chile. The strategy was twofold: to keep all attention away from the Soviet Empire, and to make deals with the Arab nations of the Middle East (on Israel) and most of the African nations (on whatever issues the Soviets needed). This is the way the Soviets had been running the Commission for Human Rights for years.

This second session was under the chairmanship of the ambassador of Bulgaria, who was painfully afraid of running afoul of the Soviets, even while he tried hard to seem—and even to be—impartial. It became clear that the Soviet plan was to run out the clock before the Poland vote could be called. On the last night, to break the deadlock between the Communist states and their friends and the Western states and their friends, the Soviets tried a maneuver to end the whole session. To the surprise of all, the Chinese delegation joined with the West on a procedural vote: to allow the final vote to be called.

Here is where our own resident Mayor Daley proved his worth. For weeks he had been in cahoots with our State Department, insisting that official representations be made in every capital to which the United States gave financial or other assistance—that it was *very* important that their delegate in Geneva receive unmistakable orders that he *must* vote to let the Polish censure go forward. Schifter had carefully counted up the undecideds and the weak sisters among our allies. Their ambassadors in Geneva each received communications from his ministry (in some cases, even from his head of state) about how serious this vote was—and how closely the United States was watching each delegation, one by one.

Sensing a Soviet loss, the Bulgarian ambassador suddenly announced that there would be an impromptu farewell reception for all at the Bulgarian embassy. How could anyone say no to that? But the clock was ticking away. It was already 6:00 p.m., and the deadline for the vote was midnight. We knew the tactic would be to fill everybody with vodka and prolong the party until 10:00 p.m. or longer. So every member of our delegation, plus a few official "observers" from human rights organizations, was given an "undecided" ambassador to invite out for coffee. The idea was to treat them with rich cakes and good coffee, in order to make sure that they drank no vodka and that no one from a Soviet delegation could get to them. Each undecided vote was assigned a sitter.

The party itself went rather well. The Bulgarian staff kept coming up to me with more vodka, but when each of them left I poured mine into a potted plant. (I bet they found a couple of dead plants the next day.) Meanwhile, I would toast every Slav delegate in my meandering path—from the Soviets through the whole Warsaw Pact—a toast "To Slavic Brotherhood!" It was an ironic joke that they enjoyed, coming from me. I would touch the vodka to my lips and then hold on for dear life until I could get near a plant.

The prearranged plan for the final vote was that one of our WEOG allies would lead the final moves toward a vote, so that the United States would not be "walking point," out in front of the line—the most vulnerable position. Richard and I scattered our staff around the room so that one of them was near every delegation we were counting on. In case the Russians made contrapuntal resolutions, such that voting no actually meant yes, we arranged a set of hand signals for how to vote, ensuring that, in a sudden reversal of direction, no one would slip up and vote the wrong way. Two weeks earlier, the Soviets had sent nine fresh UN lawyers from Moscow to assist their delegation, so we were expecting parliamentary surprises of all sorts. We knew they were not going to allow a yes vote. Such an outcome, we jokingly thought, might mean for them a quick one-way ride to Siberia. They would be playing for keeps.

But once the Chinese had broken the logjam on the procedural vote, which mandated that the Commission call the vote, we were pretty confident we could stave off everything else. However, one big thing did go wrong. The Western ambassador who was scheduled to lead the final assault had had too much vodka at the Bulgarian embassy and was unfit to come to the floor. So I asked experienced Ambassador Schifter to lead the way. To make a long story short, although there were enough delays that we had to vote to reset the clock, in order that the parliamentary midnight would arrive an hour later than the real midnight, our ragtag gang stuck together and marched toward the inevitable. Schifter had predicted the final tally almost exactly—he missed by half a vote. (At the last moment, one of the Africans who had been all set to vote with us weakened and abstained.) Nonetheless, we won. For the first time in thirty-eight sessions, a government in the Soviet bloc—in this case the regime in Poland that had put so many Solidarity members in jail—was publicly censured for a human rights abuse.

What the horrors of the Gulag had not been able to oblige the world's conscience to do, the image of Lech Walesa and all his colleagues, and behind them the watchful and quite public gaze of Pope John Paul II, made possible.

To say we were jubilant would be far too weak a claim. As I approached the escalator from the conference room, the ancient, blue-eyed ambassador for the Soviet Union, whose nickname had once been "the butcher of Prague," accosted me with an angry face. He was one of the oldest original Bolsheviks and was still a true believer. "Young man," he said, pounding with his stiffened fingers upon my chest. "You think you have won a victory tonight. But you have started World War III. You have won a Pyrrhic victory. And we had more votes than you, counting negatives and abstentions."

I was feeling sympathetic and magnanimous in the glow of the outcome. "Congratulations, Vladimir!" I said, extending my hand. "Congratulations on waging such a good fight, right to the end." But to myself I was thinking: "Oh, Vladimir! I am so going to enjoy writing my cable to Washington tonight, much more than you will enjoy writing yours to Moscow."

In my cable that night to Secretary Haig, I wrote, in effect: "Defeat is an orphan, but victory has a thousand fathers, and tonight our whole delegation, every one, played a crucial role. We won this one for the Gipper!"

The next day we received a sweet telegram from Secretary Haig, mightily commending us. We knew that Washington had given us the go-ahead to try to win, but they didn't really think we could. But, then, they didn't have Richard Schifter at their side, counting the votes. We learned that the Soviets had counted votes carefully too, and they thought they could win at the end. Their vote counters were just not as shrewd—or as watchful—as Richard. He had called it almost exactly and insisted on playing our cards tough right up until the end.

If anyone ever takes on a job like this in the future—and it is the American way to keep sending ordinary citizens, amateurs, to international conferences, while other nations send only their professionals—be sure that you have in your delegation, right by your side and with equal authority, a young Mayor Daley who knows how to shepherd every vote down to the lost sheep.

The real lesson Ambassador Schifter brought to bear, however, was to involve Washington in strong representations to heads of state and to take exquisite care that their representatives in Geneva (or anywhere else) voted as their heads of state had clearly directed them. Otherwise, the delegates would enjoy the pleasure pots of Geneva, far away from their directors, and on their own. Soviet diplomats would press upon them fine booty, occasionally paired with the most worrisome threats against their families back home.

Don't ever think that there is no steel behind the white diplomatic gloves of UN voting procedures.

18

Meetings with Lady Thatcher

Not too long after President Reagan took office, Prime Minister Margaret Thatcher gave a public lecture in Washington for the Heritage Foundation, co-sponsored by the American Enterprise Institute. Because of AEI's co-sponsorship, some of the fellows of AEI were invited to a private receiving line to greet the prime minister, exchange a few words, and have a personal photo taken with her. One of the neatest things that ever happened to me, *ever*, was her greeting. Once she had heard my name, she took my hand and held on to it. Then she stepped back a little bit and threw open her arms.

"Michael Novak," she said. "I have so wanted to meet you. I have been reading your book. You are doing the most important work in the world."

Now what really made this wonderful is that following just behind me and now standing abreast was one of the men I most admire in the whole intellectual world, Irving Kristol. Hearing Mrs. Thatcher's words to me, Irving cleared his throat. Mrs. Thatcher caught sight of him then and, recognizing him instantly, said: "You, too, Irving."

That was the kicker that made me jump over the moon. "You,

too, Irving." I felt like the little kid from Johnstown being mentioned in the same breath with one of the most brilliant, highly respected, wisest, and most commonsensical men I had ever known.

"Exposing the moral foundations of capitalism," she went on, "is so important. The fate of the poor all around the world depends on it. You must come visit me when next you come to London. I want to entertain you at Number Ten," she concluded, with her flashing eyes. She was already turning to Irving as I walked away. I was buoyant.

She got off so many good lines in her brilliant public address afterward. She was paying tribute to the oldest constitutional democracy in the world; it was as if she were trying to raise the morale of our whole nation and awaken us to all we stood for in a needy world. The tone felt a little like what she voiced some ten years later to George H. W. Bush just before the First Gulf War: "Now don't go wobbly on me, George." She was bucking us up for difficult times to come—at least, it felt that way. I could see why some people responded to her as to a headmistress; she really laid out the tasks before you and wanted you to step up and do them brilliantly.

"You have the oldest unbroken constitution in the world," she was saying. She spoke then of a friend of hers who had stopped by the public library in Oxfordshire to request a copy of the most recent French constitution. The lady librarian looked up at him over her glasses and, with a regretful smile, said liltingly: "I'm afraid, sir, we don't carry periodicals."

A bit later in her remarks, Lady Thatcher paused to describe Jimmy Carter's foreign policy. Her timing was perfect: "Lose a country, gain a restaurant." The crowd roared, all of us picturing in our minds the new Afghan, Angolan, Nicaraguan, and Salvadoran restaurants in Washington.

That quick wit was always at the ready. When she attended the G7 meeting in 1982, French president François Mitterrand was in the chair and forgot for a while to introduce Prime Minister Thatcher, as protocol demanded. At last he remembered his manners and begged the prime minister's pardon, covering his embarrassment by asserting that, after all, in the garden God had created Adam first, and then Eve to be his helpmate, and he was certain that Madame Prime Minister would be a welcome helpmate to the G7. A black cloud appeared above Margaret's head.

When it was finally her turn, the prime minister coolly thanked President Mitterrand for his courtesy, and said, "We on the other side of the Channel must read a different Bible than here. In our Bible it says that God created Adam, and then, having learned from his mistake, created Eve."

A COUPLE OF YEARS LATER, when I did meet Mrs. Thatcher at Number Ten Downing Street, she begged my pardon because an emergency had just come up and she wouldn't have time to linger for tea, as she had hoped. "But I do want to show you this. Come on in; come on in." She had turned from the hall to go back into her office. "Here, I want you to see this—it's your book. All marked up." She riffled through the book to show me underlinings and marginal notations on a great many pages. "I told you I was reading you. And I want you to believe it. There! You can see for yourself. Now I must run off. I'm afraid they are waiting to devour me in the other room. We must do this once again, when we have the time I had so been looking forward to."

It was over so soon. I was back out in the street within fewer minutes than I had expected, but I was not in the least disappointed. Her respect amazed me, and in later years, after her death, I learned how deep it was.

Recently Gertrude Himmelfarb saw a special affinity in Margaret Thatcher's and my thinking. Thatcher was not an "individualist" who held an atomized view of the autonomous unencumbered self as the alternative to statist collectivism. Instead, she stood in the line of those, like (in their different ways) Burke, Tocqueville, Acton, and the modern popes from Leo XIII to John Paul II, who emphasized the importance of the mediating structures that stood between individual and state. In Himmelfarb's words:

> It is curious that the champion of Victorian values— better yet, Victorian virtues— should be accused, by some social conservatives as well as liberals, of elevating the "self," the autonomous individual, above "society"; indeed, denigrating society in the interest of the self. Margaret Thatcher addressed this objection in her autobiography, insisting that she, like the Victorians, consistently saw the individual in the context of community, family, the other agents of society, and, not least, the nation. It was in that context, she said, that she promoted entrepreneurship, privatization, social mobility, a dynamic economy, and a limited government. She praised "the American theologian and social scientist" Michael Novak for stressing the fact "that what he called 'democratic capitalism' was a moral and social, not just an economic system, that it encouraged a range of virtues, and that it depended upon co-operation not just 'going it alone.'"

In 1992 I was summoned to England to receive the Antony Fisher Award. A war hero, Antony Fisher had turned his energies after the war to entrepreneurship. He loathed socialism, and he wanted both to open up a different path for his countrymen and to meet their immediate necessities. Meat was in scarce supply for years after the war, and many foodstuffs were rationed. Antony started some huge chicken farms, and so great was the demand that his business spread. With the money he earned from this and other investments, Mr. Fisher decided to create a fund that would support a network of think tanks all around the world (the Atlas Economic Research Foundation), spreading the ideas of enterprise, personal freedom, personal initiative, and the rule of law. He could see intellectuals everywhere turning—stupidly, he thought—toward socialism, in one form or another. He determined that although the recent war had been against the Nazis, there was now, in a different way, a worldwide war against the collectivist state whose intent was to smother personal initiative.

One of Mr. Fisher's own initiatives was to create a modest prize to be awarded each year for a book that advanced the understanding of freedom, not least economic freedom. For him that meant enterprise; it meant initiative; it meant taking responsibility. When *The Spirit of Democratic Capitalism* appeared after some delay in Britain, the jury selected it for the annual Antony Fisher Prize.

To my great pleasure, Mrs. Thatcher herself came to make the actual presentation. I don't remember her words, or those of the other dignitaries who spoke. I only remember the warmth of her presence, and the honor.

I was invited to stay overnight in the Fisher house, in which Mr. Fisher's surviving sons then dwelt. There were richly framed letters to their father on the walls, signed by Friedrich Hayek, Winston Churchill, and government dignitaries, commending Antony's bravery and his service, and several other precious missives.

MARGARET THATCHER HAD A powerful sense of tradition, with a loyalty to the giants of the past on whose shoulders we stand, as well as a deep respect for the common sense of ordinary English commoners out in the countryside—the people Agatha Christie would describe as "wearing sensible English shoes." As much as anything else, Margaret Thatcher was a teacher and an exemplar of traditional English virtues: common sense, spine-stiff respect for duty, enterprise and the tactic of surprise in debate as well as in warfare, and unfailing decency and humor. She was quite content with having been brought up as a sound British commoner.

Mrs. Thatcher also had, as any truly literate person has, an enormous love of classical high Victorian prose, as did Churchill himself, a prose elaborate and full of perfectly balanced long sentences, setting in place distinction after distinction, and contrast against contrast. Ciceronian sentences, in short. Few were any better at writing such sentences—each of them a triumph of intellect and taste—than John Henry Newman. One need not agree with him to hear the music of his sentences, to feel their rhetorical power, to admire their careful balance of temper and mind. For me, to admire a hero of the British past was not a deviation from the large-mindedness of Margaret Thatcher herself, but a form of homage to it.

Once in Washington, in the afternoon sequence of an interminable conference, Margaret Thatcher, Senator Malcolm Wallop of Wyoming, and I were scheduled to speak, one after the other—with me going first. Naturally, I felt a bit intimidated. On the other hand, I liked the challenge, and I very much wanted Mrs. Thatcher to hear me speak. I presented, I think, an eloquent defense of liberty—political, economic, and moral/cultural. The audience appreciated it with a bit more enthusiasm than anticipated. The eloquent Mrs. T. herself arose, saying in all courtesy that it was a bit intimidating for her to follow *me* on the platform. Then she gave a thoughtful, passionate humdinger herself. Senator Wallop, in his plain, self-deprecatory Wyoming manner, said his own position after those two speeches was impossible, but then proceeded in humorous fashion to make all his compelling points in an American westerner's amusing, down-to-earth way.

Later, on our way out, Mrs. Thatcher was whisked away before I could catch up to her. About five yards ahead of me, she paused to shake someone's hand. I took an enormous risk, one that made me blush, and called out over the shoulders and backs of the people in front of me, "Margaret!" She heard my voice, turned, and then, recognizing me, beckoned me to come to her. We had a fine but brief chat, while I delivered to her a message I had been charged to give her. We shook hands in very friendly fashion, and she was gone. I was amazed at my nerve in trespassing proprieties, and sounding— in a loud voice—overly familiar. I could think of nothing else to do, and she never took it in bad grace, not even for a moment, thank God. I knew then that she was as much a friend as I would ever have wished, although I would not have dared even to hope for that.

We had many other occasions together, two of which I especially remember. One was a glorious evening with a breathtaking sunset through the window of a mountain lodge in Aspen, Colorado—a long conversation, an excellent and leisurely dinner. Besides Karen and me, those present included a couple who were both musicians (and passionate believers in freedom; he a Hungarian refugee from 1956), our hostess and her husband, and Margaret and Sir Denis Thatcher. Karen as always charmed everybody with her kindness and interest, especially Denis. Mrs. Thatcher was given to asking many probing questions, so even a quiet dinner was just a little like a doctoral exam; she did not much take to inexactitude or smooth evasion. Yet it was also roaring good fun. Karen made a point of bringing Denis in on it often, even telling him (he had not yet heard of it) about the "Denis Thatcher Society," formed by a good friend of ours, a husband who had a wife more highly ranked than he in the government. Such men (in Washington at least, but in many other places, too) were forming an ever growing legion. Denis got a good-natured kick out of the Denis Thatcher Society, and Margaret loved it. It was one of the most pleasant evenings Karen and I ever spent, thanks to our great host and hostess, Stanley and Gay Gaines. We were even treated to a magnificent rainbow outside the huge window of the lodge during a late-evening misty rain shower.

The other memory was a glorious four days at the Gaineses' home in Palm Beach, Florida, with Lady Thatcher and her Secret Service attendant in residence at the time. We spent breakfast, lunch, and dinner together nearly each of those golden days. We enjoyed many good laughs, reminiscences, and speculations about the future. I told Lady Thatcher of the witticisms I had heard from her—or about her—when she was prime minister. She told stories about her American visits with "Ronnie" and about what a jolly good friend of the United Kingdom he was, an all-around good and brave fellow. "Oh, what times we had!" she reminisced. She really loved and admired Reagan.

When Reagan had been in Iceland with Gorbachev, and Gorbachev tried to bully him into giving away the idea of defensive rockets capable of intercepting incoming missiles in the air, Reagan simply walked away from the tempting offer Gorbachev was making in exchange. Reagan had guts—and principles he was not willing to trade away. And he had a stronger will than Gorbachev. Reagan saw that Gorbachev was truly afraid of "Star Wars"—that was what his game was about. Good! Let him come to me, Reagan boldly concluded.

Reagan had learned to bargain with Communists in his days in the tough Hollywood unions. Reagan was the kind of man Margaret admired. She was that kind of woman.

One final memory of Mrs. Thatcher. I was departing from London in a taxi on my way to the airport, and the radio was playing the last of her appearances before a questioning Parliament. The prime minister was even more than usual giving better than she got. Finally my driver pulled the car over to the side, laughing as though his sides ached. "You'll have to forgive me, sir," he said. "Ah never voted once for that woman, never once. But I am sure gonna miss that woman. That lady can fight, that one. She has one British wit."

19

The Helsinki Round in Bern, 1986:
Excerpts from a Diary

In 1986 President Reagan asked me once again to represent him overseas. This time he sent me for the round of diplomatic hearings prescheduled for Bern, Switzerland, as called for by the Helsinki Accords, to study past compliance on Human Contacts. This term covered everything from marriages between citizens of different nations, to tourism, international travel, international sporting events, artistic exchanges, the status of guest workers from one nation in another, and the rightful return of former war prisoners and refugees to the lands of their birth. The field was vast, and also poignant.

Deeply controversial when it was signed by President Ford in 1975, the Helsinki Accords (or Helsinki Final Act) aimed to continue negotiations toward arms control and to monitor signatories' actual behavior regarding its explicit human rights commitments. The implementation of the Accords had not amounted to much until, under Reagan, the United States began to do its duty to protect human rights in Europe.

The fact was, Reagan was a tougher president than Carter, and Jeane Kirkpatrick at the UN and Richard Schifter as Assistant Secretary of State for Human Rights and Humanitarian Affairs were granite. Premier Gorbachev had committed his government to glasnost (openness), and our job in Bern would be to press his government immediately to see how far he would go. Our lower-level work in Bern would not count for much but just might reveal some straws in the wind.

To this end, I asked the State Department if they would allow me to invite the Soviet delegation to a pre-meeting session at a location of their choice. The Soviets chose Moscow, and several of us traveled there for three days of meetings. In a whole series of daylong meetings, their foreign ministry tested me thoroughly and issued a warning or two about the "huge file" of human rights abuses in the United States they had assembled (one of them held up two large black binders). They warned me against citing cases and naming names—that was meddling by one nation in the internal affairs of another. I said, "But you have to understand. At least twenty million citizens in the United States have a grandparent from Central or Eastern Europe. For them this is a family affair, not foreign affairs."

Then I added an afterthought. I knew from advance briefings that they were expecting a "theologian"—which to their minds suggested a fundamentalist preacher. "As you know, every story in our Bible is about individuals, chapter after chapter—what happens in the mind and will of individuals. That's the way Americans think: about individuals. If I don't mention names, I will be in deep trouble from all around the United States. You need to expect that. That's the way we are," I said in my gentlest voice.

From all I had seen during our three days, I judged our meetings to have been a success. I pointed out that our goal was to build a consensus, to match the new good feelings between their government and ours. At each successive round of discussions in Moscow, with ever more significant ministers, they seemed more respectful—and more worried about what I laid out for them that we intended to do.

On the way out one afternoon, when I saw a member of their

delegation, Yuri Kashlev, reach for a cigarette, I pulled out a pack of Winston Longs I had taken care to bring (I didn't smoke) and offered him one. He gave me a brief double take, just the shadow of one, but enough for me to know what he suddenly remembered. When he had been expelled from Britain for spying, Kashlev was described in the London press as a highly Western type. Some vivid details about his preferences were added. Yuri now knew I had been shown an intelligence report on him.

When I got back stateside, I debriefed with our assistant secretary for human rights, Richard Schifter. And just before leaving to go to Bern, I was determined to meet for a minute with President Reagan. It had helped me at Geneva to quote directly from him in my press briefings there.

When I showed up at the White House moments early, I was told to expect a delay, since a sudden meeting had come up. I used my quiet time to go over the five or six lines I wanted to present. That's all I would get. A quiet phone buzzed, and I was motioned to stand at the door to the Oval Office. It was some long moments before the door swung open. The president, a bit harried but pleasant and welcoming, explained that we would have to talk right there, and deftly kept me from seeing into the room. At his elbow, ready as a witness, was Admiral John Poindexter. (I wondered weeks later if that meeting might have had to do with Libya, about which all of us were in the dark at the time. The bombing of Tripoli would occur a few short weeks later.)

From the president, I got a drawn smile and a nod, so I sped up my delivery. The meeting at Bern would cover every sort of cross-border human contact: marriages across borders, emigration, travel, migrant workers, and exchanges of cultural groups such as the Moscow Symphony. Premier Gorbachev had promised glasnost, and in Bern we would lay it on full-bore: We would dedicate the meeting to glasnost. We would demand that the opening meeting, and then all subsequent meetings, be open to the public. "But when we get as far as 'Remove This Wall,' I won't trample on that line, sir. That's yours."

With a gleam of humor in his eyes, the president gave me a nod and squeezed my arm. I felt fortified for the next few weeks. The president would not be surprised, and he didn't tell me not to press.

On March 31, TWA 890 bumped me down in Geneva. From there an embassy car drove me to Bern in a little over two hours.

During the next two months I resolved to dictate into my recorder for ten minutes before going to sleep each night, in order to keep track of the whole experience. I did that, and when I got back, my good secretary Gayle Yiotis typed up the tapes—171 pages, from March 31 through May 26. Here is an excerpt from my entry on day one of the official proceedings:

> **Wednesday, April 2.** The formal meetings began today. U.S. ambassador to Switzerland Faith Whittlesey accompanied me. Afterward, while I was speaking with Yuri Kashlev, Jerzy Nowak, the head of the Polish delegation, came up. Among other things, the latter said that the new age of communications would cause more problems for the Marxist countries than for the freer countries. [Just then a cameraman appeared, and in his flash caught the crystal chandelier above the Soviet ambassador, the Polish ambassador, and me, in friendly conversation—a front-page photo the next day.] The Polish ambassador asked Kashlev if he agreed, and the reply was a half noncommittal, half reluctant agreement. Nowak defined the issue as a conflict between a system that believed in the free-

dom of individuals and a system that believed in steering individuals. "Of course Marx said that technology cannot really change the relation between classes," he pointed out, "except only by degree. But I wonder if a sufficient number of degrees in quantity does not equal a change in quality? What do you think, Yuri?"

We also talked about human contacts and the new technology. "But the important point," Kashlev said with a broad smile, "is to make sure that the 'human' remains in human contacts."

Ambassador Eickhoff of West Germany agreed to meet me for dinner at the Hotel Schweizerhof. He had begun his foreign service career in Bern some twenty years ago and remembered it fondly. It was here he was married. The new young president of the hotel, Jean-Jacques Gauer, stopped by our table to ask how everything was going. He was pleased when Eickhoff told him of his many happy memories of the hotel and of Jean-Jacques's father.

Eickhoff and I had a very long dinner, from 7:30 until 10. He did most of the talking, and it was wonderful. The press has been besieging him a great deal lately, and I asked him what sort of questions they were after. Most relate to Germany—with twenty million Germans in East Germany, two million in the Soviet Union and Poland (if I remember the figures correctly), and several hundred thousand scattered in Hungary and other places, the Germans see the world first in terms of what happens to Germans. Directly behind that perception comes the Soviet Union. Only the United States, he says, guarantees the freedom of West Berlin and the safety of Europe. The CSCE without the United States would be heavily under the shadow of "the Colossus to our East."

This is why in the beginning the USSR wanted to keep the

U.S. and Canada out of CSCE. It cannot be, he said. Eickhoff disagrees with the U.S. proposals about the upcoming meeting. Our desire for openness during all the plenary sessions sends the wrong signals, he thinks. He would prefer to negotiate in private, not in public. One needs to work on one thing and one party at a time. In public, there are too many different parties to satisfy. I explained that we wanted to express the ideal of open meetings such as those of the United States. But our even deeper intent is to cooperate with our allies. We do wish to argue, however, for the maximum degree of openness possible. Meetings on human contacts ought to be more in contact with the public than any other meetings of CSCE. So there should at the very least be more public meetings than in any other forum. He agrees with openness at the opening and the closing. During the middle, however, in the negotiating period, he is for privacy.

FROM THAT VERY FIRST day I felt the fingers of a bad fate pressing on my neck. The Bern meetings would end in the unhappiest, most humiliating day of my life.

But in the rapid-fire days before that unhappy ending, my team had a great deal of hope and fun and excitement in Bern. I purposely met each senior officer of the Soviet delegation alone—and often—as well as every ambassador of all the Soviet client states, from Poland and Czechoslovakia to Hungary and Romania. President Reagan had already put me on the Board of International Broadcasting, which was responsible for Radio Free Europe (broadcasting to the "captive" nations) and Radio Liberty (to the Soviet Union) in the beginning of 1982, before my official swearing-in in 1983. By now I already knew a little about the territory. There was a joke from that period that I would have liked to tell then, but it was too delicate. Those interested in that period will recognize the flavor. It goes as follows:

During the crackdown on Solidarność in 1981, a Polish and a Russian soldier were on guard duty on a bitter cold night; both were very hungry. In one last attempt, the Pole found a heel of bread in his rucksack. His eyes lighting up, the Russian exclaimed: "Let's divide this in the spirit of true socialist solidarity." "Absolutely not!" the Pole replied. "Half and half, not a crumb more!"

I WOULD LOVE TO present my diary for the entire six weeks. The days and nights were amazing. Karen joined me partway through and greatly lifted my spirits, winning everybody's heart as usual. (Just to show what a great wife she was, one day she told me with a mischievous gleam in her eye that I had to go with her to the beach on the lake. I was exhausted, but we had a few hours off, and so I did. "There," she said. I saw a fairly large crowd, almost all women, some with children. All the women were bare breasted to the sun. "Knew you would enjoy it," she said. As a painter, she loved the nude figure herself.)

Near the end of the session, Max Kampelman, former ambassador to the CSCE in Madrid, and Maggie, his wife, paid a visit to say hello to old friends. They invited Karen and me up to Grindelwald, my favorite mountain spot in all the world, nestled between two great snowy peaks on either side of a deep valley, and quite high up.

Grindelwald is breathtakingly beautiful, but even more so is the mountaintop not far distant, toward whose elevated peak there is a slow, grinding train, at the end of which is an incredibly steep gondola lift going up to the top of the peak. On top of the peak is an octagonal restaurant with views on all sides that was featured in the James Bond film *On Her Majesty's Secret Service.* Over lunch there one afternoon, I confided in Max about something that was troubling our U.S. delegation: Under the NATO group's favorite rubric of "new, more precise" rules, we saw a weakening of the universal principles signed onto by all European nations in Helsinki. Each new "precision" would logically suggest that only *those* precisions really count as rights, and every other right would have to be fought for all over again as a "new precision." So the first principles would be abandoned, and all rules would henceforth be ad hoc, to be fought over one by one for all the coming decades before we won everything back that we had given away.

It was a subtle point, but quite powerful. Most of our allies seemed to get it, except that each one of them had a "precision" it wanted to be sure was mentioned. Their domestic politics demanded it. For example, the Germans deeply desired special help for the prisoners of war who had been involuntarily transplanted into the Soviet interior during World War II and were still being held there. The Germans couldn't abide doing nothing to help some two million countrymen who felt hopelessly abandoned. The Turks wanted more humane and considerate treatment for their migrant workers supplying labor to many nations of Western Europe. Et cetera. I told our allies that the United States shared their desires and rightful claims, and that I would do all in my power to win a consensus. But the United States could not surrender the universal rules.

"I fear I may have been too conciliatory with our allies," I told Max, and they had not heeded my warnings about a coming nay. I was getting more pessimistic about a final consensus.

I resolved to enjoy the magnificent view with Karen and Maggie and Max and to be grateful for the majesty and beauty of these God-given mountain ranges—whole ranges after whole ranges. Down the centuries, tens of thousands have seen this view; they are gone now and all their immense cares forgotten. Human failures fade;

the breathtaking beauty remains. That double whammy lifted my spirits a little.

The last selections from my diary pick up on May 23. According to rules set by the original Helsinki Commission, our work would not be legal beyond that date. In order to work around this restriction of time, there was a vote to stop the clock before the legal limit, and to negotiate for a few days more until starting the "legal" clock again. This entailed changing hotel and plane reservations—I was expected for a lecture in Lisbon and scheduled for others long booked for the days after our return home. Yet, in an effort to be accommodating, the United States joined the consensus to go through with this legal fiction.

On May 23, the "official" end of the conference, the vultures started circling.

> **Friday, May 23.** After the wonderful cool breezes and blue skies of yesterday, it has begun to get muggy again, although the rain is holding off.
>
> We finally got going at 2:00 p.m., with Czechoslovakia, Romania, and the Soviet Union speaking for their side, and Sweden, Austria, Switzerland, and Yugoslavia speaking for the neutrals and non-aligned [N-plus-N]. Both the Soviet side and our side accepted the N-plus-N "non-paper" as the basis for negotiations. We worked right through until 5:00 p.m., not making much progress, and simply putting brackets around the proposals that we discussed thoroughly but could not finally agree on. Of the first nine proposals we achieved agreement on three easy ones, but everything else was bracketed. From our point of view, this was a favorable development. Others were standing with us.
>
> Interestingly enough, the Soviet side seemed very eager to be accommodating, although they drew the line at some points.

The fact that they had obviously made us so depressed and pessimistic the other day seems to have obliged them to give every sign of being more accommodating today.

When we broke at 5:00 p.m., an immense thunderstorm broke out. The others all went to a reception at a restaurant outside of town, but I was very tired, and my stomach was a little off, so I came upstairs for a nap.

At 8:30 p.m., the plenary met again, in order to "stop the clock." According to our agenda, the meeting cannot continue beyond May 23, but we are not yet finished with our business. Therefore, by legal fiction it will remain May 23 for the CSCE until we actually close the plenary, probably on Monday morning.

Shortly thereafter, we met until 11:00 p.m. for another round of negotiations. We barely got through fifteen proposals out of thirty-six, before breaking off at about 2:00 a.m.

Saturday, May 24. We started negotiating again at 10:00 a.m. and went until 1:00 p.m. Then Karen and I were invited for an intimate lunch at the Czechoslovak Embassy, with their ambassador to Switzerland, Hanak, and their ambassador to the Bern meeting, Frantisek. The lunch was arranged on the spur of the moment yesterday as a gesture of "Slavic solidarity." They have a Slovak cook, and she prepared some homemade soup and a veal in a rich Slovak sauce. Also some great Czech beer. Not to mention a little Borovička. And a little dash of Becherovka at the end. Then we rushed back to get into the negotiations again at 3:00 p.m. Frantisek is on the East team with Romania and the USSR. The Romanian was left to carry the ball this morning, while we were dealing with the proposals on tourism, youth, visas, etc.—mostly proposals from their side, some of them Romanian. Frantisek was very slippery and inconsistent and did not do a very convincing job. In the afternoon, they replaced him with Shikalov, the Soviets' most veteran professional. We were still on mostly Soviet proposals.

It is curious how they have to argue. They are absolutely allergic to the words personal, personal wishes, religion, and non-governmental organizations, and at every point they have to add a reference to the legislation of the country in question, to government, or to some euphemism for governmental controls. My favorite was when they refused to accept our proposal that, in cases of emigration, "primary importance should be given to the wishes of the persons involved," and insisted on adding as an equivalent phrase that "primary importance should be given to humanitarian considerations, as well as to the wishes of the person involved." In a curious way, they meant here by "humanitarian considerations" the judgments of others, including the state, about what is humanitarian. They tried to disguise this by saying that they were thinking of a poor mother who needed support. It was crucial to them to maintain that no individual could be trusted to discern humanitarian considerations all by herself. Only the state knows what is humanitarian.

It was impossible for our colleagues on the other side of the table to allow any of our proposals in this territory to go unamended. At every point, they had to keep the principle of state control. They also wanted no verbs that could be construed as critical of the status quo. They could never accept "remove obstacles," but would insist on "intensify efforts," "increase the possibilities of," "further facilitate." Only positive thoughts allowed.

Well, we have not been getting very far.

Sunday, May 25. We had a NATO meeting at 8:30 a.m. It is a glorious day outside, and I am glad that Karen is going on an all-day outing with the Congressional Delegation [CODEL] that has just arrived from Washington. We need to be happy as we can that they have come, but we are frantic with official obligations and don't really have time for them. The Soviets and the WEOG began negotiating from 9:30 until 12:30, and I was lucky enough to get a little forty-five-minute nap and a dry, unpalatable sandwich before we began again at 3:00, and went until 7:15. I had to miss the reception at the Schweizerhof for the CODEL, for we began again at 8:00 in the evening and went on continuously until 4:00 in the morning, with brief "potty breaks." In between negotiating sessions, we had reporting sessions with our allies.

The Soviets had to stall, because they did not want to yield any more. So progress was excruciatingly slow. We did achieve some things before the 8:00 p.m. meeting. In fact, at the brief NATO caucus in the morning, it became clear that nearly all our allies were in favor of agreeing to the document as it was. Exceptions were Belgium, Portugal, and The Netherlands from the EC, and Canada and Turkey. No one really liked the document, except West Germany. Most described it as feeble and said they would assent to it only grudgingly. The reason most gave for accepting it was that it would help Ambassador Eickhoff. With the CODEL being extremely skeptical about the document, and having my instructions very clearly in mind, I had a very bad choice to make. If I accepted the document, and it was awfully weak, it would give the Soviets something of a propaganda victory, and most of all, it would not be easy to defend in substance. On the other hand, there are six or seven mildly good points in it, though it has some new and very troubling loopholes. I didn't like that choice. After 9:00 p.m., it became clear that we would not get anything more. The Soviets were crippling the proposal on religion, would not budge on minorities, and were unwilling to give primary importance to the rights and wishes of the individual in matters of visits and travel.

One of the turning points in the discussion came during the endless talk about exit and entry visas. About six or seven proposals were affected by this discussion. The Eastern bloc wanted to set up a parallel between exit and entry visas, and we could not do that. We must have tried fifty or sixty formulae, back and forth. The Soviets wanted to insert in the phrase concerning exit visas "from one participating state to another." This was aimed directly against Israel. At one point, Shikalov said: "We both know the country we are talking about. Well, if you will not name it, I will name it." His left eyebrow went up into a V. "Israel. We will never include Israel in any document."

I took that in, and after one more proposal was tried, I said that now that we knew explicitly what the Soviet proposal was aimed at, we could not in any way accept that formula, that it was impossible, repugnant, and horrible to contemplate. Therefore, we did not see how any further progress on exit visas could be made. And if no progress on exit visas, then no progress on entry visas.

In the end, at about 4:00 a.m., the Soviets saved us from having to make a decision. By design, Sir Anthony [Williams of the United Kingdom] put into his remarks the fact that the NATO nations had put on the table another document, our contingency final statement, in case the contact group did not succeed in reaching agreement. He did not describe it, but only wished to mention it so that on the morrow the USSR would not be surprised. They pretended to be surprised, although they must have known about it through one of the translators the minute we sent it to be processed by the executive director. The Soviets took a little time while deciding, but then decided that they would walk out. They ostentatiously put on their jackets, but then they sat down again for a while. Until they saw the new document, they said, they did not want to continue negotiating. They threatened to put on the table their own final statement.

It was 5:00 a.m. before I got to bed, and I had to set the alarm for 7:45, in order to be at breakfast with the congressmen. Two hours of sleep seemed worse than none.

Monday, May 26. At 9:00 a.m. there was a plenary, and after it, I had to duck out to go over to the Casino to introduce the showing of a twelve-minute film on the divided spouses in Moscow, which the CODEL wanted very much. I got back about 10:10 for the NATO meeting.

By now the N-plus-N had copies of their "take it or leave it" version of a final document. EC met first, and the remaining five of us found ourselves unable to support the "national minorities" paragraph in the poor document that faced us, because it was worded in terms of "citizens from participating states," which again meant excluding Israel. We had heard that same proposal the night before and had decisively rejected it. Apparently, the N-plus-N had failed to note our hostility to it.

After the NATO meeting, Spencer Oliver of the Helsinki Commission attacked the draft in graphic language, saying he had found seventeen passages in which the document fell below the standards of the Helsinki Final Act. Many in the Western delegations disputed him vigorously. But Oliver did point especially to the same recurrent phrase that had also worried me: limiting the right to travel to "when personal and professional circumstances permit." Such circumstances can easily be manipulated by a government so as to deny travel to anyone. I knew that an argument could be made for every Western proposal showing how it went beyond the Final Act, at least by a little. But I also knew that such arguments would be scholastic, and that common sense could hardly discern any effective, practical progress. Any clear eye could see several potential dangers in some new phrases. So I requested that our embassy get Assistant Secretaries of State Rozanne Ridgway and Richard Schifter on the phone, and they caught Schifter first, at home. It was extremely early in Washington, on Memorial Day, a holiday. I read the document through to him, and he said that we should not accept it; it was weak and seemed to him to fall short of the Final Act at several places. I pointed out the political reasons for agreement at our end, and I said that his arguments on the relation to the Final Act could be countered, but that the reason I was calling him was that I, too, had my doubts.

We next reached Rozanne Ridgway. After hearing the text, she had the same opinion as Schifter. She asked my own opinion, and I said that I believed the document could be defended, and that I would be willing to defend it, but I thought that this defense would be difficult, that the text was weak at best, and that it raised too many troubling questions. I favored "No," but I wanted to be sure Washington understood the probable uproar in Bern. The dismay sure to be felt by the Allies, and the fact that the U.S. would probably be the only party at this point to break consensus, might make going with the document more prudent. She said, "Forget the politics and the public relations—what do you think about the substance?" I said that judging the document merely as a document, it would be too weak. Just after this call I would have to go down and announce our instructions to the contact group, I told her. She told me we should reject it, since Richard Schifter also agreed. "Those are my instructions, then?" I asked. "Those are your instructions," she said. I was relieved, but I now had to face the music.

I hurried downstairs to find Ambassador Torovski, the coordinator, and gave him the word. I also passed it along to Sir Anthony, when at last I could isolate him from the others, and to Canada. The other hesitating states, Romania and Poland, had not received their instructions yet, so they requested another delay. NATO was to meet immediately, and this gave me an opportunity to explain our decision to NATO.

Ambassador Eickhoff was white in the face and trembling. He asked for time to get to his foreign ministry, to make a demarche to Washington, to get in touch with Foreign Minister Genscher who wanted to appeal to Secretary of State Shultz, personally, etc. We telephoned Washington to report.

Meanwhile, at about 2:15 p.m. we received a "nyack urgent" cable from Moscow, telling us that our consular officers had been called to the foreign ministry in Moscow that morning, and then were told to come back in two and a half hours. On their return, our team in Moscow was handed a list of thirty-six families for which permissions to reunite had been given, and we were promised another thirty-six more. Thrilling news for me—at least our work had one real result for real people.

Meanwhile, Romania and Poland received instructions to join the consensus, and it was now clear that the United States was the only party holding out. The next meeting of the contact group was scheduled for 5:30 p.m., and I called Ridgway and Schifter again (they had told us to keep calling). It was time to bite the bullet. They said to go ahead.

But just as we went out the door and down the hall, Ambassador Eickhoff met us with the neutral coordinators and the Swiss and requested another delay, for humanitarian reasons, until German Foreign Minister Genscher got through to Secretary Shultz. I agreed. Within a short time, though, we received another phone call, informing us that Genscher had gotten in touch with Shultz, that Shultz had ordered another review, and that, meanwhile, text at last in hand (by cable), the department again concluded that the document was simply too weak, and allowed damaging loopholes. I was delighted— except for the ugliness I would soon face in the meeting.

The disappointment of many of our colleagues at the last Western meeting was keen, especially that of Eickhoff. He was desolate. This was especially painful to me. He was my friend. He was flawlessly loyal to the United States. He had counted on getting consensus on freedom for World War II prisoners, as a final crown of his career.

When word came from State about the Genscher telephone call and the review requested by Shultz, I had to go back to the Allies at the next NATO meeting and tell them the situation was now definitive. At 8:30 p.m. Kashlev approached me and handed me a list of the names of the remaining thirty-six families. I wondered how long he had had them. He seemed a little forlorn, and asked me if we could not change our minds. I said that I was very grateful to have received the cable from Moscow early in the day, but that it had come too late. The decision had been made. It is never too late, he said. But it was. His earlier list had proven to be less than reliable, and there was no way I could be certain that this one would hold up under examination. If only the Soviets had acted earlier during these eight weeks. If only the final document had been unambiguously stronger.

I then went to a press conference, where I sat at a table before eighty or ninety journalists. Under bright lights, I spoke slowly and explained our position in terms that I would use the next day, pointing to the deterioration in compliance in recent years and the seriousness of words in the Helsinki process. I explained our worry about the original, robust proposals having been weakened and loopholes having been introduced into others. The United States had agreed to the most easily achieved compromise proposals at this conference in good faith, pending a review of the cumulative weight of the whole. Alas, the whole was too weak to accept in that form. I expressed hope that by the time of the next CSCE meeting, six months later in Vienna, a stronger document could be developed, and the degree of compliance by signatory states sufficiently improved, so that we could join in consensus. Meanwhile, we must show our respect for words about human rights by saying no to words we found to be too weak, and to emphasize that such words are empty, unless they are given meaning by compliance.

That day was the unhappiest of my life. I knew I had failed to achieve the task that I had set for myself, one that my government was expecting of me. I felt humiliated. I thought the press would have a field day deriding me. I didn't want to face my colleagues at AEI. I dreaded facing the news stories. My best hope was that the story would slide away into the pit of forgetfulness.

All the way home on the plane, I felt dejected.

Imagine, then, my shock when, upon arrival, the editorial of the *Wall Street Journal* European edition fell into my hands:

BREAKTHROUGH IN BERN

Michael Novak, American ambassador to the Bern Conference on Human Contacts, brought considerable credit to the U.S. at that gathering by refusing to sign yet another agreement for the Soviets to violate. Critics who charged that he jeopardized the Helsinki "accord" couldn't be more wrong. . . .

When you take in the total picture you begin to see that Mr. Novak's refusal to sign amid mounting pressure was a courageous decision made in the best interests of the people for whom the conference was called. Together with . . . Mr. Reagan's own refusal in Geneva to be pressured into another meaningless agreement, it points to a new resolve in American policy: The U.S. will no longer agree to anything just for the sake of agreement. This will strengthen the hand of the negotiators the next time round, e.g., the general review of Helsinki scheduled for November in Vienna. Most important, it signals that the Americans are serious enough about negotiation to reject language that doesn't represent progress.

BACK AT AEI, AMBASSADOR Zimmerman, star diplomat to the Eastern European region, top aide to Kampelman at Madrid, and already appointed to lead the next CSCE meeting in Vienna, telephoned to say I had just made his upcoming work infinitely easier. Surely the Soviet Union would watch seriously every intonation of his voice and never again take a U.S. vote for granted. A "No" had never happened before. It heightened the power of future words from the United States.

Senator Jackson's office called to tell me that Moscow had been publicizing the U.S. *nyet* for domestic readers. A photo showed the day's news display in the Kremlin with citizens gathered around my photo as I broke consensus with all the other Europeans. The news of the United States saying *nyet* to the Soviets was being banged around on the pipes of the Gulag as another bit of hope from Ronald Reagan.

Alexander Ginzburg, the first of the Soviet dissidents and founder of the first samizdat publication, attended a discussion of glasnost at AEI in the summer of 1987. Ginzburg had suffered for two years in a Soviet labor camp, and was released in 1979 in an exchange for Soviet spies (a cruel practice in itself). After the discussion, I moved to the back of the room to shake his hand and express my admiration. Instead, he told me of a telephone message he had received the night before from Moscow from a colleague who told him to thank me for the "brilliant refusal" to sign the Bern document. Ginzburg told me that this action "had saved the Helsinki process."

These words made all the agony of confronting the negative reaction in Bern disappear. I had known then it was the correct judgment; I would not have wanted to live with the thought that I myself had signed a bad document. I dreaded the thought that some of its phrases might later be used by Soviet officials to justify rejection of the claims of dissidents, refuseniks, and others to basic rights. But on the day of the decision, I could not know for sure whether our "No" might lead to greater closure than before. Our clear aim was to convince Gorbachev that the United States was serious about compliance. In any event, later that summer the Soviets began to take the large steps toward openness that we had urged them to take. It was quite a joy to see so many persons whose names were mentioned in Bern in freer circumstances than before.

20

The Project on Social Invention:
Welfare Reform, 1985–86

Four main inquiries drove me in the 1980s: (1) how to rethink capitalism in a moral and religious language; (2) regarding my work at the UN, what are the root concepts of human rights and how are they best protected?—not by "parchment barriers" (Madison) but by strong associations in free societies; (3) in my work on the board of Radio Free Europe and Radio Liberty, how to concentrate reliable information to defeat communism in the Soviet Union and China; and my personal favorite, (4) how to break the chains of poverty throughout the world.

My brilliant and effervescent friend Michael Horowitz came to AEI as a visiting scholar for three years or so, after distinguishing himself in the Office of Management and Budget under Ronald Reagan and David Stockman. Horowitz generated a lobbying effort to nominate me as the new Secretary of Health and Human Services. I didn't think that was the work I was made for or that I would get the nomination. But Horowitz spread the word around pretty extensively. Soon *The New Republic* editorialized on my behalf. In the end, I was put forward at the White House as one of the two finalists for the job.

Clare Boothe Luce called me to say she was praying that I would not get the job. "Every man I know cannot resist the lure of public service, and once they are in it they can never say a completely honest word again—they owe too many loyalties and share too many personal confidences. I don't want you to get it, Michael." I didn't, thank God.

The indefatigable Horowitz immediately pressed another project upon me: the "social invention project" at AEI, meant to carry forward AEI's widely acclaimed "project on mediating institutions." This project had two main underlying ideas. The first was that the Great Society was almost exclusively a matter of the state, to the neglect of all the mediating institutions of civil society, so that the state grew stronger and the family and other associations atrophied. The second was that the era of social invention had not ended with the War on Poverty.

Then Horowitz hit me with this: "*You* should lead a committee on what worked and what didn't work in the War on Poverty during the past twenty years." Horowitz was big on new ideas for finding more successful ways to eliminate poverty. We convened some twenty top experts on the left and the right, to see if after a year of probing discussion, the group could come to a consensus on practical suggestions for the future. "It has to be a consensus document by the Left and Right together." Horowitz was firm. "It cannot be a conservative point of view or a liberal point of view. Its power depends on consensus."

"But, Michael," I argued back, "I am no expert in any of this stuff." He then appealed to my vanity, sort of. "All the more reason why everyone will trust you. You have no record in this area. They will see that they have to teach you. They already think of you as fair-minded. You are probably the only man in this town who can do this." In other words, I was incompetent in this area, a blank slate. Therefore, I was perfect for the job. (Thanks a lot!)

When we went to the Bradley Foundation in Milwaukee for potential support, they suggested we bring in Marquette University and also hear from the University of Wisconsin, so we might take advantage of Wisconsin's leadership in regard to poverty and welfare. Horowitz took charge of bringing in all the top experts—at OMB he had worked with all of them. Like me, he was still a Democrat from birth, but romantic about new ideas and possibilities, whatever their source.

A young scholar, Karl Zinsmeister, prepared materials for the first thin draft of our report, consisting mainly of brilliantly arranged statistical tables. He taught me how to read them and how to fix on what was new or unexpected. His enthusiasm was contagious. He had been a researcher for Senator Pat Moynihan and Ben Wattenberg, who with Richard Scammon had written best sellers on the enormous data assembled by the U.S. Census Bureau in each decennial, books such as *The Real Majority* and *The Good News Is that the Bad News Is Wrong*. Zinsmeister explained each chart to me and why he had included it, breaking out with excitement at what he had found.

The main thing Zinsmeister taught me was that poverty is not a fixed state but a dynamic one. Many individuals move through every statistical level of poverty and income, from the bottom to the top—and then down again as they retire without an annual salary. It's important to distinguish *individuals* from statistical profiling. The generic profiles might stay relatively fixed, but individuals moved up and down between the levels with amazing fluidity. He taught me to keep an eye on individuals. The help many of them require while down for a bit might be needed for only a couple of years. This was typical for divorced persons, students, individuals launching new businesses not yet generating cash flow, college grads taking a year off to travel, newly arrived immigrants, and many others.

As an example, Zinsmeister taught me that the children of the wealthy who were now in graduate school, living on a teaching fellowship, might be counted statistically among the poor for several years. To be careful not to make this mistake, one had to differentiate between individuals who would end up being poor year after year and individuals who might be in the statistical ranks of the poor in any single year but rise out of that grouping very fast once they got a job in the profession they were studying for. (It suddenly occurred to me that I had been ranked among "the poor" when I was in graduate school at Harvard, and even after our marriage Karen and I together probably fell into the ranks of the poor, until Stanford hired me.)

Zinsmeister also showed me that there was a difference between having no more than the income of a poor person and having additional savings to draw on. Some retirees, for instance, have low annual income, yet also have access to a mortgage-free property, a pension, and savings that keep them well removed from what we think of as poverty. Main point: Hidden in cold statistics is an awful lot of drama, even pain, but also hope. There is a great array of other factors to consider.

For instance, in every decade since 1950, as many as 5 million immigrants entered legally into the United States. On entry, nearly all of them fell into the category of the poor. But by the end of a decade, a large majority of every annually entering cohort was out of poverty. A great many of them opened small newspaper and magazine kiosks, fruit stores, and other businesses, employing all able-bodied relatives to help them out. All these income earners pooling their incomes together as one household normally climbed up steadily out of the bottom two ranks. Different ethnic groups tended to choose different strategies: some pushed for higher education for each of their children, while the first priority of others was helping each new household in the family put a mortgage on a home of their own, and still others encouraged their children to open lucrative small businesses. In the mid-1980s, upward mobility still worked in America—not equally for all, because success is strongly influenced by hundreds of years of family experiences and learned skills. The most valuable inheritance is not money; *sound habits, skills,* and *family-encouraged tendencies* are of more value.

With the benefit of Zinsmeister's instruction in the best up-to-date thinking on these matters, my job was to come up with rhetorical strategies based on what I was learning and to develop the most conciliatory prose I could produce, so as to induce bipartisan consensus. For over a year there were many, many joint meetings, commissioned papers, and much haggling, sentence by sentence, statistical table by statistical table, page by page, over my early drafts. I have remembered this project ever since as my "thirty-Excedrin project." At the very first meeting, I had promised everyone that I would do my best to include each participant's point of view in every sentence and every paragraph. If we could not all agree, we would drop that sentence altogether, or point out the main lines of divergent judgments. My motto was "As all of you know, I am no expert. You are going to have to guide me. We want a bipartisan consensus—that's the only thing that will have any political power in the Congress and the White House."

It took us a year, during which I was given many homework assignments in order to come up with lines of argument that included everyone's views. One or two experts quietly told me that in conscience they had to bow out, because they found me too sanguine in pinning as much hope as I was on government programs, no matter how carefully attuned these might become. They pointed to many years of experiences that had proved to them this hope was a chimera. They thought government was just not capable of doing such a delicate human job.

Our "Working Group on Family and Welfare," as we agreed to call it, soldiered onward. We put *family* front and center as the main

factor in poverty research. And in the end our gang achieved a remarkable degree of consensus and a broadly persuasive book. Disparate individuals such as Alice Rivlin, Robert Reischauer, Franklin
Raines, Charles Murray (before he dropped out), Glenn Loury, John
Cogan, Blanche Bernstein, Barbara Blum, and Lawrence Mead
united in ways that are rare in Washington, D.C. We produced a
final document, got it approved by the (mostly Democratic) Marquette Institute for Family Studies and the Marquette University
Press, in cooperation with the AEI Press, and began sending out
final drafts—and, eventually, printed galleys—for review. The comments were amazingly flattering. In fact, the British *Economist* somehow got a copy, pirated all our main points, made it a cover story,
and discreetly gave the Working Group very little credit. But our
group wanted influence, and the flattery of imitation by the best
magazine in the English-speaking world did not in the least hurt us.

Later on a committee of some of us was asked to present our findings to the president and the relevant portion of his cabinet over at
the White House. The White House said they could accept our conclusions, but they didn't think Congress would. When we took our
consensus document to the Senate, amazingly both parties said they
liked it. Senator Dole looked around with his eyes full of amuse-
ment and said, "Well, if all you farmers and ranchers can be friends,
I guess Republicans and Democrats over here might be able to do
something together. Don't you think?" There was mostly universal
nodding—not too confidently, but nodding.

Nothing would have warmed my heart more than to see welfare
reform enacted into law. I thought it would be immensely liberat-
ing for the young poor, and sounder for the elderly, too. Our group
had come up with some fifty suggestions for making welfare work
to greater practical effect. Those proposals were our answer to the
second question we had agreed to face: How could we make the

nation's programs to help the poor and elderly work better? What could we propose better than the 1960s War on Poverty?

It is fair to say that the War on Poverty had massively succeeded in improving the condition of the elderly. Not only were they more prosperous and more active, but many were soon living as much as two decades longer—so that a new problem was emerging, a happy problem for those who loved them: the emergence of the "elderly-elderly," that is, those over eighty-five, not sixty-five. The fiscal challenges this improvement entailed would one day have to be solved, but the progress was real.

By contrast, the condition of the young between eighteen and thirty had visibly deteriorated. In previous generations the number of young males who abandoned young women to rear children by themselves was not such a huge proportion. After 1965, criminal acts of violence among the young increased by 600 percent, and the number of the young who died by violence was heart wrenching. There are diverse positions on the morality of having children out of wedlock, for sure. But the social damage to children (and even their parents) was growing ever more intense and personally painful. That damage was measurable in the statistics about high-school dropouts, protracted illiteracy, an unusually large number of low birthweight infants (condemned to long-term health problems), antisocial behaviors, unemployability, and imprisonment for crimes. The picture was heartbreaking—it was so unnecessary, and so often exacerbated by well-intentioned but humanly destructive new "reforms." Too many programs had made matters not better but worse.

This had a huge effect on my own way of thinking about cures for our worst social problems as a nation. Below are some of the findings that most shocked and sobered me, borrowed loosely from *The New Consensus on Family and Welfare: A Community of Self-Reliance*:

- Since 1965, the fastest growing segment of the poor (30 percent) has been single mothers with children under eighteen.

- Children living in poverty have become nearly four times more numerous than the poor among the elderly.

- Forty-six percent of children on Aid to Families with Dependent Children (AFDC) in 1983 were born to parents not joined in marriage.

- More out-of-wedlock children are now being born to whites (often in rural areas) than to blacks; the concern is now nonracial.

- Among the poor, blacks suffer most: Among poor blacks concentrated in high-poverty areas of central cities, single-parent families have come to outnumber married-couple families by more than three to one, and illegitimacy rates in some poverty tracts have surpassed 80 percent.

All these developments led Senator Moynihan to declare: "An earthquake has shuddered through the American family structure." Some conclusions: Poverty in America was no longer characterized solely by low income but also by self-damaging behaviors. For instance, those involved in drug trafficking, prostitution, or other off-the-books and life-threatening activities may not suffer from low income at all. The sharp distinction between these two types of poverty—merely monetary deficiency versus behavioral dependency—is an important key to reducing poverty. The first is easy to address—just give sufficient additions of income to lift every single family out of poverty. The total cost of these additions would be much less than is now spent annually by government to reduce poverty. The second requires help in changing habits, and often creating new human networks in which to do so. Poor people are not just like cattle to be fed and housed. They are human subjects in need of their own self-fulfillment in high achievement and in appreciative communities.

I saw that conservatives on the right had come to acknowledge that the nation must do something about the increasing numbers of vulnerable ones—women and children chiefly, but also men who in more normal times would have stood by their women, not abandoned them. Liberals on the left had come to see that money is not enough; behavioral dependency must be replaced by the pride of high achievement.

The main point is that for welfare programs to do their proper job, they need an ethical component, a signaling function, a call for a bond of mutual obligations between helpers and helped. The community must reach out to suffering individuals; the recipients must do what they can to contribute to the community. In a word, Right and Left can establish new common ground, just as the nation is taking on anew the challenge of breaking the chains of poverty.

American society demands much of individuals, because it expects them to be free. The source of the nation's beauty, and of the love its citizens bear it, is that it asks so much of them.

It turned out not to be practical to achieve welfare reform until the nation had a Democratic president. As it took President Nixon to open up a new era of cooperation with China, so it would take President Clinton to lift a finger against the settled habits induced by the untouchable War on Poverty. Not altogether enthusiastically,

Clinton was forced into cooperation with the new Republican majority that swept into the House of Representatives by the Gingrich-led landslide of 1994. In that year the Republicans picked up a stunning fifty-four seats. Then Clinton signed the welfare bill, and his practical political instinct in doing so is very much to his credit.

To the discomfort of its severe critics, who predicted unmitigated disaster for the poor, Clinton's welfare reform turned out to be an astonishingly happy and positive success. Persons who had been living on welfare just a few months earlier were telling the press about a new pride and sense of achievement they felt, which they had never expected to attain. Welfare rolls shrunk almost overnight by about 30 percent. The results were far better than those who had worked long for this result had dared hope.

Except for one thing: The number of households headed by a single mom with no male partner present continued to creep up. This painful pattern remains a tragic wound in the nation's midsection even in 2013.

21

1989: A Year that Will
Live in History

Beginning in 1982, for ten years I had the privilege of serving on the board of Radio Free Europe (for Eastern and Central Europe) and Radio Liberty (for the vast Soviet Union, including its soft Muslim underbelly in "the 'Stans"). President Reagan declared it the goal of the United States to win the Cold War, not just accept it as our long-term fate.

With Reagan's wholehearted approval, we at the Radios set out to bring ideas of individual rights, equality under the law, and justice into analyzing the news of local events in each region. Our job was to turn Western standards of truth and open inquiry upon Soviet life from within, in the native languages of all its captive peoples, including Russians themselves. Reagan was confident old intellectual habits would spring back to life. Common sense would be emboldened. The universal craving for truth and personal responsibility would grow. The great novelist Aleksandr Solzhenitsyn was pressing much the same point in his Nobel Prize address: "One word of truth shall outweigh the whole world." Yes, it does.

There was an old joke in those days: The name "Union of Soviet Socialist Republics" contains four lies: It is not a union but many conquered nations annexed by superior power; these were not republics, but dictatorships; and these so-called republics were neither soviets (local deliberative bodies) nor socialist, but oligarchies based on party favor.

The new board leading RFE and RL was composed of nine members, four from each political party, with its chairman named by the sitting president. Each of the nine had to be individually vetted and approved by the Senate. In forming the new board, Frank Shakespeare, the former very successful president of RCA, put forward what some said was "the most powerful board in Washington." Next after Frank was Ben Wattenberg, the internationally known demographer and former White House writer for Lyndon Johnson. Then came one of the most powerful Democrats in the country, internationally famous (specifically in the Soviet Union) Lane Kirkland, president of the AFL/CIO; and the great novelist James Michener, world-renowned for his then new novel, *Poland*. To these stellar lights of the Democratic Party, in order to have at least one public theologian of Central European roots, known to be on the wavelength of the new Polish pope, John Paul II, was added the least known of them all: me.

On the Republican side were Congressman Clair Burgener, five-term huge vote-getter from California, who had promised his wife he would retire after ten years and did; he was a straight shooter and gave us strong credibility on the Hill; also Arch Madsen, the most genial and warmhearted executive you'd ever want to meet, president of Bonneville International Corporation, one of the biggest chains of private broadcasters in the world, and world-class expert on broadcast technologies of all sorts, a Mormon bishop, a devout man, brilliantly informed about various parts of the world (partly through the work of Mormon missionaries worldwide); the head of the largest and most successful public relations and advertising firm in the world and future U.S. ambassador to Canada, Ed Ney, adviser to top-level Republicans; and Steve Forbes of *Forbes* magazine.

Shakespeare exaggerated a lot when he introduced me as a theologian experienced in human rights and the idea of America, and a necessary bridge to the deeply religious people of Central Europe and in Russia itself. I still remember with great pride our group photograph. When the board visited the great museum in Prague (in early 1989), we were led by U.S. ambassador Shirley Temple Black through surly and unpleasant lines of the regime's Communist guards at the traffic barriers. There in the museum were two special displays all were quite proud of—first there was the display on American jazz, with wonderful photographs, memorabilia, and wax models of American icons of the 1920s and '30s, and full surround sound. The second was a display honoring Radio Free Europe, filled with memorabilia and newspaper clippings about us, and there, at the end, a group photo of our board. There, behind the Iron Curtain. That museum display was the clearest possible proof of how dear RFE had become to the whole region—even the regime, which dared not block it. (They, too, perhaps, saw the handwriting on the wall.)

To underline the quality of our staff in Munich (our longtime broadcasting center), I must mention our chairmen in residence there. There was former Senator James L. Buckley, a true gentleman, diplomat, and brave pro-American patriot. After him came Gene Pell, whose deep and mellifluous voice I used to hear on Boston radio; he was the former president of the Voice of America and a skillful, resourceful, and inventive leader. Next came the equally creative Ken Tomlinson, also a highly experienced and sharply focused broadcaster and editor, later editor in chief of *Reader's Digest*.

When the creative and much-loved Frank Shakespeare retired to accept an ambassadorship to Portugal (homeland of his dear Shrine of Our Lady of Fatima), he nominated Steve Forbes to replace him. Steve stepped up and demonstrated his abilities as leader right off the bat. He came to every board meeting extremely well prepared, ready with new ideas and initiatives, and with boundless energy. He spent an immense amount of time in the Munich broadcasting offices, as well as in briefing members of the House and Senate in Washington. He sponsored a new program to enlist "stringers" who worked on the ground in the Soviet Union, and he opened up toll-free numbers to take calls from citizens in all the broadcast areas. These initiatives bore especially rich fruit when the famous nuclear disaster hit Chernobyl and its fumes spread across Europe. RFE/RL had reports from eyewitnesses on the ground early, yet, unlike other broadcasters reporting the disaster, RFE/RL held off putting out the first (largely erroneous) descriptions of ground zero until they had two reliable sources to confirm the information.

One of the later but shrewdest members to join the board was Karl Rove, who in our regular meetings with the broadcast journalists in Munich was especially quick and adroit. Many of the RFE/RL journalists were citizens of the Iron Curtain countries—and a surprisingly large number of them were from the British Commonwealth countries, rather to the left of American liberals and a fortiori of Reaganauts. Rove was unusually good at giving them the real lay of the land concerning public political opinion in the United States. He helped make U.S. election results, exit-polling, and public opinion polls intelligible to non-Americans. We each saw one of our tasks as helping our editors and broadcasters in Munich to understand many facets of the American electorate that were otherwise unfamiliar to them. The importance of religious faith to many Americans, for example, was far beyond its importance to Western Europeans. Most people in Europe took their reference points on religion from the France of 1789, not from Boston and Philadelphia of 1776.

By late 1987 or early 1988, RFE/RL had a toll-free number for calls in most parts of our two regions. Telephone calls poured in: calls of increasing daily frustration, anger at local injustices, descriptions of the conditions of loved ones in named local hospitals, fresh examples of lies from local officials, accounts of local outbreaks of protest. Almost half of all hospitals had no hot water; patients were frequently assigned two to a bed; relatives had to bring in food to sustain them. Before broadcasting any snippets (which delighted and inspired other listeners), we took pains to double source them. These calls gave us great leads.

At our spring meeting in Munich in 1989, our key people reported that all signs pointed to the lid blowing off the Soviet Empire before the end of the year. The huge volume of incoming calls and their despairing tone, plus detailed reports from our growing number of stringers in the whole dispersed broadcast area, made even our most hardened and jaundiced editors believe that an eruption was coming.

One story our people reported was the appearance of a novelty among street vendors in Moscow: a market in burned-out lightbulbs. Why buy burned-out bulbs? Hardened Muscovites took them to the office, unscrewed bright, live bulbs to take home, and screwed in the burned-out ones in their offices.

As soon as I came home I wrote a short magazine article conveying this prediction and warning readers that, whatever they were hearing from most of the media and university Russia experts, the end was nigh. My pieces usually got into print quickly in the religious journals I chose. This time no editor would believe me. At least five times the piece came back.

Thus, I turned to Steve Forbes at *Forbes* magazine. I worked my longer piece into three one-page articles, using new information as it unfolded. My intention was to help readers anticipate the coming events and grasp the unfolding larger narrative. *Forbes* began publishing the short series on July 24, 1989.

By the spring of 1989, it had at last begun to be said openly—even Gorbachev said it—that the USSR might have a First-World military, but much of the rest of the economy was Third-World, even Fourth-World, well below the level of India. And this could no longer be disguised. Even the manufacture of soap was unreliable. Food shortages were being reported by Russian journalists, with worse to come during the winter months. Some internal experts predicted pockets of famine.

A story was also being told in Central Europe (recycled from earlier times) of General Jaruzelski of Poland being summoned to Moscow. When he came back, his secretary noticed a large bandage on his cheek. He said nothing. She hesitated to ask. Finally, by day's end she summoned up the courage to mention it.

"The dentist," he explained. "In Moscow I had to go for a filling."

"But the big bandage?"

"You think I open my mouth in Moscow?"

THE FIRST GIGANTIC EXPLOSION against the Empire was struck—where else?—in Poland. The breakthrough came when Lech Walesa, an electrician and cofounder of the labor union Solidarity, launched a massive outbreak of public protests throughout the nation, and General Jaruzelski was obliged to bow to the demand for parliamentary elections, which this time could not be rigged. In August, democracy worked its peaceful magic in a stunning transition of power. The new leaders of Poland came out proclaiming their vision as "democratic capitalism."

The real magic had arrived ten years before, when the new Polish pope, the young and vigorous John Paul II, through his own unrelenting insistence, was invited by an unwilling Polish Communist government to make a pilgrimage to his native land. When the crowds, sometimes in the millions, gathered around him, a stunning awareness pierced Polish hearts: *There are more of us than there are of them.* "Be not afraid!" was the pope's repeated theme. It turned out that the pope had a great many more divisions than Stalin—and that the arms of the Spirit are more empowering than military weapons. Alas, many in the West still could not believe that the whole Soviet Empire was falling down.

And then the center of the action shifted to Czechoslovakia. In 1977 more than two hundred courageous writers, priests, and physicists had signed a charter of human rights that landed many of them in jail or got them booted out of their jobs. One physicist with a highly promising future was sentenced to shoveling coal in the basement of an apartment building—he discovered that during most of the day he could read (and pray), and years later he told of his punishment's paradoxical benefit—all the potent books he read. (He particularly liked *The Spirit of Democratic Capitalism.*) The future cardinal of Prague, Cardinal Vlk, was sentenced to wash the windows of apartments and office buildings—and when years later people finally saw him on television after his elevation, many remembered having seen his face outside their windows with a squeegee.

I witnessed a tiny bit of this history in my office at AEI in 1983, when a young Pole materialized suddenly at my office door. He looked over his shoulder as he spoke and was hesitant even to enter the room completely, keeping the door open. He lowered his head humbly and told me that he had come from Solidarność to ask my permission to publish a Polish translation of *The Spirit of Democratic Capitalism.* I smiled broadly but said that I would need to charge royalties. His face fell, and he began to stammer that that was not possible—until I told him what the royalties were: "One copy for the pope, and one for me." He broke into a large grin and extended his hand thankfully.

"The first will be easy," he said. "The second will take a lot longer."

By very early 1985, *The Spirit of Democratic Capitalism* had been illegally published underground in a tiny, black-covered pocket edition. News of it soon spread all through Poland, and on into Czech and Slovak lands. (Still later I learned from Václav Havel that he and four or five of his best friends from Prague used to meet at his home in the mountains every month or so to discuss that book chapter by chapter. Some used the Polish translation, some the English.) Until that book, there had been hundreds of others predicting the transition from capitalism to socialism. This was the first to describe the transition from socialism to capitalism. That was its utility just then.

BY THE LATE FALL of 1989, under the charismatic leadership of the former prison inmate and dramatist Václav Havel, protests in the old part of Prague, particularly in Wenceslas Square, increased in numbers and intensity. Finally, on a day that will live in history, November 17, 1989, the demonstrations reached a climactic point. A young worker in a brewery near Wenceslas Square stood on a box inside the small factory and urged his fellows to join the protests. He was reported to have declaimed in a dramatic flourish, "We hold these truths to be self-evident, that all men are endowed by their Creator with certain inalienable rights, among these are the right to life, liberty, and the pursuit of happiness!" The workers moved rapidly outside to join the protestors in the square. Students and poets protesting is one thing, but when workers join the demonstrations, all proletarian pretenses of Communism collapse. The government eventually resigned, Havel was acclaimed interim president, and the great ugly wall that had separated Christian Europe into two branches (as the pope put it) sprang a thousand leaks, and scores of thousands streamed to the West. The Wall in Berlin was soon pounded down, hammer blow by hammer blow, and the roots of Christian Europe were once again nourishing a single tree.

I remember that glorious day in Prague with great warmth and joy. We celebrated outside my office by pouring champagne. I got out the Red Army's bright red battle flag, which RFE friends in Prague had saved for me a few months earlier after it was left behind in their building's hallway by rapidly departing Soviet troops. It was huge, and unfurled it all but covered up one of my bookcases. My friends at AEI helped me hang it there, and together we celebrated it like a battle trophy taken on the battlefield.

What was especially beautiful about that day was how peacefully Communism fell in most of Eastern and Central Europe. That peaceful ending seemed to vindicate all those long years of restraint under Mutually Assured Destruction, that seemingly mad policy—the policy that actually did work. Every hour, every day, there were U.S. bombers in the air, poised in airspace near Soviet territories, as a deterrent against any surprise attack. Scores of thousands of U.S. airmen (and women) maintained large nuclear forces day and night for more than twenty-five years, without ever using them. These were, in that sense, the most successful military weapons system ever—because best are the weapons that are never fired.

Those of us who had long been anti–Communist empire really partied that day. What a sweet victory it was! What a sweet, sweet day, which (we thought in our excitement) would be remembered by schoolchildren for a thousand years to come: *1989—The Year the Wall Came Down*.

It was altogether right that day that champagne should flow, and from a few eyes should trickle tears of joy.

22

Looking Forward

Ronald Reagan left office in 1988 with world-changing momentum. The communist idea *was* thrown on the dustbin of history. The fantastically expensive deterrent to the Red Army's intercontinental weapons had, in fact, *deterred* (despite so many voices that said it could never work). A huge peace dividend fell into the hands of Bill Clinton and subsequent American presidents after the Soviet Union dissolved.

Meanwhile, its own inadequacies ate away socialism's innards. Since the early 1980s, no serious person behind the Iron Curtain (or in China) any longer believed in socialism as an economic dream. The Soviets had held the belief that the only true socialism is *real, existing socialism*—its empire, massive marching armies, weapons, and spy networks. The real thing. But it wasn't only the raw reality of power that tumbled stone on top of stone before our eyes. What tumbled was the socialist *idea*—and with it a whole morality-denying system. Soviet socialism's only morality had been "What helps socialism succeed is good; what weakens socialism is evil."

For an entire century the world had been testing two propositions, one political, the other economic: *dictatorship is better for the people*

than democracy; and *socialism is better for the people than capitalism.*
The bloodiest century had shown that the answer to both propositions was no: democracy is better, and capitalism is better. The Nazis
exterminated some 16 million people, the Soviets upward of 53 million (for further readings, consult *The Black Book of Communism*).

What had been neglected for a century was the third component
of the free society: the *moral and cultural* system. That is the deepest system, and the inner dynamic within the two others. A good
economy is indispensable for human flourishing; a sound, limited,
law-abiding government is necessary for such an economy; and a
truly humanistic cultural system is the indispensable life support for
the other two systems. Economics begins in the mysticism of creativity. Politics begins in the mysticism of common action. Culture
supplies the mysticism for both.

At one time in human history, the highest value was the silent
contemplation of the inner light of creative truth at the center of
everything that is. No human could know all that truth. But in the
search for each fragment of it, evidence beyond the power of human
altering became the judge of who was closer to, or farther from, the
truth. In short, there is truth to be uncovered—intersubjective, du-
rable truth. Humans are not masters of that truth; they are only able
to glimpse it, expand their comprehension of it, hold to it in tough
times, and reverence it. As Jefferson wrote, the mind may rightly
bend the knee only to evidence, and be bound only by evidence.
Only down that way of seeing reality is the advance of science possible. Only down that way is the inner realm of individual conscience
seen to be inalienable. Evidence can animate action only when it is
grasped and pursued by individual conscience—each conscience at
its own pace and in its own way. How else can evidence shape the
soul of individuals?

Toward the end of the twentieth century, however, it seemed that
hardly anyone in the world knew how to talk about such things—

even to set out the basic terms for whole societies, let alone a plural-istic world.

No wonder the world has foundered a bit since the Wall went down in 1989.

In several drafts of this book prior to this one, I tried to tell the story of the last five presidential terms following Ronald Reagan's—those of George H. W. Bush (Bush 41), Bill Clinton, and George W. Bush (Bush 43). The problem with that plodding strategy was that my narrative began to sound like a series of newspaper summaries, too close in time to be really reflective, too bogged down in concrete stories to indicate what in the news was actually changing *me*. And a lot of deeper stuff was, in fact, churning within me.

So here I have decided to concentrate on ideas distilled from the past twenty-four years of the political life of the United States, from the only point of view I am responsible for: my own. This viewpoint might not be shared by anybody else. But it does embody an argu-ment that kept changing me.

The Reagan administration had come into existence by surprise and a bit prematurely. Neoconservatives (those former leftists who had been knocked around by reality) had begun uncovering the self-contradictions of socialism—or, in our case, statism. They had begun to limn the outlines of an alternative governing vision—but had not done nearly enough to complete that vision. *Newsweek* de-clared that the neoconservatives in the small circle around Irving Kristol ("the Godfather") were now the "red-hot center" of the new conservatism being ushered in by the new administration.

The older, traditional conservatives who had labored in the heat of the vineyards day after day for so many decades did not much like the interloping Kristol gang, who had arrived just in time to share the spoils. The older, traditional conservatives, the paleoconservatives (as they styled themselves), positively loathed neoconservatives. Yet neither one was the real enemy to the other. Even though Reagan had won, the forces of statism were not dead. The clients of the welfare state grew. To pay for government pensions, the cities, states, and federal government needed massive amounts of money. The cry for "equality" grew louder. What that meant was "tax the rich and middle class" more—but one could not, of course, say that the middle class must be taxed more. So the focus was put on the really rich. From deeper still, the contradiction in statism reared its head above the waters and arched its back in the air. One cannot have both a Leviathan welfare state and a large, modern military. Statists became more and more demanding: There must be cuts in the military budget. The trouble with the welfare state is that it eats everything in sight.

In the practice of politics, events govern. Events come so fast that there is little time for theory—little time for reading, little time for big ideas. So by 2013 this nation found itself hopelessly at odds with itself, two sides hardly able to talk with each other, separated by a huge no-man's-land where "ignorant armies clash by night." Let me review a few highlights.

The Two Bushes

Who [have] the milk of human kindness by the
quart in every vein.

The two Bushes: kinder and more considerate men never served in the White House. And they showed uncommon bravery by taking huge political risks in going to war first against Muslim aggressors in Iraq after Saddam Hussein invaded Kuwait, then in Afghanistan after al-Qaeda struck the United States with support from Afghanistan, then back in Iraq, which had brazenly violated the conditions for peace agreed to a decade earlier. By late 2002 Saddam failed to account for more than 5,000 liters of anthrax which, in order to secure conditional peace just a few years earlier, his government had registered. Not included in the tally were thousands of liters of botulin and other forms of biological weapons, including sarin, reported by UN inspectors to have been present in his arsenals. Nor did it include the stockpiles of mustard gas the UN reported were in his possession. Chief UN weapons inspector Hans Blix of Sweden commented to the Associated Press (*New York Times,* November 22, 2002): "The production of mustard gas is not like the production of marmalade. You're supposed to keep some track of what you produce. There must be documentation, records of what was produced."

By the year 2000 there were something like thirty-two active armed conflicts across the globe, and more than two-thirds involved Muslims, as Samuel Huntington reported in his book *The Clash of Civilizations.* Bush 41 got his war over with quite abruptly, despite brooding public fear about "the mother of all battles"; in 1991 Senator Edward Kennedy had warned the Senate that 50,000 caskets would have to be prepared for the early American dead. Yet that First Gulf War under General Stormin' Norman Schwarzkopf ended with casualties on the scale of English losses at Agincourt, as depicted in *Henry V.* The First Gulf War concluded in less than two months.

Poor Bush 43—the Second Gulf War ten years later began with lightning success in Afghanistan, even in the first four weeks of fighting in Iraq II. But then the two wars dragged on for years. (And then, as Bush was bringing Iraq II to a fragilely successful end, quite gratuitously President Obama made a big thing about the "necessary" war in Afghanistan, dropped Iraq prematurely, and ramped up in Afghanistan, intending to drop it soon, too.) Democracies, especially now that there are so few sons per family, cannot fight long wars.

As George W. Bush himself must have calculated in advance, his brave vision of lighting fires of liberty across the Middle East cost him a huge slide in popularity, especially during the last year of his presidency. Both the press and the Democrats attacked him incessantly—and unscrupulously. George W. thought that vigorous resistance against the "asymmetric warfare" preached by Osama bin Laden was necessary, and I concurred. This cost Bush dearly—although not as much as it cost Saddam Hussein, who was hanged for his crimes by an open and reasonably fair court, to widespread applause throughout the region.

All over Iraq, newspapers, magazines, political parties, radio stations, and civic institutions multiplied. Throughout the Middle East, democracy and rights and liberties were more widely and openly discussed than at any time during the previous two hundred years. A brand-new argument erupted in the core of Islam when the ideas of liberties, rights, and democracy faced emotional resistance throughout backward-looking parts of the culture. In 2011 the radicals of the Muslim Brotherhood in Egypt, buffeted by the new power of the idea of democracy, succeeded in deposing the much flawed president of Egypt, Hosni Mubarak. Still, the same radicals, born around the same ideas that spawned Osama bin Laden, dumped the idea of democracy. This was not the first time that radical Islamists pretended to embrace the democratic ideal only to dump it after their victory: "One man, one vote—*one time*!"

The end of the story of the battle for natural rights in the Muslim world is far from finished. Onrushing history will prove that. Certain inalienable rights are natural to all humans—Muslims included, of course. Even doused fires smolder—and then reignite later in the night. Muslims in that part of the world have suffered so much torture and imprisonment at the hands of the state police and the religious police that their natural longing to live free of torture and arrest will drive them on until they fulfill it. That is my bet. Not in this generation, but incrementally and not too long from now.

In domestic politics, Bush 41 flashed a bright light on the two different conceptions of community in American life and history, a theme that 43 duly carried forward during his own two terms. If you will, allow me to return to this in the next chapter, for it is pivotal to the deepest argument that wracks our time.

Bill Clinton's Two Terms

Quickly now, I must say a bit about Bill Clinton, too. The most striking achievement of Bill Clinton is how cleverly he stole Reagan's clothes, especially in regard to taxes and economic growth, even while most Republicans thought of him (as he was in some areas) as a far leftist. His choice of Wall Street's Robert Rubin for Treasury Secretary was brilliant. Take job growth, for one thing. Under Reagan, from the depths of stagflation some 16 million new jobs were created—a staggering performance. In addition, by 1988 a higher proportion of working age adults were working than ever before (just over 64 percent).

Clinton, while raising high-income tax rates to 39 percent from 28 percent, did even better. Under Clinton, some 23 million new jobs were created, proving that low taxes and high job growth were a bipartisan recipe for success. I was one who predicted that by raising rates as much as he did, Clinton would diminish job creation and employment. But I was wrong. I learned that there is no one fixed tax rate that is perfect for all times. A leader must make prudential judgments and adjust by trial and error. Clinton did this better in his second term, when against Democratic ideology he cut capital gains tax rates back toward Reaganaut levels—and then watched as new capital investments and the turnover of profits from old areas into fresh areas doubled the revenues his Treasury took in from capital gains.

Clinton is often given credit for balancing the budget and producing surpluses. He deserves great credit. But so does Reagan, whose policies Clinton mimicked. In fact, the new Gingrich majority in the House—through an unprecedented gain of fifty-four seats in the 1994 election—fairly forced Clinton to commit to a balanced budget. Dick Morris usually mentions that he helped persuade Clinton to balance the budget, and thus advance the Democrats' cause by stealing the Republicans' clothes on this policy while attacking them elsewhere. No matter, the job got done: a balanced budget,* surpluses. In 2013 Democrats are still boasting about how Clinton raised taxes over Reagan's levels. Clinton did so, but only modestly. Compare:

	Highest income tax rate	Capital gains tax rate
Carter, 1980	50%	70%
Reagan, 1981	28%	20%
Reagan, 1986	28%	28%
Bush, 1990	31%	28%
Clinton, 1993	39.6%	28%
Clinton, 1997	39.6%	20%**

*In Chapter 15 above, I criticized the "green-eyeshade" approach to balanced budgets for two reasons: first, it seemed punitive ("it isn't good for you unless it hurts"); second, it did not add incentives for growth (lower tax rates). By contrast, President Clinton made use of lower capital gains tax rates as a means to cultivate significant economic growth, both in the number of jobs and in GNP, and from these came a burst of new incoming revenues.
**Note: The 28 percent capital gains tax rate of 1993 produced $36.1 billion of revenue; whereas at the lower rate of 20 percent in 1997 the revenue was $79.3 billion, more than twice as much as in 1993.

In addition, the huge peace dividend from the Reagan victory over Communism fell to Clinton, not Bush 41. With lower military spending, surpluses became a lot easier to achieve for Clinton than for his predecessors.

Clinton made vividly concrete an old lesson I learned from Jacques Maritain, one of the architects of the Universal Declaration of Human Rights—namely, that a certain amount of pragmatic jibbing and tacking, even from cynical motives, may achieve good outcomes for the public. Put otherwise, cynical intentions do not necessarily undermine good policy, and good intentions may at times produce bad outcomes. The difference between intentions and results can be vast—the plunge into hell is often enough driven by good intentions.

As Maritain teaches, in art the morally good man can produce an ugly work, while the morally bad man may produce a brilliant one. The same goes for politics. That rule is a caution against overemphasizing the need to elect men of good character in order to achieve good outcomes in politics. There is a crucial point in praising moral character, of course. But the results are not always good, and not necessarily good in all ways. Achieving the higher common good through politics takes more than a good character and good intentions. Jimmy Carter helped make that truth vivid. There are a million ways in which actions can go wrong and produce unintended consequences.

The biggest fault I found with the Clintons was that their support for abortion was absolute—it brooked no contradiction, no matter how minor. They did not approve of parental consent requirements, nor of a quite modest test to be sure a woman had at least a basic knowledge of the consequences before blindly going in for an abortion. The Clintons did not show much concern about prior information before the weighty, life-and-death choices made by teenage mothers. Any slightest deviation from an absolute right to have an abortion by anyone at any time was for them out of bounds. Their speeches to pro-abortion groups made one wonder about the slogan "Abortion should be safe, legal, and rare." Why rare? They actually treated abortion like an unquestionable sacred rite, *not* to be closely examined and monitored.

The official Democratic absolutism on the issue of abortion may be undermining the essential premises of the welfare state. This is not a new insight, and admittedly it is but a utilitarian one, in spite of the fact that the issue at hand goes much deeper. But it's a plain fact: the higher the number of future workers who are aborted, the fewer workers there will be to fund each recipient of old-age benefits and Medicare. Has the total of 54 million abortions in the United States since 1973 not blasted a gaping hole in the projected funding for Social Security and Medicare? Exactly how much revenue has abortion already stolen away from funding for the elderly and the sick?

A Brief Word on Steve Forbes

Steve Forbes has never really gotten credit for the intellectual substance of his contributions to practical public policy in America. I loved helping him out a little in his presidential campaigns of 1996 and 2000. I learned from him much more than from any other campaign.

Imagine where our national debates about tax rates in 2012 would have been—and would now be—if the Republicans and Democrats had much earlier accepted Steve's proposal of the "flat tax"? Without the complaint by one of the richest men in the world that he should not be paying a lower effective tax rate than his secretary, the Obama campaign of 2012 would have lacked one of its most dramatic talking points.

Under the Forbes flat-tax policy, rates for both capital gains and income would long since have been equal. The more income a person received, the more taxes that person would pay. Warren Buffett, that richest of men, would have paid vastly more than his secretary. At the 2013 National Prayer Breakfast in Washington, D.C., noted Johns Hopkins neurosurgeon Ben Carson commended the flat tax loudly and clearly. He recalled that the Bible announced one single rate—tithing on all. And he went on: "You make $10 billion, you put in a billion. You make $10, you put in $1. . . . But some people say, 'That's not fair because it doesn't hurt the guy who made $10 billion as much as the guy who made $10'—but where does it say that you have to hurt the guy? He just put a billion dollars in the pot. We don't need to hurt him."

The flat tax is an idea of far greater scope than first meets the eye. Most of its critics miss its most important effect. Agreeing to a flat tax that could be filed on a one-sheet form—postcard size, if you will—would render unnecessary a huge chunk of federal bureaucracy. An enforcement arm at the IRS would of course remain at work. But how much simpler their work would be! Millions of man-hours would be saved both in government, and vastly more in every business (and every family) in America.

Now that Democrats have plumped for the flat tax—the "Buffett Rule" by another name—we may all be Forbesians soon. At the very least, Congress and the press should study already existing national experiences with the flat tax, such as those in Chile and Slovakia and some three dozen other nations. Chile has reduced the percentage of its poor quite drastically. Slovakia has become a magnet for safe investment from abroad; it is already producing so many vehicles for French, German, and Korean automakers that it has become the largest per capita producer of cars in the world.

There is another wrinkle to the flat tax as Steve Forbes proposed it. It gives a solid incentive for intact marriages and having children. The device Forbes was first to imagine is wonderfully simple: Exempt each adult from paying any income taxes on the first $13,000 of income, so that a married couple could earn $26,000 tax-free. Similarly, allow for an additional $5,000 exemption for every child. Thus every family of four would have $36,000 of income tax-exempt. Retaining that much income tax-free would be a solid, bankable incentive to marry, as well as for parents to stay together and raise children. It would balance out the many perverse incentives of current federal policies.

There are two other ideas Forbes proposed for dealing with the huge demographic crisis accelerating today. The first was for Medicare, the second for Social Security. For two reasons, Medicare costs are growing much faster than are the funds necessary to cover them. Because of the increased longevity of the elderly, each year the proportion of the population eligible for benefits grows. In addition, technological and pharmacological advances make standard medical care for the elderly more expensive each year. For example, a single weekly chemotherapy treatment might cost $10,000 or more, and that cost is multiplied by many weeks of treatment. These are huge costs.

In a sense these problems have come about for two happy reasons: our elderly are living longer, and the standards of their care are leaping upward year by year. These are among our great successes as a nation. But the decline in the numbers of the working population may soon make caring for these dear ones close to impossible. No matter how you regard it, huge bills are inexorably arriving, for which we already have no money. Which will be the last age cohort to receive good care? That time is coming soon.

In regard to the looming Medicare crisis, Forbes proposed personal health savings accounts held in individuals' own names and under their own control, with funds increasing tax-free until they are used. These personal savings are then backed up by a high-deductible catastrophic insurance policy for major diseases, car accidents, and the like. Funds could be withdrawn from the account, as an individual decided, for routine visits to her doctor and other health-care expenses. Whatever she didn't spend would stay in the fund under her own ownership, and the account would be completely portable if she ever left her current employer. Lucky people in good health (and all now would have an incentive to keep healthy) would watch their kitty grow from year to year. Less healthy people would be just as well covered as before, by their supplementary insurance for more costly expenses. Anyone who wanted to could just stay on the current system.

The outspoken Ben Carson, at the same prayer breakfast just mentioned, proposed health savings accounts as his own favorite reform: "When a person is born, give him a birth certificate, an electronic medical record, and a health savings account (HSA) to which money can be contributed—pre-tax—from the time you're born to the time you die. When you die, you can pass it on to your family members so that when you're eighty-five years old and you've got six diseases, you're not trying to spend up everything. You're happy to pass it on and nobody is talking about death panels." He added: "For the people who are indigent, who don't have any money, we can make contributions to their HSA each month because we already have this huge pot of money. Instead of sending it to some bureaucracy, let's put it in their HSAs. Now, they have some control over their own health care."

As an alternative to Social Security, Forbes proposed the option of personal, heritable retirement accounts. The existing system would still remain an option for those who prefer it. Forbes pointed out that presently all those who die before they reach the age of sixty-five lose every dollar they have ever paid into the system. He proposed, for those who wanted them, accounts that would be personal and that they could pass on intact to their children. Thus each new generation might receive at least a small capital fund on which to build its future.

Forbes paid a lot of attention to details, but this is not the place to describe them. (The reader might, for example, Google "Steve Forbes health care" for more information.) The point is that Forbes some years ago already foresaw the demographic tsunami currently wreaking havoc among us. More of the elderly are living longer. Many more women are choosing not to have children, and many others are having significantly fewer. And 54 million human individuals once living in the womb have been aborted in the United States since 1973. Those missing millions have left a shortage of workers to support Medicare and Social Security. Both programs are great and humane ideas, but their funding mechanisms need to be thoroughly rethought.

It meant a lot to me that Steve called my attention to these enormous needs.

I learned from Bush 41 how a true gentleman conducts himself in office. For years afterward, the hotel staff at the Waldorf Astoria remembered him from his stay there when he served as ambassador to the United Nations. All received handwritten notes from him when new children were born, or death struck their families, or even just in recognition for some service they had rendered him. And I loved Bush 41's stress on community.

I learned from Bill Clinton the great range of talents he had for empathy and emotionally moving people, and his smooth and eloquent talking, keen mind, and willingness to compromise and meet opponents halfway. He may have been the greatest natural political leader ever to hold the presidency. He liked to play "the good bad boy." He was full of cheer and optimism. He had a charming wit, whipped out like a rapier against his foes and deployed with a warm, triumphant smile. He was shrewd and adjustable. He maintained the Reagan prosperity.

From George W. Bush I learned how a brave man keeps on course under the most relentless invective hurled against any president in my lifetime—and how a brave man keeps calm, steady, and cheerful withal. He may have also been the most prayerful man (after Lincoln) ever in the White House. He won huge popularity for his handling of the immediate aftermath of September 11, 2001, and for his firm and crisp leadership for some years following. He won great victories both in Congress and at the United Nations in gaining backing for his strong stand against Saddam Hussein's flagrant abuses of the conditions of peace agreed to at the end of the First Gulf War. Hussein's mass tortures and massacres of his own people, horrific mass abuses against the Kurds and his own Shi'ite subjects, and attempted subversions of his rivals in the region awakened a large coalition against him. Bush's second inaugural applied to the Muslim world Lincoln's arguments for natural rights—the same arguments Lincoln had made for the sake of America's former slaves. "With malice toward none, and charity for all." Some thought Bush's support of freedom in the Middle East utopian, and he was ridiculed in important circles, even conservative ones.

But on that point I side with Bush. The cry for the vindication of natural rights for people in that part of the world (and people in other parts of the world who continue to undergo terrible abuse) has been heard all around the world. I am proud an American president issued it, and I regret more than words can say that our people at last became too weary to stick with the task until it was done. Perhaps that was too much to expect. Bush's words were in line with the view of natural rights I expressed in my own way in *The Universal Hunger for Liberty,* and I am sticking with those words. I continue to thank President Bush steadily for his fidelity to natural rights and will be thankful forever for his taking me aboard Air Force One for the funeral Mass for Pope John Paul II, my dearest and deepest friend.

Now to the fuller discussion of community that I promised earlier.

23

Community Springs Only from Honest Argument

One of life's most time-consuming tasks is to achieve disagreement with an ideological opposite. Without blinking, you might object: "It's not hard to disagree. Heck! Most people do it all the time."

Still, most apparent disagreements, wouldn't you agree, are a matter of inevitable human differences—different understandings of terms, different perspectives on history, different estimations of the road ahead, contrary and angular temperaments, different sets of fears and rosy scenarios. (That beautiful girl, Rosy Scenario—have you met her?) But these are not disagreements, only misunderstandings. We are most often like ships passing in the night.

Sometimes, Manhattan's wise old Jesuit John Courtney Murray once said, two people cannot come to real disagreement without sticking to the argument for a very long time—maybe long enough to work through a case of brandy together as they ruminate. Patience and time. Careful dissection of differences, endless goodwill. And, if possible, infinite good humor.

It often seems that humans, given our immense variety, are *intended* to be in disagreement, and at certain points where patience and humor fade out, to allow rising passions to block the road of reasoned argument, at least for that night.

Oh well, in politics we have to try. We have to find ways to live together in painful toleration of each other. Every one of us is a heavy burden to some others—and they have to carry that burden. That is the Latin derivation, the image embodied in toleration, *tolerare:* to bear the burden of the opinions of the other. We give each other a pain in the neck from this burden. Imagine the headaches Ronald Reagan and Tip O'Neill gave each other.

There are a few things that, after some back-and-forth reflection, we can all agree on; other things we recognize that, in the limited time we have, we just cannot agree on; and for still others we can over time narrow some of our differences. We do this by finding the point where we began missing each other. I like the lesson of my teacher Reinhold Niebuhr: In my own views, there is always some error; and in the views of those I disagree with, there is always some truth.

Still, I am more discouraged in 2013 than I have ever been over the determination of so many to refuse to talk with those with whom they disagree. I seldom hear pro-life people, for example, make an effort to understand what those who are pro-choice are actually thinking, or try to probe their reasons for that position. The reverse is also true. And I believe I have never watched a television news program in which the time is taken to hear out both sides calmly. On such matters the temptation is to be absolutist: yes or no.

It is the same with other issues. Conservatives do not try often enough to grasp the motives of those who disagree with them, and liberals very seldom see the good and responsible reasons why conservatives think as they do. Worse, each side too easily tends to stereotype, even demonize, those on the other side. Neither you nor I would consider any of this honest argument. At its best, it is simply mudslinging. At its worst, it is outright disrespect.

The defining characteristic of civilization is the willingness of its members to engage *in conversation,* that is, in the effort to persuade each other through speech. It bears repeating over and over: Civilized people converse with one another, offering counterargument for argument, and try to follow the evidence where it leads. Barbarians club one another. The contemporary form of using clubs is ridicule. Mutual ridicule has by now been developed into a high art form. And, yet, we must do better. The freedom of our civilization lies in the balance.

We may agree, at least to a large extent, that together we face several huge and perhaps unprecedented crises. However, we disagree mightily (polls and voting patterns show) about how to *describe* these crises, even before we get around to talking about what to *do* together to face them. Perhaps we should start by putting our crises on the table, one by one, and working at describing each accurately. Maybe then we could take a few steps toward forming a majority shaped by respectful mutual understanding. Neither side gets everything it wants, but it is still a modest yet impressive negotiation. Then we might be able to fashion some broad strategies for addressing what we agree on, and discussing further what we do not agree on. One baby step at a time—tiny, confidence-building steps. *Anything beats sitting passive while crises shoot at us by the dozen!*

LET ME MENTION JUST some of these crises. We cannot go into each because that course would take several whole books. One of the most serious is the rapid decline in births in almost all parts of the world. Populations are shrinking at remarkably rapid rates. These low birthrates necessarily mean a serious diminishment of the future labor force. In the United States this translates into not enough workers to support those whose Social Security and Medicare benefits depend on approximately a seven-to-one ratio of wage earners to benefits recipient. The current ratio is down almost to two to one.

In the United States the depopulation crisis also ratchets up the immense pressure exerted on our grandchildren when we constantly increase our national debt. I feel sorry for future generations. They will not have a strong military at their call—and rebuilding it would be an immense task once it is gone. The struggles ahead for our grandchildren from ever heavier taxes and ever shabbier services will place them in an America immensely inferior in its promises and opportunities to what previous generations have known.

Another crisis we face together is the widening chasm of moral convictions about what we mean, morally and legally, by "marriage." In Western civilization the word has long meant only the specific union between a man and a woman in which, normally, children are nourished and instructed in good moral and civic habits. The state has had a great interest in man-woman marriage, since it is the one institution that guarantees the state a future and sustains the law-abidingness of its citizens. Such marriages are not simply contracts for two individuals to love each other. They are contracts for openness to bearing children and nurturing in them civic virtues and skills.

If the meaning of marriage is now widened to include a social contract between a man and a man, or a woman and a woman, the word no longer means what our civilization has meant by it for thousands of years. I do not see how or why the state has an interest in contracts for individuals who love each other. But if some persons want certain protections for the permanence of their love, then for the sake of civil peace, I might agree to accept a new legal institution to do that job. Without disturbing the subtle wisdom of ages by re-defining marriage, gays and lesbians might find legal shelter in other social contracts recognized by the state, and such support for long-term mutual love has much to recommend it. For humane reasons, such contracts might well include provisions for hospital visitation, inheritance, and other benefits.

This whole argument is vastly complex, and many have written brilliantly on it. I recognize how inadequate my few comments are. We need honest conversation, honest argument. It won't always be easy to maintain.

Then there is the crisis over the proper place of the traditional religious heritage of the nation's institutions and morals. Should this element of society be forced out of the public square in order to make that square solely secular? The problem is that while some seem to imagine that "secular" means neutral, in fact it does not. Secularism is also a commitment of mind and soul, a particularly totalitarian one at that, which seeks to remove statues and symbols dearest to the souls and minds of so many in order to sweep out anything but its own ideological flatness—unquestioning, empty of meaning. From public life it bars the question "Why are we here?" Most human beings since the dawn of history, and still today, regularly experience the presence of an ordering and, when all is said and done, good and progress-favoring Intelligence. Some version of this experience, Alfred North Whitehead pointed out, undergirds the project of science and its hopefulness about human advancement. The world around us does not usually seem to be mad, perverse, and hostile, but quite amenable to endless questioning.

I have met persons who call themselves neither atheists nor agnostics, just people "who wait for others to produce some evidence for the presence of God." They have not found such evidence yet. But if you ask them what sort of evidence they want, they say "empirical" or "scientific." That is to say, they want their God to be physically observable. They are not searching for God at all, but only for a pathetic idol of clay or bronze or gold. Do they really expect God to be just another object in the physical universe, classed among the rest?

Have these people not considered even one or two of the hundreds of books about where and how to become aware of the presence of God all around them? Are they serious seekers—or just lazy?

The top hundred founders of our country—the eighty-five who signed either the Declaration of Independence or the Constitution or both, plus any other fifteen or so influential figures, such as Abigail Adams and Tom Paine—deserve close inspection for their religious practices, beliefs, activities, and passions. Even Tom Paine, though despising the Bible, believed in God and took ship to France to persuade Robespierre and the others that without God French rights would be unprotected and impossible to argue for. Paine believed in a Creator, a free, governing Providence, and a final Judge. He was sent to prison in France and risked death for his beliefs. Jefferson believed much the same, within the confines of Unitarianism. Yet Paine and Jefferson are outliers. Nearly all the other top one hundred founders were active Christians. Several held that Christianity is the best religion a republic could have, for more than any other it inculcates habits of liberty, that is, republican virtues. Contemporary scholars studying the religion of these founders—for so many years a neglected topic—are increasingly opening up these lines of historical inquiry. In twenty years we will know much more about the religion of the founders than we now do. I invested my own five years of study into this question, as witnessed in *On Two Wings: Humble Faith and Common Sense at the American Founding* and *Washington's God* (requested by Mount Vernon).

On yet another issue, climate change, we might all try at least to agree that there are measurable variances in temperatures, even for the world as a whole (although that's a lot trickier to measure than most news stories would have you believe). The argument is really not about climate *change*. Passions tend to explode when people have very different ideas about the *reasons* behind such change. The first instinct of many is to blame human beings for what goes on in nature. Why do some people seem to love nature but hate human beings? Why the joy in finding humans guilty? At least, *other* humans.

Since maybe a hundred years from now all this will look different from how it does today, it wouldn't hurt each of us to step back for a moment and try to imagine the shortcomings or downsides of our own position. What if the world becomes colder during the next hundred years, as people were predicting just thirty years ago? What if it does become hotter, but not quite so much—or maybe a bit more—than the worriers now believe? Don't forget that there are mighty self-interests behind each and every predictor. The Italians have a saying: "Greens are like tomatoes. They begin the summer Green, but by the end they are Red." Meaning that the ultimate goal of environmentalists is state control. On the other side, Greens blame the forces of greed and stasis.

Maybe a little caution before we make up our minds definitively is actually wiser, more prudent, humane, and appropriately cynical. Maybe the other guys are right. But "make haste slowly" is usually sage advice. There are a number of reasons for doubting the so-called scientific consensus reported in the media. Is it not curious that this point of view so neatly fits into the characteristic disposition of the Left to increase the powers of government enormously and with severe coercion? And that it also fits the Left's caricature of business and industry?

THERE ARE AT LEAST ten other public choices to make, on which a lot more human kindness and a deeper capacity for human sympathy might actually sharpen our minds. The worst thing is to let ourselves imagine that our side is the side of the angels, and that the other side is the side of stupid and evil spirits. It really is always a little better to imagine that the other side may be in some part right. That willingness forces us to think harder, and to look at problems in more than just one way.

Unless we can bring back to life honest argument, along with honest, open disagreement and lively conversation, we can never enjoy a pluralistic community.

Community: Defeating Envy and Poverty

Arguably the most pressing crisis concerns the growing number of our poor. It is crucial that they be helped to break the chains of poverty. Further, if Jewish-Christian and humanistic societies are to maintain self-respect, they have no option but to help the poor. But our serious disagreements over rival strategies about *how* to do so makes helping the poor difficult. Nonetheless, over the last thirty years we have reduced the number of the poor in the world by nearly one billion persons. Nearly half a billion persons in China and India alone have moved out of poverty in that time.

But poverty is not the only ill to be overcome. Envy—or covetousness—is another.

The founders of our country studied why all previous experiments in building a republic were fragile and usually short-lived. We should also try to figure out why this pattern repeats itself over and over again in history. Republics usually fail, our founders discovered, because of envy and covetousness. Sometimes one powerful family envies another; one section of a city resents the behavior of another; the poor covet a larger portion of what the rich have, the middle class resent the poor, and the rich are indifferent to all below themselves. Sometimes two powerful personalities despise each other, and each will be satisfied with nothing but bringing down the other. In the Ten Commandments, the Lord forbade covetousness seven times (count them). It is the most pervasive sin—far more dangerous than, say, anger. Anger openly displays its destructiveness, while covetousness presents itself not as a capital sin but as the pursuit of "justice." Its battle cry is "Equality!"

A fundamental task of a republic, therefore, is to defeat envy, to the degree possible for humans. For that, the "pursuit of happiness" by each individual is indispensable. In societies in which self-improvement is impossible and social stagnation is universal, individuals rejoice when evil befalls their neighbors. After an honorary degree ceremony, the great conductor Rostropovich once told me the story of a Frenchman, a Brit, and a Russian under sentence of death on the coming Wednesday. As a temporary reprieve, each is given a long weekend to do whatever he wishes. The Frenchman wishes for a weekend in Paris with his mistress, no strings attached, no promises made. The Brit wishes for a weekend walking the fields of Oxfordshire with his collie, reading Keats and Shelley. The Russian wishes that his neighbor's barn will burn down.

A similar story is told in other peasant societies. When individuals have no individual future to forge for themselves, they do not compare where they are now with where they are working hard to get to. They are going nowhere. So they compare their lot today with that of their neighbor. In Serbia, for instance, there is the tale of the genie who appeared to one peasant and promised him anything he wished—except, the genie said, whatever you get, your neighbor will get twice as much. Instantly the man said: "Take out one of my eyes!"

Consider by contrast a republic in which each brother and sister finds happiness in a different area of life, and each lives and works in quite different ways to make a success of his or her preferred lifework. Consider Sarah and Elizabeth, two sisters from Kansas born in the Depression, both now living near Washington, D.C. Neither is married; both have modestly high-paying jobs. Sarah is a bon vivant, loves to dress well, eat out as often as possible, travel to a beautiful world spot for her annual vacation—she hardly keeps a penny in the bank. Why should she? In fact, she chides her sister, "Neither one of us has children or any other relative to leave anything to. I believe in living to the hilt. I have only one life to live; I intend to live it." Elizabeth worries about Sarah, living so close to the edge as she does, and Sarah feels sorry for Elizabeth: "All you do is put money in those darn mutual funds. You aren't even living." The sisters do not envy each other. Each feels sorry for the other.

When Sarah dies, she leaves some $2,320 in her bank account. When Elizabeth dies a couple of years later, she has, to everyone's amazement, some $2.3 million in her mutual fund account. Any sociologist looking at that comparison might use it as proof of how unequal American society is. Yet neither Sarah nor Elizabeth was envious of the other; they loved each other and worried about each other. Each died happy. The choice of how to pursue one's own happiness does not eliminate envy, but it does make it rather pointless.

All of this brings us to the central issue of poverty. Envy clearly destroys community, and the deepest issue underlying the poverty crisis concerns the very nature and responsibilities of human community. Which form of community better helps the poor? The question is hotly contested in our national politics today.

In order to make my account succinct, let me stipulate one fairly strong position—which will take me two sentences. (1) Historically, the Left has been better, more up-front, more dramatic, in focusing attention on the poor. (2) Conservatives have the better argument concerning which form of community best helps the poor. Each of these propositions is an indispensable point. Let us give serious attention to both.

Which party speaks more often and more dramatically about the poor is all but self-evident. The main political strategy of the Left depends rhetorically and in policy terms on justifying almost all basic moves on the grounds of compassion. Everything is *said* to be for the sake of the needy and the lowly. Even the very form of community to which the Left turns for carrying out this main purpose—the federal government—is dictated, they say, by the needs of the poor.

This issue, more than any other, seemed to me to have been the subtext of the Reagan administration and the first Bush administration. From 1932 until the 1980s, the Left (there being more big government than ever before) had higher moral prestige in the public square. The New Deal . . . Compassion . . . Big Government. For fifty years those were the governing terms of the dynamism within our public life. President Johnson, with his Great Society and the War on Poverty, launched the second stage of that particular rocket into our national skies.

But then Ronald Reagan deftly ridiculed the way the New Deal and the Great Society actually played out. He pointed to the huge rebirth of a new kind of poverty—often taking more virulent forms than in previous generations. More murder, more crime of all sorts, more family breakups—even the new inability of families to form—and the unprecedented irresponsibility of men toward women and their own progeny.

As I mentioned, the Democratic Party has typically spoken more often and better about the needs of the poor than conservatives have. But reality keeps mugging good intentions. I've come to think that the analysis of poverty made by the Left—for many years, my own analysis—is not deep enough. Not empirical enough. Not self-critical enough.

It is worth re-inspecting the public arguments on community in the years after Reagan. The most dramatic change of all occurred in the underlying political philosophy of the community within each party. At the 1988 Democratic National Convention in Atlanta, presidential nominee Michael Dukakis described the new central philosophy of his party:

It is the idea of community. The kind of community that binds us here tonight. It is the idea that we are in this together; that regardless of who we are or where we come from or how much money we have—each of us counts. And that by working together to create opportunity and a good life for all—all of us are enriched—not just in economic terms, but as citizens and as human beings.

The idea of community. An idea that was planted in the New World by the first Governor of Massachusetts. "We must," said John Winthrop, "love one another with a pure heart fervently. We must delight in each other, make each other's condition our own, rejoice together, mourn together, and suffer together. We must," he said, "be knit together as one."

Now, John Winthrop wasn't talking about material success. He was talking about a country where each of us asks not only what's in it for some of us, but what's good and what's right for all of us.

In most of human history, however, the idea of community has been tribal, familial, clan centered. The Democrats tried to evoke the emotive power of this ancient communal past, while yoking it to an activist federal government. The party spoke the language of personal love, but its actual programs were quite impersonal. To some extent Dukakis drew examples from all those mediating structures formed by private citizens, such as the Denver priest who helped the homeless. But the unmistakable emphasis of his conception was on larger federal funds, more federal programs, new government initiatives.

Because of four inherent weaknesses, this Democratic conception fell on hard times. It is extraordinarily expensive. Its spending is disproportionate to its actual results. It generates self-defeating incentives and unintended negative consequences. And its reliance upon large government weakens all other social strengths and practices—family, neighborhood, local institutions, and the "little platoons" of which Edmund Burke wrote—that are the historically most effective locus of social justice. "Social" does not only mean "state." But Democratic programs typically do supplant local incentives while at other times weakening them by federal regulations, requirements, and oversight.

These fundamental flaws in the new Democratic Party—which were not characteristic of the party of my youth—offered Republican presidential nominee George H. W. Bush a perfect foil for framing his own public philosophy, which was actually far closer, not simply to American history but even to the history of the Democratic Party, and his son, Bush 43, inherited it and sharpened it. Here is how Bush the elder articulated it in New Orleans in his own acceptance speech at the 1988 Republican National Convention, after speaking of the American tradition of intellect and learning—of building colleges even on the edges of the frontier:

> And there is another tradition. And that is the idea of community—a beautiful word with a big meaning, though liberal Democrats have an odd view of it. They see "community" as a limited cluster of interest groups, locked in odd conformity. In this view, the country waits passive while Washington sets the rules.
>
> But that's not what community means, not to me. For we are a nation of communities, of thousands and tens of thousands of ethnic, religious, social, business, labor union, neighborhood, regional and other organizations, all of them varied, voluntary and unique.
>
> This is America: the Knights of Columbus, the Grange, Hadassah, the Disabled American Veterans, the Order of

Ahepa, the Business and Professional Women of America, the union hall, the Bible study group, LULAC, Holy Name [parish]—a brilliant diversity spread like stars, like a thousand points of light in a broad and peaceful sky.

Does government have a place? Yes. Government is part of the nation of communities—not the whole, just a part. I do not hate government. A government that remembers that the people are its master is a good and needed thing.

Years before, Republicans spoke incessantly of the individual. They sounded, especially regarding economic rights, as libertarian and individualistic as the ACLU. But no longer: The new Republicans speak the language of "work, family, and neighborhood." They glory in their own newfound philosophy of community. They have been mastering the concepts of mediating structures and subsidiarity, and they are striving to bring social healing to lonely individuals. They want to invent ways for citizens to act socially, without necessarily acting governmentally. They observed the distinction between society and state.

I gained a lot of respect for the first President Bush—and also for his speechwriting team, especially the often lyrical Peggy Noonan, who put these things so well. Even though until 2010 (after I moved my legal residence to Delaware) I thought it necessary to stick with the Democratic Party until it came to its senses, I was also seeing evidence before my eyes that, in practice, the Republican Party better represented where I thought the country should go.

Democrats tend to circle the wagons to hold on to the welfare state of the past, fatal flaws and all. Republicans are aiming for a new future, different from the administrative state, and better connected to the nation's animating spirit. Not socialism, not individualism, but the community commitments of our founders. Without much stress on unity—"United we stand! Divided we fall"—this nation could not have won its independence. In order to save the Union at the cost of immense carnage, Lincoln prevented the young nation from being broken into four or five blocs, each in alliance with a different European power—which would have sown the seeds for another divided, war-torn Europe in this battered world. The American model remains: the pioneer villages of the Midwest, the inventiveness of new immigrant neighborhoods in the East, and the adaptability of our units in the field in World War II. In battle, I learned from veterans of the armies they faced in the field, the American military was a unique mix of individual initiative and large-unit military cohesion that evoked a certain wonder.

The new Republicans believe there is a better way to overcome poverty than the administrators of the federal welfare state dreamed of. That way is economic growth, new small businesses on every local level, opportunity, and vast social cooperation voluntarily leaping in to help in one small needy group, then another—the original American way. The federal program, designed by social engineers far from the action on the ground, has a penchant for screwing up all the human incentives that lead to creativity and personal responsibility and the desire to "give back" to the community that has so well nourished each previous generation.

But federal action must always be involved in the mix. Federal involvement was required in the Rural Electrification Act, the Federal Highway Act, the Social Security Act, even some sectors of the War on Poverty, for example. The debate over community is not about which type to choose exclusively. It is about putting the right mix together, each part making the other parts stronger—not weakening them by taking over their functions. Both parties need to be honest about such things.

Four generations ago there was an old Tammany Hall saying: "The fella wot said that 'Patriotism is the last refuge of scoundrels' unner-istimated th' possibilities o' compassion."

Compassion may be the most beautiful of all virtues. It is the new possibility that Christianity added on to Greek and Roman virtues. It has captivated the imagination of the modern, pagan West: "Liberty, *Fraternity*, Equality." These are not directives of Greek or Roman philosophy, but the teachings of the carpenter Jesus Christ. They have captivated the Left.

Without "compassion," what would be left for the Left? Yet like every other good ideal, compassion is often used in a fraudulent way. Instead of being blinded just by the name, take a look at the actual, real-world effects of any given policy. The Left leads off with the correct word, but it is not watchful enough over the unintended consequences its policies (said to be in the name of compassion) often dump onto history.

AS I SAID EARLIER, I am very discouraged about the possibilities of conversation today in the face of radical divides about what this nation was founded to become, and what future it ought to aim for today. The country seems hopelessly split on such matters, and too tired to have honest discussions.

In short, this nation desperately needs honest argument. That means overcoming our weariness and treating our partisan opposition with respect for their dignity and love for this country. I wish our president would lead the way, as sometimes he suggests that he might. Up to now, though, he speaks with contempt for people who have views like my own, and for many others who have views different from his.

Lest we begin to feel sorry for ourselves, however, let's think of Eastern Europe (from Poland through Ukraine to Siberia) thirty-five years ago, under the heavy gray smog over the Soviet lands. In that grayness, amid the ugliness of "socialist-style" architecture, the young new Polish pope, Karol Wojtyla of Kraków, had the nerve to say that Europe was one tree with two branches—East and West—and that both were already, perhaps invisibly at first, in the process of reuniting. Or again, that Europe was one house that would not remain divided. His words seemed so utopian, so naïve, that I for one felt a little sorry for the pope. Yet a decade later the Wall between East and West had been broken down, stone by stone, and people from around the world took chips of that Wall as souvenirs of a bad dream. Next the Soviet Union came apart at the seams. Nuclear arsenals were significantly reduced, and placed in new, better, more honorable hands; the weapons that remained seemed not nearly so menacing. East and West turned their energies toward creativity and building anew. (Well, until Putin they did.)

No one was more responsible for this than Pope John Paul II—although he could not have done it without the foresight, courage, and persistence of Ronald Reagan and Margaret Thatcher, those two great transatlantic soul mates.

In my lifetime I have been favored to meet and often work with many great political leaders, presidents, artists, and builders of brand-new industries in new technologies of the Electronic Age. I especially prized working with Reagan, Thatcher, and Václav Havel. But of all the great human beings I have met—and even been invited into friendship with—none is closer to my heart than John Paul II.

No one better represents my dreams for the future than John Paul II. Thus I want to close this book with some memories of that good man, full of humor, electric energy, and grace.

24

The Pope Who Called Me Friend

In the autumn of 1991 I was in Italy for a conference on economics and religion in Foligno, a beautiful town south of Florence. One morning I was driven to Rome where, as I often did, I was staying overnight with the U.S. ambassador to the Vatican. At dinner a phone call came for me, for which I had to leave the table. It was the Vatican, inviting me to have dinner with the Holy Father the very next evening. I was to enter at the bronze door next to the Basilica, and the Swiss Guards would show me up. Back at the table, everyone was excited—no one more than I was, although I did my best to look suave and cool.

In a way, the background of the pope's invitation to dinner was, it seemed, the publication of my book *The Spirit of Democratic Capitalism* in 1982. That book made two points that seemed useful to those around the world who helped Pope John Paul II in the drafting of his historic encyclical of 1991, *Centesimus Annus*—commemorating the "Hundredth Year" since the first of all social encyclicals, *Rerum Novarum,* was published. The first point grew from my experience as a grandson of immigrants to the United States from Central Europe. In the United States they found "capitalism" (the economic system), but they simultaneously encountered a political system that protected their individual rights and a cultural system that strengthened the rights and duties of the free public exercise of multiple religious traditions under the protection of law. The United States also allowed for each people of the world to sound distinctive notes in the one national cultural symphony: English, German, Irish, Latin, Slavic, Jewish, etc. The tripartite definition of this free system—economic, political, and cultural—showed up very clearly in paragraph 42 of *Centesimus Annus*.

My second political thesis was that the most underreported fact of the twentieth century was the death of socialism as a plausible idea for the future. In practice, it did not work. More than that, socialism's underlying theories made it impossible for it to work. The best hope of the poor in the world was not socialism. The actual history of my own family and millions of other poor families showed Marxism to be the opiate of intellectuals and students. The much despised "capitalism," combined with a polity of law and rights and a culture of spirit, routinely turned workers into middle-class families, with positive attitudes toward personal initiative and personal responsibility.

Two of my closest colleagues who expressed gratitude for my work (without necessarily agreeing with all of it) were John Paul II's own immensely talented papal secretary, Monsignor (later Archbishop of Kraków, and in 2006 elevated to cardinal) Stanislaw Dziwisz and the philosopher and Italian political leader Rocco Buttiglione.

When I arrived for dinner, after the very long climb up three flights of stairs, accompanied by a serious Swiss Guard, my lungs were burning with the strain (but my tall young guard was not even red in the face). I was ushered into the reception room where Monsignor Dziwisz met me. "Welcome, welcome," he said; "we know who our friends are." He told me Rocco was to be a guest, too, and should arrive shortly, which was great news to me.

Back in 1985 Rocco had raised very difficult questions for me (especially about the "common good") when I first lectured on capitalism and democracy at the Catholic University of Milan, but over the years as he read more of my work, he had come to grasp the good parts of it better than I did and incorporated them into his own vision. Later, having become good friends, we made plans to begin a summer program to bring Eastern European and American students together to study economics and democracy, preferably in the West.

Rocco arrived, and then the pope silently entered, with his trademark smile, slightly ironic, in a white papal soutane. A bishop from Poland who worked in the Vatican and whose English was fluent also joined us, so we were five. I was so awestruck that I hardly said a word at first. One thing I noticed was that Monsignor Dziwisz wanted to keep the conversation light, and he instigated some bantering between Rocco and the pope. Rocco was a professor at two Roman universities as well as the International Academy for Philosophy in Liechtenstein, but the pope had come to know him well in Kraków, where Rocco had gone to study the famous Polish phenomenologists. There Rocco learned Polish passably well, and he became a good friend of Wojtyla, a fellow philosopher.

In the autumn of 1978, the election of a man from behind the Iron Curtain as the new pope was a startling choice. It sent shockwaves throughout the lands on the Communist side of the Iron Curtain. The Communists immediately started laying plans to limit Pope Wojtyla's influence, to undermine him, and if necessary to wipe him off the chessboard of European leadership.

They feared Wojtyla, but they did not fear him enough. Wojtyla was a lot cleverer than they, and he was nearly always a move ahead of them on the chessboard. By natural talent a warmhearted and eloquent communicator, an actor who enjoyed being in crowds large or small, a skier, a poet, and a very brave man, Karol Wojtyla seized the imagination of the world almost immediately. He was young, vital, vigorous, and handsome, with a flair for dramatic action and swift repartee.

When I had first seen him in Washington, D.C., on his first papal visit to the White House, standing alongside President Jimmy Carter, I was struck by the pope's naturalness and ease. It was a beaming Carter who seemed a little stiff.

Later the pope stood on the balcony of the priests' house at St. Matthew's Cathedral on Rhode Island Avenue, just east of Connecticut Avenue. Karen had brought my excited mother with us, and we stood right below him, across the street. The happy crowd all around us filled to overflowing the street below him and began to shout very loudly: "JOHN PAUL II, WE LOVE YOU! JOHN PAUL II, WE LOVE YOU!" After a little while the pope held up his arms to ask for a pause. He smiled and then shouted into the microphone: "JOHN PAUL II—*I* LOVE *YOU*!" Laughing, clapping, and with not a little weeping, the crowd picked up as before. I was glad my mother and my wife were at my side, drinking it in and enjoying every moment of it.

SO THERE I WAS, seated at dinner with the man who had seized my imagination ever since the day of his election. It thrilled me that he was Slavic, as my family was. Moreover, it was said (I believe apocryphally) that the pope's mother was Slovak. One thing is certain: both his southern Poland and our northern Slovakia were for some centuries thought of as one people (a tough mountain people).

On this point, some years after this dinner, the pope in fact told George Weigel, his great biographer: "Michael Novak says he is Slovak. But he is actually Polish." Coming from him, I took this as a great compliment. Later I wrote him a letter that said: "By the Magisterium I may be Polish, but by family, genetics, and geography, I am Slovak." A few weeks later, on an inner wall of the castle where my ancestors had labored for centuries, I ran into a map that showed clearly that the eleven northern counties of which we were a part did belong to Poland for three centuries. So I had to write again: "Darn infallibility! You are right again, and I was wrong." But all this was years later.

At this first dinner in 1991, while I remained fairly quiet, Rocco and Monsignor Dziwisz kept the banter going. Much later, at yet another dinner, the pope asked me what I recommended to help the millions of poor whom he had just seen in Latin America. I don't recall his being terribly convinced by my three points, which were raising the level of universal education from the third grade (on average) to the twelfth grade; changing the law to make the formation of micro-enterprises quick, cheap, and easy; and introducing new, small, local banks (like the U.S. farm credit bureaus) specializing in making loans to poor people on farms and in new businesses.

I remember fondly how much like dinners at my grandmother's these dinners were. A hot chicken broth and, then, in a nod toward Italian cuisine, a small antipasto of fettuccine Alfredo, followed by lightly roasted pork with little round potatoes and cabbage. Dessert, as I recall, was usually fruit, sometimes a little lemon cake from Kraków that the pope liked so much. The wine was an inexpensive local white wine, probably Frascati from out near Castel Gandolfo, the pope's retreat from the summer heat of Rome.

I resolved that if I ever was invited back to dinner, I would come armed, like Dziwisz and Rocco, with some good jokes or funny stories, which the pope seemed to love. Most of the time his blue eyes twinkled merrily like those of Saint Nicholas of old. But when I congratulated him on his part in the unexpected "miracle" of the fall of the Berlin Wall and the collapse of Communism, he looked at me with a certain pity. He waved his hand as if my ignorance was too much for him. "Getting rid of that Mickey Mouse system was no miracle. It was a matter of time. It was built to fail." (I cannot swear from this distance that the pope actually used the words "Mickey Mouse"—we may at that point have been speaking in Italian—but he said something remarkably close to that.)

Then, after dinner, just before we took our leave, the pope took my hand for a moment and looked me directly in the eyes. "Monsignor Dziwisz showed me your article for this week in *Tygodnik Powszechny*" (the Kraków Catholic weekly). The theme of the article was the remarkable change in the pope's thought since his encyclical *Laborem Exercens,* in which he had written that labor is superior to capital because labor always involves persons, and capital is inferior since it is always composed of things. In his 1991 encyclical, *Centesimus Annus,* by contrast, he wrote that the causes of the wealth of nations were knowledge, science, and practical insight—he called such habits "human capital." In any case, after mentioning my article in *Tygodnik Powszechny,* the pope said kindly, in a slightly accented voice, "You understand my thought pritty *gut.*" I replied that I had planned the article to appear just as I was to meet him. He recognized the irony with a smile. He well knew that when I was writing the article, I had had no idea of ever seeing the pope at dinner.

Wow! What an exhilarating evening. I could hardly breathe, and I felt like I was walking on air. I thanked Rocco profusely in case he had had something to do with the invitation, as he drove me to the ambassador's residence after dinner before heading to his home on the other side of Rome. Rocco kept me guessing: He neither denied nor claimed responsibility. Rocco always loved keeping a wisp of mystery and behind-the-scenes maneuvering about him. He enjoyed pretending to the realism of Machiavelli, and he affected the habit of playing three-corner billiards—it would be only after the third bounce that you could see what he had been up to all along.

The Man of Prayer

Four or five times, sometimes with my wife at my side, I was invited to attend Mass with the pope in his miniature chapel. Crowded in, there was barely room for sixteen people. When one entered the chapel some moments before Mass, the pope had already been at prayer for a long time. He knelt bowed over on his prie-dieu, so rapt in prayer that his demeanor produced in all of us a kind of awe. The pope seemed caught up in a world far deeper and holier than ours. It was not that he seemed devout; rather he seemed transported out of himself. One could feel it in the air. I have never felt such a presence.

Over the years I heard several different cardinals, some of whom were not among his admirers, say how moved they also were by his posture at prayer. Some spoke of him as "our mystic pope." They did not say this with particular respect, nor with disrespect either; they were reporting what they saw. They wondered at it.

Almost always when I was at Mass, Monsignor Dziwisz asked me to be the lector. I remember trying to read in a steady, linear voice, while praying that the Holy Spirit would gently inflect this flow of words with the quiet power of their meaning—none of me in the reading, only the Holy Spirit. This is probably self-deception, but that is what I prayed for. One felt obliged to be decreased in the presence of a pope who was so deeply immersed in God, as if only God and he were present. One did not want to interrupt that silence.

On one such occasion, my beautiful and soft-spoken Karen was carrying in her arm a bronze corpus of Jesus dying on the cross. She had cast it herself, and she wanted to present the piece to John Paul II, whom she had always loved from a distance. Seeing the heavy bronze as we came out from Mass, Monsignor Dziwisz led us to the rear of the line that was forming around the large table in the center of the ample room outside the chapel. He encouraged all the other participants to go first. "So you will have more time with the pope," he whispered to Karen.

When the Holy Father approached us, he took in the beauty and gentleness of Karen, as he reached out for the heavy bronze on her arm. He immediately pointed to the heavily arched back. Slowly he said, "Exactly at the point of death." Karen was touched that he grasped so instantaneously the point of what she was striving for. Just as quickly she fired back at him, "Crossing the threshold of hope," the title of his most recent book, which she had loved. He burst into an appreciative grin, and it was clear that she had gone straight to his heart. Many times thereafter, whenever the pope spotted Karen in a group, even in those later days when his face had fallen into a kind of mask that he was no longer able to control because of his steadily advancing disease, the sight of her caused him to relax and break into a smile and a pleased nod.

At another time, for example, the pope welcomed all our Liechtenstein and Kraków alumni and faculty of the summer institute *Tertio Millennio* (On the Third Millennium) to a private audience. It was the very first day of the new millennium, January 1, 2000. Just over a hundred of us gathered in the high Clementine Hall, marvelously painted and cleanly laid out, where a small dais and papal chair had been set up at the front. We milled about in a semicircle, excited and a bit in awe at the paintings on the walls and the high ornate ceiling. We were more excited still about the soon-expected entrance of the pope, and we hoped he would stay for at least a few moments. We had practiced a Christmas song for him, in Polish, as a surprise. Meanwhile, there was plenty to chat about as we waited. Karen and I sidled toward the rear of the group, so the younger people could be up front. We didn't know it at the time, but the door near us on the right was the one through which the pope would enter, instead of the main door to the left.

When the door opened, Karen saw him first, a few steps down the hall. When he reached the door, the first face he recognized was Karen's, and once again his drooping mask broke into a lively smile as he nodded to her warmly. He walked to the front, said a few jolly words, and then our Polish leader, Father Maciej Zieba, OP, whom the pope treated almost as a son, told him we had a surprise. Our choir leader stepped forward, and we sang our Polish song of Christmas greeting. (About half those present were Polish, and they carried our uncertain Polish vowels along safely to port.) The pope joined in the song, beaming with pleasure. He said a few kindly words of welcome, and expressed gratitude for all the time we were putting into studying his social thought every summer. ("I wish some of the bishops would study as you do," he once wrote us in a letter while we were in Kraków.)

Next he invited everyone in the room to come up individually for a blessing. Scott and Erica Walter, who had recently been married, came forward in their formal wedding attire. Then Catherine and Michael Pakaluk approached, with their youngest son in Michael's arms and their next child, in his eighth month, bulging out beneath Catherine's navy blue maternity dress. The kindly pope blessed the couple and their babe in arms, and then, with a great smile, he made a blessing over the child in the womb. Some of us smiled, and some shed tears. The pope laughed with Father Maciej and spoke with Father Richard John Neuhaus, then George Weigel for some time, smiling all the while and joshing with them. They were our most distinguished faculty members, already well known to him. He blessed every single one of us.

It was a heckuva way to begin the millennium! Our hearts were exultant.

Leading Up to *Centesimus Annus*

Everybody in the world knew that there would be a papal encyclical in 1991 to mark the hundredth anniversary of Pope Leo XIII's justly famous *Rerum Novarum* (On the New Things of Our Time). There had already been encyclicals on the fortieth (Pius XI) and eightieth anniversaries (Paul VI). At the American Enterprise Institute I had been running monthly seminars on just this subject since at least 1981, asking the question (from many points of view, not only religious), "If you were asked to give advice, what would you recommend should be included in the coming encyclical?"

It's just as well that we started thinking about it early. In late 1990 and early 1991 I encountered several front-page newspaper articles in Europe, supposedly based on interviews with those who were busily drafting the upcoming document. These screaming articles announced that, with this new letter, the pope would take his place decisively as the foremost leader of the social democratic left, with Willy Brandt, François Mitterrand, Neil Kinnock, and others. This new letter would put "capitalism" and "free markets" to rest once and for all. In social democratic Europe, both "capitalism" and "free markets" were nearly always uttered as terms of opprobrium. Some newspapers also reported that there were at least two, maybe three, drafting groups, and all were tending in the same direction. An American monsignor, who claimed to have visited in Rome and been shown the drafts, warned a conference at Notre Dame (and I was in the room) that "people like Novak" would be cut off at the knees.

But there was another drama afoot that journalists involved in the prepublication leaks were not aware of. In 1987 the pope had issued his second encyclical on the social question, *Sollicitudo Rei Socialis* (In Solicitude for Social Reality Today). The Associated Press announced in its first reports about this new text that the encyclical had as its main theme the moral equivalence of the two systems that then menaced Europe, the Eastern Bloc's communism and the West's capitalism. This report left me sick at heart. I could hardly wait to get the original text in my hands.

True enough, there was a passage in the encyclical that seemed to justify such reports. "Each of the two blocs," the pope wrote, "harbors in its own way a tendency toward imperialism, as it is usually called, or towards forms of neo-colonialism." And again: "The Church's social doctrine adopts a critical attitude towards both liberal capitalism and Marxist collectivism." Yet it was impossible to believe that this pope from Kraków, where he had suffered keenly under Communist oppression, could see no difference between Kraków, say, and Columbus, Ohio—let alone Florence, Aix-en-Provence, and present-day Coventry. In fact, the complex and well-argued text thoroughly undermined the prevailing early interpretation in the press. Alas, however, William Safire, the bright, usually fair, and acerbic columnist of the *New York Times,* had hammered that early interpretation home, bitterly accusing the pope of a despicable doctrine of moral equivalence between East and West.

Slowly I worked on a close textual examination, which showed rather devastatingly how the encyclical's praise of "enterprise" and "economic initiative" as a fundamental human right of the person went beyond any other papal document ("Beyond 'Populorum Progressio': John Paul II's 'Economic Initiative,'" *Crisis* [March 1988]). The letter also went decisively in the direction of the kind of capitalism that Americans have experienced in small town after small town, from sea to sea and even in big booming cities. The encyclical also made a sophisticated counterargument to the many Communist arguments (well known to this pope) against democracy and those vital civil societies (uncontrolled by the state) that are its lifeblood. The pope laid out his case point after point, in fact, as a manifesto in favor of a liberal society, articulated against the rival totalitarian alternative. The style, alas, was Italianate, without the bluntness of English. But even so, the meaning was unmistakable.

It so happened that just then the first President Bush was scheduled to travel to Rome for a visit to the Vatican and an audience with the pope. At the time I didn't know this, but Secretary of State James Baker asked the U.S. ambassador to the Vatican to request a reliable interpretation of the encyclical, with which the president might accurately inform himself. The U.S. ambassador brought the matter up with Cardinal Ratzinger, then prefect of the Congregation for the Doctrine of the Faith ("The Holy Office"), and after some reflection the cardinal recommended my article for the president's reading.

In any case, it was obvious in 1991 that the pope had been rather distressed by the journalistic misreading, especially in America, of *Sollicitudo,* which he had had reason to think would be a widely applauded document. The pope was also upset at the facile anti-Americanism so commonly expressed in certain organs of the Vatican, which repeatedly buckled under the pressure of European "political correctness."

Thus the pope resolved in 1991 to undertake personally a final revision of the drafts he had been sent, with which he was notably unhappy. He also sent an emissary to America to go over the main points of the final draft with a number of Catholic thinkers who had some feeling for American intellectual opinion. For this task there were a number of priests and laypeople in Rome who knew the work of the drafting committees thoroughly and also understood where and why the pope was unhappy. This emissary was instructed not to show the final revision (which was secret), but to convey its main points orally, especially those points that might be unwittingly controversial (in the way that errant passage in *Sollicitudo* had been). I do not know how many other people were consulted, but I do know the emissary had two long conversations with me.

After I had heard the emissary through, never interrupting him, I told him that essentially I liked the document very much—it was a big step beyond anything in the past—but I thought there were at least three points that could evoke a huge backlash in America. I mentioned them briefly, and just as briefly gave him new language as I thought it ought to be. My intention was to clarify, for an American audience, the points it seemed the pope wanted to make, but to note that in these three places the final words (as rendered to me) came out in ambivalent and possibly inflammatory language. The person asking my opinion was very bright; there was no need for pen and paper. I deliberately limited my remarks to three—in my mind the most crucial three.

In 1991 the pope also saw to it that the first distribution of the final draft would be much more thoughtfully carried out. Someone near him ordered that three separate sources send me the document two days *before* publication. My task was then to copy it immediately to two other knowledgeable lay writers closer to the pope than I was. We planned simultaneously to have articles on the encyclical in the hands of three key American publications ready for print as soon as the embargo on the texts had expired. The only problem was that two of the official sources charged with getting me an advance copy failed to cooperate with their instructions. I got a call from the emissary to see if I was pleased, as he hoped I would be, that all three of my suggestions were incorporated into the final text. I told him that the actual text had *still* not arrived on my desk. He was quite upset, but he calmly told me to telephone the third source, whom he knew already had the text. I phoned and asked the person to read three specific passages to me. There my three points were. Perfect!

Within an hour or two the document was in my hands, and then copies were on the way to my associates. The next morning my friends and I published articles on the main points of *Centesimus Annus* before anybody else. As a result *Centesimus Annus* received the fairest welcome in the press of any recent encyclical. This time, the opening introduction was not a hostile misreading in need of months of straightening out.

Years later Peter Hebblethwaite, the former Jesuit and leftish British writer on the Vatican, asked me at a party in London how "that" had happened. He insisted that he had been sure the final draft was the way *he* had wanted it. He had seen *two* drafts that had him excited, and how they failed to get by the pope he could not understand. He seemed to have been drinking at the party for some time, so I was more than usually careful. "I'm just an American," I said (or something like that), "and I don't know quite how these things are done in the Vatican." To myself, I thought, "I'll bet it was much more fun for me to write about the final draft than it was for you." But I kept on my mask of innocence.

Centesimus Annus—the "Hundredth Year"—turned out to be a huge hit in both America and the Third World (but not among Marxist-leaning liberation theologians), and it made European social democrats uneasy. Their habit was to sound rhetorically as if they were more on the socialist side than they actually were, and to say as little as possible in favor of capitalism. Most of them never really took to *Centesimus*. But some of them were sons of entrepreneurs, and they really liked it—and got in touch with me to say so.

A papal document on contemporary social questions deserves plenty of criticism and examination. There are a vast number of contingent judgments to make, several steps removed from any biblical texts. But these are intended to be redolent with the wisdom of the Gospels; they are meant to stand as serious attempts to interpret the present time in their light—as, for example, the interpretation of that highly contingent and complex year, 1989, in the third chapter of *Centesimus Annus*. Devout Catholics of good will may well disagree over the meanings of key words and the interpretation of particular events. Just the same, the dozen or so important social encyclicals of the last hundred years since *Rerum Novarum* in 1891 make a sobering impression on most who read them, even those who at first came to mock.

For instance, such passages as *Rerum Novarum*'s long list of reasons why socialism *must* fail from internal weaknesses read far better today than the descriptions by many Western intellectual eminences of rosy hopes. *Rerum Novarum* reads a lot better in retrospect than the paeans to socialism penned by major writers from John Stuart Mill to Jean-Paul Sartre to Antonio Gramsci. In addition, all the popes over many long decades made a consistent defense of both labor and private property—labor and capital *both*—which mattered a great deal in Europe's political upheavals after World War II.

I HAVE MANY OTHER precious memories of John Paul II. Among these are the great struggle of conscience I faced when in 2003 the pope did all he could to avert the second war in Iraq—whereas my own conscience told me that, while everything might go wrong, still, this war was indispensable to getting an example of a working democracy in the Middle East. I felt it was necessary to inspire a profound rethinking in all those other Middle Eastern nations that had so far been utterly resistant to democracy.

I hated to take a position different from that of the pope, which might mean I would lose his friendship, one of my most precious treasures. I reread the passage on just war from the *Catechism* (#2309), which made clear that such a decision is a prudential one, which persons of good will might measure differently. In addition, it said that a decision to go to war, after thinking through the principles of a just war, belonged above all to the political leaders closest to the facts.

In the following years, there was no diminution in the friendship and support shown me by the pope, Archbishop Dziwisz, and

Vatican press secretary Joaquin Navarro-Valls (who was, in fact, of great assistance to me). I was glad that the pope opposed the war, thus blocking any intimation that it was *religion* that was the *causus belli*. To have turned a political question into a religious war would have been horrific. At the same time, I was also glad that President Bush maintained the honor of the UN by following through on its formal threats to Saddam Hussein and by working so mightily over the next few years in nourishing the slowly burning coals of democracy underneath Arab nations.

A final vivid memory is of being invited by President Bush to fly with the presidential party to pay homage to John Paul II, who was lying in state in St. Peter's Basilica. The next morning our group was in attendance at the dramatic funeral. At one point a sudden breeze turned the pages of the open book of the Gospel highly visible on the central lectern. Then, as the varnished wood casket was slowly being lifted to be carried into St. Peter's, the breeze nudged the clouds away from the sun, and for the first time that day a beam of sunlight fell directly upon the casket and the pallbearers. The contrast between the early grayness and the sudden rays of the sun is vividly caught in photos taken before and after the ray of sun broke through. (I tracked down these photographs myself several months later, after a couple of hours of searching the archives at *L'Osservatore Romano*.) I am not saying an act of God occurred; natural causes could explain it. But these signs expressed what we felt when we shouted into the great roar of the throng, *"Santo Subito! Saint Soon! Declare him saint soon!"*

Index of Names